THE HOLIDAY WHICH? GUIDE TO

The Scottish
Highlands

THE HOLIDAY WHICH? GUIDE TO

The Scottish Highlands

including the Inner Hebrides

Published by Consumers' Association
and Hodder & Stoughton

The Scottish Highlands
First published in Great Britain by
Consumers' Association
14 Buckingham Street, London WC2N 6DS
Hodder & Stoughton
47 Bedford Square, London WC1B 3DP

Written by Kenneth Lowther, with contributions by Val Campbell
Editor: Stephen Brough
Designer: Sally Smallwood
Cover illustration: Jim Robins
Cover design: Fox + Partners
Illustrations: Sheilagh Noble
Maps: David Perrott, Machynlleth

First edition 1984
Second edition 1986
Copyright © 1984 and 1986 Consumers' Association
Maps copyright © 1984 Consumers' Association

Typeset by Gee Graphics, London EC1
Printed and bound in Great Britain
by R.J.Acford, Chichester, West Sussex

ISBN 0 340 40403 5

Also available – *Holiday Which?* Travel Tapes
A twin-cassette pack, also entitled *The Scottish Highlands*, is
available as a companion to this book, featuring four half-hour
programmes on the Highlands, produced by *Holiday Which?* and
presented by Derek Cooper. Included in the pack is a full-colour
fold-out map.
The cassette pack is available from booksellers or from
Consumers' Association, Castlemead, Gascoyne Way,
Hertford SG14 1LH.

Contents

Preface

For me, the wild and lovely region of the Highlands is like a gigantic mountainous lodestone which attracts my emotional magnet, pulling me again and again past the Lowland towns of Glasgow, Edinburgh, Dundee and Stirling to the empty straths and glens across the Highland line.

I was imbued early on with a deep fascination for the Highlands and in particular Skye. My home is in the Hebrides now and when I reach the western seaboard my pulse beats more strongly and my temperature rises. A state of euphoria suspends my critical faculties, so be warned – nothing that follows is to be believed because I am in thrall to the beauty of these northern parts.

It's not so much a region, this, as an experience: 14,000 square miles of moorland, mountain, tumbling burns, silver beaches and enchanted islands. It doesn't matter that the weather can be appalling, that it rains far too much, that the wind blows the blossom off the trees and sometimes the slates off my roof. God in his infinite fair-mindedness has plagued us in the summer months with small, winged dive-bombing midges and, while the rest of Britain may be suffering from 'Phew! It's a heat-wave official', we're still in sweaters. But to my mind that's a small price to pay for the serenity, the calm, the Kodachrome beauty of blue seas and the greener than green grass of the moors. Even in high summer you can find solitude and a tranquillity that is almost tangible.

The Highlands came into social prominence when Victoria and Albert built Balmoral Castle. After that, every lordling and brewer had to have his fishing and shooting lodge for the autumn slaughter of deer and grouse. It's still a sporting place to go for salmon and trout fishing, sea angling, stalking and sailing. But don't miss the natural history – all those seals and seabirds, even a golden eagle or two if you're lucky. Don't miss the social history, either – the megaliths, brochs and forts, castles and keeps. The Highlands and Islands have had a tempestuous past and the relics of Viking occupation, clan feuds and the struggle to survive lie all about you.

Though the area is vast – one-fifth of the United Kingdom – its population is not much larger than that of Hull. It's an independent population, too; the majority of Highlanders, although not averse to doing a little B&B in the summer, are not particularly anxious to alter their way of life. Their independence of spirit often manifests itself in eccentric ways, not all of which seem calculated to fill the Scottish Tourist Board with enthusiasm. In parts of the region, buses, ferries and planes don't move on the Sabbath. Mealtimes are less elastic than in the south, shops less well-stocked, petrol pumps few and far between, gastronomic temples even more thinly scattered. Inconveniences, certainly – but you'll soon forget them in the face of such awe-inspiring views. Even in the rain, the magnificence takes your breath away.

DEREK COOPER

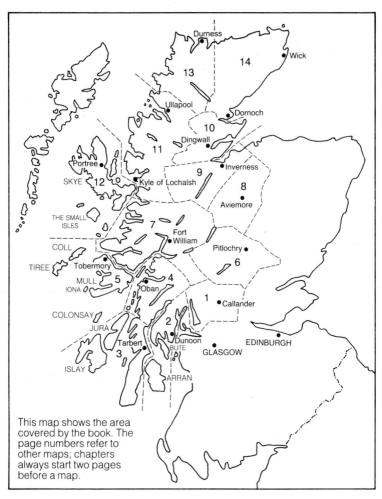

This map shows the area covered by the book. The page numbers refer to other maps; chapters always start two pages before a map.

Introduction

No other British area can match the splendid scenic combination of the Highlands. It is classic touring country, and not only because of the scenery – there is much more for the holiday-maker to enjoy than the million and one views. Rich in history, it has a wealth of prehistoric sites and ancient remains to puzzle over, innumerable castles to explore, and a great deal more to absorb – clan history, the Clearances and the story of the 1745 Rising when Bonnie Prince Charlie attempted to recapture the crown. The range of good walking country is almost unlimited; geologists can enjoy some of the oldest and most fascinating rock formations in Britain; and for lovers of bird and wildlife, the Highlands offer plenty. The fishing is famous, and there is no shortage of other activities and things to do – from loch cruises and sailing to pony-trekking and golf.

The Highlands are defined in various ways. The most common dividing line between the Highlands and Lowlands is the Highland Boundary Fault, cutting north-east from the Firth of Clyde to Stonehaven, south of Aberdeen. For administrative purposes the Highland Region, though it includes many of the Hebridean islands, is much smaller. This book covers the area shown on the map on the opposite page, and includes islands in the Inner Hebrides. In the east we have kept roughly to the official regional border but have gone as far south as Dunkeld, in the old county of Perthshire, and Stirling. In the west of the mainland we have gone as far south as Loch Lomond and the Kintyre peninsula.

We have set out not only to paint the marvellous Highland picture, but to provide – for both the uninitiated and those in the know – a book of great practical help in deciding where to go, what to do and where to stay.

The book has sixteen chapters: two are general, the other fourteen each deal with a specific area; the map opposite shows the divisions we have made. The first general chapter deals with the Highland background – history and heritage, wildlife and weather; the second is concerned with practical information – on getting there and around, accommodation, food and drink and activities; and tells you where you can get further information.

Each area chapter follows a standard pattern. We start with a two-page introduction summarising the area. Following that is a map. Then we describe a centre which is either the main community of the area, or is well placed for touring. These centres, however, should not be seen as our recommendation of *the* place you should make your base; for many people the countryside and villages outside the main towns are the most appealing places to stay. Next there are a number of tours, all of which begin and end at the centre described earlier. Few people will find themselves in position to start and finish the tours exactly as described – and some of the tours would be difficult to accomplish in a day – but the text should help you determine which scenic gems and places of interest will most suit your tastes and schedule, as well as ensuring you find them. In two chapters which cover a particularly large amount of ground, we have used two centres for our tours.

★ Within most tours there is usually one section, occasionally more than one, highlighted as this one is. We have done this to pick out the highspot(s) of the tour. ★

We finish each chapter with accommodation and general information. In the accommodation section we give a brief run-down of how well supplied the area is with hotel and bed and breakfast accommodation. (The chapter on practical information gives help on self-catering, camping and youth hostels.) We also give comments on recommended hotels, ranging from the extremely luxurious (and expensive) to more modest and reasonably priced establishments. Places where we recommend hotels are underlined on the maps. We have included only hotels which we consider out of the ordinary in some way, reliably comfortable and which serve good food. All the hotels have been stayed in and inspected by our own inspectors or have been included on the strength of recommendations from *The Good Food Guide* and *The Good Hotel Guide*; we are very grateful to the guides for their help.

In the general information section we give details of leisure facilities in the area, give a brief summary of the entertainment possibilities, list the major events and give details of summer ferry services and tourist information offices. The latter can give you more precise details of where to go for particular leisure activities, as well as information on all holiday aspects.

Places of interest
In our tours and in our descriptions of touring centres we have included all the main and many of the minor places of interest. With some – cairns, hill-forts and some ruins, for example – there are no restrictions on when you can visit. Others, such as museums and most castles, are generally open only in season – from Easter or early April to September or October. Opening hours are usually from 10am or 10.30am to 5pm or 6pm. In the text we give details of opening hours only when they are more restricted.

NTS means run by the National Trust for Scotland. Members of the NTS or the National Trust get free admission to all properties in Britain owned by either trust which are open to the public. For details contact:
National Trust for Scotland, 5 Charlotte Square,
Edinburgh EH2 4DU, Tel: 031-226 5922
National Trust, 15 Queen Anne's Gate, London SW1H 9BU,
Tel: 01-222 4856

AM means ancient monument in the care of the Scottish Development Department; generally open mid-March to mid-October 9.30am to 6.30pm, Sun from 2pm, rest of year to 4pm. An annual season ticket gives you free admission to all ancient monuments in the UK. For details contact:
Scottish Development Department, Ancient Monuments Division, 3-11 Melville Street, Edinburgh EH3 7QD; Tel: 031-226 2570

Hotels
Details are those confirmed with the hotels in summer 1986.
Price categories (see below) are based on the cost for one person sharing a double room for one night in 1986, inclusive of tax and service. Many hotels give reduced terms for stays of three nights or longer.

GFG means in the 1986 edition of *The Good Food Guide*
GHG means in the 1986 edition of *The Good Hotel Guide*
GPG means in the 1986 edition of *The Good Pub Guide*

Dinner, bed
and breakfast

£15 to £30	£
£31 to £40	££
£41 to £50	£££
£51 to £60	££££
over £60	£££££

We're very grateful to all those who helped us with this book, in particular the departments of Scottish History at the universities of Edinburgh and Aberdeen, and all the local tourist offices who filled in questionnaires or provided other help.

Our apologies to any clan members who feel we should have used an alternative spelling of their name.

Also available as a companion to this book are the *Holiday Which?* Travel Tapes, also entitled *The Scottish Highlands*. This twin-cassette pack features 4 half-hour programmes on the Highlands; a full-colour fold-out map is included.

The land and the people

Beginnings

The whole of Britain is geologically the worn remnant of a turbulent past; and in the far north-west the sandstone peaks of the Highlands are Britain's most ancient rocks. Suilven and Stac Polly were formed over 600 million years ago – and the Lewisian gneiss under the moorland from which they rise is some of the oldest rock in the world, a yet more inconceivable 2,000 million years old. The Great Glen, created by a huge slide of mountain masses, is comparatively a recent event of 350 million years ago; and geologically it was only yesterday that Ben Nevis was created and volcanic basalt lava poured across Scotland, leaving as its most dramatic outcrop the columnar cliffs of Staffa. For more millions of years rains shaped the rocks, and then came four swift ice ages: the jagged Cuillin resisted the smoothing process of the glaciers. Climate changed again, to something warmer than today's, and covered the Highlands in forest; in turn it grew wetter and the forests decayed into peat. Peat still covers vast areas but the forests have returned, according to climate and contour.

Landscape

As well as ice and lava, shifts and thrusts seldom apparent to the ungeological eye mapped the Highlands into the many variations of its magnificent scenery – spectacular mountains, rugged cliffs, wild sea lochs, majestic inland lochs, tumbling waterfalls, sparkling rivers, and a landscape of vivid greens, browns and purples. The north contains the greatest contrasts. North-east, fertile flat promontories lie below the Dornoch Firth and above it a stern line of cliff coast edges the rolling plateau of East Sutherland and Caithness; in the remote west a beautiful amalgam of mountain, loch and woodland stretches far north along a coastline deeply riven by lochs and a seaboard full of islands.

Less remote, the Central Highlands – Loch Ness, the Spey valley, Loch Lomond and the Trossachs, Tummel and Rannoch and Atholl – have their own contrasts. Pitlochry is pastoral, the Trossachs utterly picturesque and the River Spey bubbles through the green fields of the broad valley floor; yet the mountains are never far away. The Monadhliath range is massively inaccessible, the Cairngorms a winter playground, and Ben Lomond's fine peak above its legendary loch is the beginning of the west again.

The Western Highlands and the islands off their coast are the concentration of classic Highland scenery. The highest mountains, the finest lochs, the most dramatic glens are all designed to romantic extremes: the Road to the Isles – and every other – threads through splendour. The islands are yet another range of contrasts: gentle Bute next to rugged Arran, Mull's layered moors and mountains, Skye's challenging verticals, and so many smaller islands each with a note of its own.

History

The earliest occupants of the Highlands left a wealth of archaeological remains. Vitrified forts are the oldest inhabited constructions: they were strengthened with timber, which tended to catch fire, and the intense heat partially melted and fused their stone walls. Stone Age (from 5000 BC) flint tools and mounds of shellfish detritus were found; there are Bronze Age (from 3000 BC) stones, cairns and graves, Iron Age (from 500 BC) duns and brochs to be seen, sometimes in great concentrations. The brochs were round towers with passages contained in their immensely thick walls, built mainly during the first century BC, probably as protection against later Celtic immigrants or the earliest marauders from the sea.

While the Romans occupied Britain – in the first and second centuries AD – the land north of their Antonine wall belonged to tribes they called Picti: painted people. The Romans fended off their raids, but never occupied their territory; only when the tribes fought Agricola at Mons Graupius in AD 84 were they considered more than nuisance value. Three hundred unchronicled years later, Gaelic Scots came over from Dalriada in Ulster, and colonised Kintyre and the islands off Argyll. By the mid-sixth century they occupied all the land between the Firth of Clyde and Ardnamurchan. St Columba came to Scotland in 563 to begin his work of converting the northern Picts to Christianity. However, confrontation between the Scots and Picts continued for two hundred years, until in 843 Kenneth MacAlpin united the two peoples. Unification was helped by the constant threat of Viking invasions. The Norsemen gained control of the Hebrides, of nearly all Argyll and of the whole of north-east Scotland as far south as Inverness. The sway of the Norsemen was not finally ended until 1263 when Haakon IV of Norway was defeated at Largs. In the following century, a deep cultural division between southern Scotland and the Highlands was becoming apparent. While the Lowlands adopted English as the normal language and feudalism as their social organisation, the Highlands retained the Gaelic language and a social system based on the clan.

A clan was at once a group of kinsmen and a term applied to all adherents of a particular chief – kinsmen, hired retainers, lesser chiefs and all those bound by the half-tribal, half-feudal tradition of 'manrent': support and service, rather than money. During the 14th century the Clan Donald Lordship of the Isles, centred on Islay, grew enormously in power. It strongly supported Robert the Bruce's fight for Scotland's independence, which culminated in his victory at Bannockburn, and its rewards were great. As the Scottish political scene expanded, the Scottish crown had always to subdue the Highland powers – or use them. For a long period Clan MacGregor was deprived for its rebellious activities of all civil rights, and even their name abolished. Clan Donald was too strong;

James IV removed their Lordly title and appointed other chiefs as 'sheriffs' to control the Highlands. Argyll was one – the Argyll Campbells too had aided the monarchy since Robert the Bruce, until their chief became the strongest man in Scotland. Several clan battles took place during the 16th century, but the quarrels had virtually died out by the 17th and the Highlands went through a period of calm and stability – apart from Montrose's divisive campaign on behalf of Charles I, which after a string of victories ended in his defeat, his capture at Ardvreck Castle in Assynt and his execution in Edinburgh. In 1692 the Massacre of Glen Coe took place, when Macdonald of Glencoe delayed taking an oath of allegiance to the new king, William of Orange.

The Act of Union in 1707, which united the parliaments of England and Scotland, did not end the Highlanders' support for the Jacobite cause and their hostility to the Hanoverian succession. Personality counted – 'the Highlands loved a man'. The lack of enthusiasm for the Old Pretender's rising, compared with the support for Bonnie Prince Charlie, is partly explained by James III's lack of charisma. Sentiment counted too – 'the King over the water'; Highlanders had supported the Stewarts through good times and bad, through French imbroglios and religious ferment, and the Jacobite cause by the end was hopelessly romantic. The Bonnie Prince left France and landed near Arisaig on 25 July 1745 on an adventure that lasted 14 months, and saw his fortunes rise to a peak of expectation only to drop to a trough of despair. The Prince raised his standard at Glenfinnan, proclaiming his father King James III. Within a month he had 2,000 followers; they swelled to 5,000 after his victory at Prestonpans. The army marched south to Perth, Edinburgh and Carlisle, winning several victories. But at Derby the Prince was advised that he had no hope of succeeding in his planned march on London, and the Jacobite force turned back to the Highlands. The Prince blew up Inverness castle and stayed in the town for seven weeks, until he learnt that the Hanoverian army under the Duke of Cumberland had reached Nairn. Eager for battle, the Prince insisted on confronting the enemy on Culloden Moor and on 16 April 1746 the Jacobite army was completely crushed. The Prince was pursued throughout the Highlands and Islands, taking refuge in various parts of Lochaber and in the Hebrides, safe from betrayal in spite of the £30,000 reward on his head. Flora Macdonald helped him to reach Skye and eventually he escaped back to the mainland to re-embark for France, from a point close to that of his ill-omened arrival.

'Butcher' Cumberland's brutalities after Culloden were only the beginning of a long purge of the Highlands: every attempt was made to destroy the area's political unity and culture. The victorious government resolved to eradicate the Highland way of life. By a series of punitive laws, Highlanders were forbidden to

carry arms, to wear the tartan and to play the bagpipes. The chiefs lost their powers of jurisdiction and the Gaelic language was virtually proscribed. By the 19th century the area was over-populated and hungry; the chiefs were mere landlords now, stripped of their traditional powers and requiring increased rents rather than service. Clan loyalties disappeared as they found it more profitable to sell out to farmers from the prosperous south. The Highland Clearances began: in the Hebrides, Caithness and Sutherland, Inverness and Ross, tenants were evicted to make room for sheep. Crofters went to the towns or – often with assistance from their landlords – tried to make a living round the coast; hundreds of thousands emigrated to America and Canada, often lured by false prospects even over there. Evictions were enforced if necessary, by burning crofts and by use of troops and police; the government 'assisted' emigration. The process continued for over 40 years.

Economic distress for those who stayed in Scotland was worsened by natural disasters – the vanishing herring shoals in the 1830s, potato blight in the 1840s – and the discovery that sheep farming too was uneconomic in view of the fierce competition from imported Australian wool. In many places the sheep in turn were 'cleared', to make way for Victorian sporting terrain – 'deer forest' and grouse moor. Riots in Skye in 1882 led to the 1884 Crofting Act, giving security of tenure and attempting to fix fair rents. Emigration, now voluntary, was often still the only solution to hunger. Even now the Highlands remain seriously underpopulated, particularly in the interior, in spite of the efforts made by the Highlands and Islands Development Board.

Landmarks of Highland history

500-800	**Kingdom of Dalriada** in modern Argyll, founded by Gaelic-speaking Christian 'Scots' from Ireland
563	St Columba arrives at Iona
794,801	Viking attacks on Iona: Columba's shrine removed to Ireland
843	**Kingdom of Alba**: Kenneth MacAlpin unites Picts and Scots, moves seat of power to Scone
9C, 10C	Alba defended against Vikings, Lowlands, Northumbria
1005-1034	**Kingdom of Scotia**: Malcolm II fends off Norse attacks, defeats Northumbrians
1034-1040	**Kingdom of Scotland** under Duncan I, uniting Scotia and Strathclyde
1040-1057	Macbeth opposes the 'anglicisation' begun under Duncan
1057-1093	**English influence** under Malcolm III (Canmore): marries devout English princess (later saint) Margaret
1093-1249	**Feudal system** develops in the Lowlands; the Highland clan system remains intact and Gaelic-speaking
1098	Magnus Barefoot of Norway confirms Norwegian rule throughout Hebrides
1156	Somerled of Argyll defeats Vikings at sea and becomes King of the Isles: descendants Clan Donald, Lords of the Isles
1249-1286	Alexander III: stable reign, 'golden age'
1263	**Battle of Largs**: Vikings' final invasion defeated
1286-1296	Disputes over the succession: Edward I of England ('Hammer of the Scots') claims sovereignty
1296	**Edward I** removes Coronation Stone to Westminster
1297	**William Wallace's** rebellion: rules one year as 'guardian'
1306	**Robert the Bruce** crowned but fails for lack of support
1307	Death of Edward I; Bruce 'tries again', against Edward II and Scottish rivals, for seven years
1314	**Battle of Bannockburn**: Robert the Bruce defeats the English
1329	Death of Robert I leaving infant son and powerful nobles
1329-1371	**French influence** begins with alliances against Edward III
1371	**Stewart Kings** begin with Bruce's grandson Robert, who had been High Steward of Scotland (spelling 'Stuart' later introduced by Mary)
1506	James IV takes 'Lordship of the Isles' for the Crown
1513	**Battle of Flodden**: disastrous defeat of Scots helping French against English
1538	James V marries French and Catholic Mary of Guise, alienating Henry VIII
1542	**Battle of Solway Moss**: with James' death soon after his newborn daughter succeeds as Mary Queen of Scots
1554	Mary of Guise, Queen Mother, takes over the Regency of Scotland

1558-9	Mary Stewart marries French Dauphin and becomes French Queen
1559-60	**Protestant Reformation** in Scotland inspired by John Knox
1561-1567	Mary Queen of Scots' turbulent reign, from widowhood to abdication in favour of infant James VI
1603	**Union of Crowns**: on the death of Elizabeth I, James VI of Scotland becomes also James I of England
1638-1651	**The Wars of the Covenant**
1638	**The National Covenant**: a return to strict Presbyterian church, rejecting James VI's bishops and Charles I's new prayerbook
1638-41	**The Bishops' Wars**, ended by a constitutional settlement with the King, the Scottish Revolution
1643	**The Solemn League and Covenant** with the English Parliament brings Scotland (under the Earl of Argyll) into the Civil War
1644-5	Montrose's campaign against the Covenanters, in support of Charles I
1649-51	On the death of Charles I, his son Charles II signs the Covenants and before his exile is proclaimed King of Scots, and crowned by Argyll
1651-1660	Cromwell's military occupation of Scotland
1660-68	**The Restoration**: Argyll hanged; church legislation annulled, bishops re-appointed; Covenanters suppressed
1688	William of Orange summoned by the English in preference to Roman Catholic James II, who is exiled. William and Mary accepted as Sovereigns of Scotland
1689	**Battle of Killiecrankie**: Jacobite Highlanders rout William's troops, but are promptly defeated at Dunkeld
1691	Highland chiefs take oath of submission to William and Mary
1692	**Massacre of Glencoe**
1707	**The Treaty of Union**: English and Scottish parliaments combined into that of the United Kingdom
1715	First Jacobite rising on behalf of 'The Old Pretender', James III
1719	**General Wade** begins building roads for use in controlling the Highlands after small second rising
1745	**Bonnie Prince Charlie** raises the clans again
1746	**Battle of Culloden Moor**: the Prince's defeat and escape
1746-1780	Military control and reprisals after the 1745 Rising lead to effective destruction of chiefs' powers and clan system, abolition of Highland dress and pipes
1770-1860	**The Clearances**: eviction of crofters as chiefs let their lands go to sheep farmers from Lowlands and England; beginning of depopulation of the Highlands

The Highlands Today

Three organisations created in this century have had an important effect on the outward face of the Highlands and on the way of life of its people. The Forestry Commission was founded in 1919. It now owns about two million acres of forest and has established forest parks with information centres, picnic areas, campsites and forest trails and roads. There has been a massive afforestation programme but, sadly, it has often resulted in gloomy ranks of conifer covering the bare hillsides where once there was fine mixed woodland.

The North of Scotland Hydro-Electric Board, founded in 1943, has built more than 50 dams and hydro-power stations and is now concentrating on pumped storage schemes, two of which have been completed, at Cruachan on Loch Awe and at Foyers on Loch Ness. The board's operations have transformed the countryside in many areas, creating new lochs and enlarging old ones, building massive dams and erecting buildings where none previously existed. Unfortunately the government has not allowed cables to be taken underground because of the expense involved, but in general great pains have been taken to preserve the environment.

The third organisation is the Highlands and Islands Development Board, founded in 1965 to encourage the development of industries appropriate to the area. The Board has had its disappointments: the closure of the pulp mill at Corpach and the aluminium smelter at Invergordon. But a major success has been the revitalisation of the sea fishing industry, which now employs considerably more people than it did 10 years ago. Tourism has also made an important contribution, giving employment to more than 11,000 people.

The Highland Heritage

The ban imposed after the last Jacobite rising on all the outward ceremony of Highland life – banners and gatherings, pipes and tartan – was lifted in 1782. By then the Jacobite cause had completely evaporated and Highland regiments had distinguished themselves abroad with the British Army. The Highlands began to enjoy a romantic revival – notably in the novels of Sir Walter Scott – and an influx of literary visitors. In 1822, George IV made a State visit to Edinburgh and Scott organised a complete Highland revival at Holyrood; when the monarch appeared wearing Royal Stuart tartan, the vogue was established.

The kilted plaid, a long rectangular blanket of woollen cloth, was the Highlander's main garment for 800 years. Immensely practical, it could double up as a sleeping bag; heavy and loosely hitched, it was generally thrown off before a clansman charged into battle. In each area the plaid was woven in a different way. By the 17th century the patterns and the vegetable-dyed colours had become quite elaborate; in the 18th, military tartans were coming into formal use by Highland regiments; in the 19th, the new sentimental interest in all things Highland created something of a 'tartan myth', exaggerating its antiquity and hierarchical distinctions. The main tartan divisions are by clan: within these there are 'dress' and 'hunting' tartans, and tartans for chiefs, regiments and other more doubtful claimants.

That other characteristic Highland phenomenon, the bagpipes, had been proscribed as an instrument of war – there had been sufficient demonstration of the rousing qualities of its music for marching men. But the pipes' repertoire also includes dances and slow Gaelic airs; serious classical music, the *ceol mor*, takes years to master. Bagpipes began to supplant the harp and fiddle in the 16th century. Soon every clan chief had his hereditary pipers – the most famous were the MacCrimmons, pipers to the Macleods. Today piping contests are very popular: the most famous takes place each year at the Cowal Highland Gathering at Dunoon.

Highland Games and Gatherings great and small are held in all areas, usually in July or August. They were probably originally organised by chiefs as a mixture of entertainment and the means of selecting the strongest men for their fighting forces: the stars are still the 'heavies', the men who toss the caber and put the stone. Highland dances too are an integral part of any Gathering. The earliest were developed from Celtic originals, possibly with ritual significance; many modern ones were introduced by the regiments, who vied with each other in piping and dancing prowess. Games and Gatherings received their greatest encouragement from Queen Victoria, and the reigning sovereign is still a regular visitor to one of the oldest, the Royal Braemar Gathering.

A Highland tradition less easy to revive is its language. Gaelic, brought to Argyll from Ireland by the original settlers in the 6th century, is spoken by most of the people in the Western Isles and also by many on the mainland, particularly in the coastal regions of West Ross, Argyll, Sutherland and Inverness-shire. *An Comunn Gaidhealach* is devoted to fostering the Gaelic culture and language, and some Gaelic is taught in schools.

Wildlife
In the vast emptinesses of the Highlands – some inaccessible to man, some preserved by man, some with both advantages – live over 30 species of wild mammal (and innumerable birds). Red deer are most likely to be seen; the herds keep to high ground in summer and move down to the glens and moors in winter. Walkers and climbers may meet rarer inhabitants – serious naturalists sit still and wait. The polecat now is rarest of all; the pine marten, almost exterminated during the last century, thrives again in the north and in nature reserves.

The bird population is provided with enormous variety of habitat. Along the coasts the seabirds teem and colonise; inland there are the species of lochs and streams, of moor and mountain and of woodland. The famous ospreys (killed off 70 years ago because of their taste for trout) have reappeared, at Loch Garten and Loch of Lowes; the golden eagle is not uncommon, but hard to find in its high mountain territory – that impressively big bird spotted in the middle distance is probably a buzzard and only half the size. The peregrine falcon is seen less and less.

The smallest flying creature in the Highlands is also the greatest nuisance – the midge. Unless like the deer you keep to the high tops in summer, this is an example of wildlife you will certainly encounter. Novelist Neil Munro's Para Handy was bitter about them: 'Look at Tighnabruaich! – they're that bad there, they'll bite their way through corrugated iron roofs to get at ye!... There iss a spachial kind of mudge in Dervaig, in the Isle of Mull, that sits up and barks at you ...' The midge problem is at its worst in July, August and September, spanning the tourist high season.

Weather

Sometimes second only to the midge as the Highland menace, the Highland climate is not subject to safe generalisations. Like everything about this land, it has infinite variety. The finest mountain scenery, on the west coast, attracts the highest annual rainfall – but only on the heights: Ben Nevis collects twice as many annual inches as Fort William four miles away. The scenery anywhere may be blotted out for days on end at any time of year; or within the space of hours waver in and out of view among sunlit cloudscapes; or stay illumined for a week in wonderful clear light. The prevailing westerly winds bring Gulf Stream warmth, making possible the lush vegetation in western glens and sea lochs; further north, gales can blow for days – seemingly from any direction – making the sea hostile and the land desolate.

The eastern seaboard generally lives up to the theory that it must be drier – though overall statistics are no consolation if your week happens to be wet. In the far north in midsummer months, the longest hours of daylight and twilight let you appreciate the changing skies and sunsets, the colours of the open land and sea.

Temperatures are fickle too: rather lower in the east, especially in winter. The Cairngorms get more snow than western mountains, and it may lie all year in the north-facing corries of Ben Wyvis above the Cromarty Firth: Clan Munro's tenure of the area included payment of a snowball to the King any time he passed. In summer, whatever the comparative sunshine records, the west feels warmer.

Practical Information

Getting there and around

Driving The main road routes into the Highlands are the A9, which skirts the Trossachs and heads north, through Pitlochry and the Spey valley to Inverness, continuing as far as Wick, and the A82, which leaves Glasgow and heads up along the western shore of Loch Lomond. Main roads are good, the A9 is excellent. But some of the roads to the most spectacular parts of the Highland scenery are winding, narrow and steep; in fact many roads in the Highlands are single-track with passing places.

Remember that in parts of the Highlands petrol is relatively dear and garages few and far between; many close on Sundays.

AA centres for breakdown assistance: 24-hour, Tel: Glasgow 041-812 0101 or Edinburgh 031-225 8464. Centres open to 7pm: Tel: Aviemore (0479) 810300; Elgin (0343) 46450 (closed Sun, Mon); Fort William (0397) 2099 (closed Sun); Inverness (0463) 233213; Oban (0631) 62854 (closed Sun, Mon); Perth (0738) 23551.

RAC centres for breakdown assistance: 24-hour, Tel: Glasgow 041-248 5474 or Edinburgh 031-229 3555. Centres open to 5.30pm: Tel: Inverness (0463) 231640; Perth (0738) 23717.

Public transport If you plan to make much use of public transport, you'll find *Getting around the Highlands and Islands*, published by the Highlands and Islands Development Board, invaluable, and you can buy a *Travelpass*, which gives unlimited travel on most bus, train and ferry services for up to 12 days.

Train The maps in each area chapter show the rail routes. Motorail services run to Stirling and Inverness. Even if you are travelling mostly by car, it is worth considering making the odd rail journey: the Highlands possess some of the finest rail routes in all Britain, notably the line to Kyle of Lochalsh. There is an observation car (with commentary) on some services to the Kyle and from Fort William to Mallaig. Steam trains travel along the Strathspey Railway between Aviemore and Boat of Garten.

Coach and bus National Bus, Scottish Bus Group and Cotters are the principal coach operators for services from south of the border. The bus network is fairly comprehensive but services aren't very frequent in remote areas. The main operating company is Highland Omnibuses Ltd, Tel: Inverness (0463) 237575 or 231816. Post buses operate on some local routes.

Ferry In the general information section of each chapter we give details of ferries. Most services are run by the state-owned Caledonian MacBrayne; head office, Tel: Gourock (0475) 33755.

Air From south of the border you can fly direct to Aberdeen, Edinburgh, Glasgow and Inverness. Loganair has built up a very extensive network of services in Scotland. Air Ecosse, British Airways, Burnthills Highland Helicopter Service and Dan Air operate other internal Scottish services.

Hotels and bed and breakfast

The Highlands aren't littered with outstanding hotels, but scattered through the region are some amazingly good ones: a couple of luxurious baronial piles, a number of comfortably converted country houses and former shooting lodges; and the occasional atmospheric old inn.

Modern hotels are few in the Highlands: there is a concentration in the Spey valley resort of Aviemore and the occasional motor hotel. Among the older hotels there is no shortage of grand-looking establishments in fine settings; unfortunately, many of these don't live up to the promise of their exterior.

Guest houses or private houses which offer bed and breakfast are widely available in most parts of the region, and for holiday-makers B&B can be a good way of finding out more about the Highlands and the Highlanders themselves. **Help** in finding accommodation is provided (for a small fee) by tourist offices in the region, through their 'Book A Bed Ahead' scheme.

Guide books include our own publications – *The Good Food Guide*, *The Good Hotel Guide* and *The Good Pub Guide*. The AA and the Scottish Tourist Board (STB) publish a number of useful accommodation guides. The Michelin *Red Guide* is perceptive, the British Tourist Authority's *Commended Country Hotels, Guest Houses and Restaurants* is excellent, and the *Guestaccom Good Room Guide* is useful in finding good value places to stay; Tel: Brighton (0273) 722833 for a free copy. The tourist offices for individual Highland areas also produce guides to accommodation.

Self-catering accommodation

There is a wide range of properties for rent, from purpose-built chalets to cottages, flats and houses on vast estates. The standard of a lot of chalet accommodation in Scotland is higher than in many other parts of Britain – often stylishly designed and on very attractive uncrowded sites. There are also several **time-share** developments in the Highlands – around Aviemore and near Aberfoyle. On the whole the standard of accommodation is high and units are sometimes available for rent.

Agencies which have quite a large number of self-catering properties to rent in the Highlands include:

Blakes Highland Cottage Holidays, Wroxham, Norwich, Norfolk NR12 8DH; Tel: Wroxham (06053) 2917

Forestry Commission, 231 Corstophine Road, Edinburgh EH12 7AT; Tel: 031-226 5922

Hoseasons Holiday Homes, Sunway House, Lowestoft, Suffolk NR32 3LT; Tel: Lowestoft (0502) 62292

Mackay's Agency, 30 Frederick Street, Edinburgh; Tel: 031-225 3539

Scottish Highland Holiday Homes, Wester Althaurie, Abriathchan, Inverness; Tel: Inverness (0463) 86247
Summer Cottages, 1 West Walks, Dorchester, Dorset; Tel: Dorchester (0305) 66877
West Highland Holidays, 33 High Street, Fort William, Inverness-shire PH33 6DJ; Tel: Fort William (0397) 2433
Useful publications include:
Association of Scottish Self-Caterers' list of approved operators available from Mr T Smyth, 58 East Trinity Road, Edinburgh EH5 3EN; Tel: 031-552 4823
Scotland: Self-Catering Accommodation, published by the STB.

Camping
There are campsites scattered all round the coast and in the popular central and southern inland areas. Many are in lovely settings – by a deserted beach, or surrounded by mountains beside a loch. Useful guides include: *Scotland: Camping and Caravan Sites*, published by the STB; and the AA's *Camping and Caravanning in Britain*.

Youth hostels
There are about 50 youth hostels in the Highlands; you don't have to be young to use them. Some arrange activity holidays.
For details contact: Scottish Youth Hostels Association,
7 Glebe Crescent, Stirling FK8 2JA; Tel: Stirling (0786) 72861

Food and drink
A number of the hotels we recommend serve excellent food, often making skilled use of raw materials which are home or locally produced. But restaurants without accommodation where you can be sure of culinary expertise are almost non-existent; even cafés are rare in some areas. Breakfasts are frequently hearty enough for you to do without lunch. High tea is an institution, and evening mealtimes are often earlier than you may be used to. If you want to try traditional Scottish fare, look for hotels and restaurants displaying the 'Taste of Scotland' sign; the Scottish Tourist Board produce a booklet listing places in the scheme.

Although Scotland is not a country for lovers of real ale, it is the home of the malt. Several of the distilleries in the area covered by this book will take visitors on tours and give them a dram; to the east of the Spey Valley the 'Whisky trail' takes you to five distilleries. There aren't many pubs with the kind of olde-worlde character you find south of the border but, on the other hand, there are many which are open all day. Useful guides to food and drink include our own publications, *The Good Food Guide* and *The Good Pub Guide*, as well as some of the others mentioned earlier.

Activities

The general information section in each area chapter gives details of activities; local tourist offices and the Scottish Tourist Board and Highlands and Islands Development Board can tell you more.

Climbing and walking The Highlands offer an almost unlimited range of good walking, from demanding hill-walks to gentle strolls, as well as climbs for both the beginner and the accomplished mountaineer. Scotland has more than 500 peaks over 3,000 feet, of which 282 are classified 'Munros' after H.T. Munro who began listing separate mountains in 1889. The hazards of mountains cannot be underestimated: it's important to be properly equipped and know how to read a map and use a compass; you should always leave written word of when and where you are going and check in when you get back.

The STB publish *Scotland for Hill-Walking* and *Walks and Trails in Scotland*; and many local tourist offices can give you information on walks in their area. The Ramblers' Association publishes an information sheet on *Walking in Scotland*: s.a.e. to 1-5 Wandsworth Road, London SW8 2LJ. The Countryside Commission publish a free leaflet on the West Highland Way. Also: *A Guide to the West Highland Way*, by Tom Hunter, published by Constable, and *The West Highland Way*, by Robert Aitken, published by HMSO. For details of mountaineering clubs contact the British Mountaineering Council, Crawford House, Precinct Centre, Booth Street East, Manchester M13 9RZ; Tel: 061-273 5835

Fishing Our general information sections give some idea of where you can fish for trout and salmon. No general licence is required but local permits must be obtained; available from clubs, estate offices, hotels, tackle dealers. The trout season is from mid-Mar to early Oct, the salmon season is longer; dates can vary from area to area.

The STB publish *Scotland for Fishing*. Other publications include: *The Fishing Handbook*, published by Beacon; *Where to Fish*, published by Harmsworth/Black; and *The Sea Angler's Guide to Britain and Ireland*, published by Butterworth/Ventura.

Golf There are courses throughout the Highlands with many on the east coast. The STB produce a map, *Golf Courses in Scotland*. Other publications include: *Good Golf Guide to Scotland*, published by Canongate, and *The Golf Course Guide to the British Isles*, published by Collins/Daily Telegraph. For a list of clubs contact the Scottish Golf Union, 54 Shandwick Place,
Edinburgh EH2 4RT; Tel: 031-226 6711

Pony-trekking Pony-trekking is possible in several Highland areas. A leaflet, *Riding Holidays and Trekking*, is produced by The British Horse Society, British Equestrian Centre, Stoneleigh, Kenilworth, Warwickshire CV8 2LR; Tel: (0203) 52241

Sailing and watersports There are many places where you can charter yachts on the west coast, and there are watersports centres in some of the central and more southern Highland areas. For information contact The Royal Yachting Association, 18 Ainslie Place, Edinburgh; Tel: 031-226 4401

Skiing There are four main ski areas in Scotland: Cairngorm, near Aviemore; Glen Coe; Glenshee, between Braemar and Blairgowrie; and Lecht, near Tomintoul.

Other useful addresses
Our general information sections list local tourist offices. Here are some other organisations which provide information.
Countryside Commission for Scotland, Battleby, Redgorton, Perth PH1 3EW; Tel: (0738) 27921. Books and leaflets on walks and country parks.
Forestry Commission, 231 Corstophine Road, Edinburgh EH12 7AT; Tel: 031-334 0303. Useful maps and guides to forests.
Highlands and Islands Development Board, Bridge House, 27 Bank Street, Inverness IV1 1QU; Tel: (0463) 234171. General and regional information on the Highlands and Islands; their publication, *Holiday Ideas*, is particularly useful. They also run a computer holiday booking service; Tel: Dingwall (0349) 63434.
Nature Conservancy Council, 12 Hope Terrace, Edinburgh; Tel: 031-447 4784. Various publications – eg, on nature reserves.
Royal Society for the Protection of Birds, 17 Regent Terrace, Edinburgh EH7 5BN; Tel: 031-556 5624. Details of bird reserves and holidays.
Scottish Sports Council, 1 St Colme Street, Edinburgh EH3 7AA; Tel: 031-225 8411. Wide range of leaflets on specific sports, also brochures of courses available.
Scottish Tourist Board (STB), 23 Ravelston Terrace, Edinburgh EH4 3EU; Tel: 031-332 2433. A wide range of information.

Loch Lomond
and
the Trossachs

Loch Lomond

Parallel to the line of the Great Glen (but much less sharply defined
and visible) runs the Highland Boundary Fault, the geological
demarcation between the Highlands and the Central Lowlands. It
marks the base line of the Grampian mountains, running from the
foot of Loch Lomond in the south-west to Stonehaven on the
north-east coast. Above it, typical Highland scenery begins; Loch
Lomond lies across it. Much of the terrain covered in this chapter is
not even geologically 'Highland'; but some of the 'Lowland'
attractions to the east are so easily explored from our centre,
Callander, and the Trossachs that it would seem wasteful to omit
them. At Stirling, Scotland's history took a new direction when
William Wallace first drove out her southern invaders, the English,
in 1297 – only 34 years after her northern invaders, the Norwegians,
had been finally repelled after the Battle of Largs.

While several lochs are contenders for the title 'loveliest in
Scotland', Lomond has its supporters as the most beautiful stretch
of inland water in all Britain. 18th-century novelist Tobias Smollett,
born a few miles south, declared: 'This country is justly stiled the
Arcadia of Scotland; and I don't doubt but it may vie with Arcadia

in every thing but climate'. Loch Lomond is certainly the largest Scottish loch and it must be the most visited and most celebrated. The old song *Loch Lomond* – 'Ye'll take the high road, and I'll take the low road' – was reputedly written by a supporter of Bonnie Prince Charlie, awaiting execution in Carlisle: the speedier 'low road' would be that of the spirit, after death. The high road that serves Loch Lomond today is often slow, as travellers absorb the scenery. Over 30 islands and islets dot its southern waters, bearing traces of castles and monasteries, prisons and graveyards. The MacGregors took their oaths by their burial-place on Inchcailloch; the Buchanans' war cry was 'Clairinch'. Little lochside bays are fringed with varied woodland; the waters are full of trout and pike and busy birdlife. Above the eastern shore rears Ben Lomond, Scotland's most southerly Munro (see page 24).

Here begins the country of Rob Roy MacGregor, the early 18th-century freebooter romanticised in the 19th into a Scottish Robin Hood. Several parts of the Highlands have Sir Walter Scott to thank for their initial tourist appeal; the publication of his poem *The Lady of the Lake* began it for Loch Katrine, and in *Rob Roy* the scenery of the Trossachs ('the bristly country') was more significantly evoked. People came in droves to follow the hero's movements through his native wilderness. Coleridge, Lake poet, compared it with his beloved Borrowdale: 'the only thing that really beats us....all the mountains more detachedly built up, a general Dislocation – every rock its own precipice, with Trees young and old'. In Scott's time the only exit from the short defile of the Trossachs proper was a rugged scramble: now a little road takes visitors from Loch Achray to Loch Katrine, its car park and its cruise. Rob Roy's route to Aberfoyle has been opened up – a magnificent road winds up through the forest. But his cave by Loch Lomond is as inaccessible as ever: there's room for only the narrowest footpath between water and steep mountainside.

Beyond Rob Roy's grave under the Braes of Balquhidder, busy and beautiful Loch Earn lies among mountains; east of here the scenery opens out along Strathearn. Comrie and Crieff, Doune and Dunblane, and Stirling itself are within easy reach.

A Highland area with broad appeal, it's popular with day-trippers – Loch Lomond's southern banks are just a half-hour's drive from Glasgow. There's a whole range of things to explore – castles, museums, cathedrals and historic sites – as well as walks and climbs, golf, fishing and watersports; and the Trossachs excel in forest walks and viewpoints. There is a wildlife park near Balloch and a safari park near Blair Drummond. Loch Katrine is best seen from its steamer cruise. Loch Lomond, too, can be enjoyed by steamer or the ferries which connect its busy western side with its much quieter eastern shore; small boats are popular too, but remember: it's cold, its dangerous, don't swim.

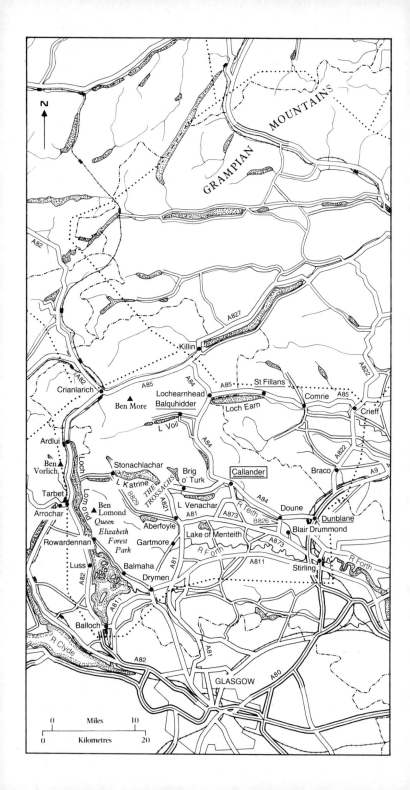

CALLANDER

At the foot of the Highlands, Callander spreads hospitably between the winding River Teith and wooded hills; behind rise mountains to the north and west, with **Ben Ledi** (2,873 feet) near at hand. The town is both bracing and sedate, with broad streets of shops and clean stone-built houses, a tall church dominating the centre and an air of dignity and commonsense. It was the 'Tannochbrae' of television's *Dr Finlay's Casebook*, which perhaps increased its tourist trade. Callander and Aberfoyle are the main centres for the Trossachs: Aberfoyle is closer to the heart of the area but in many ways Callander is a preferable base – it is bigger and has retained more of its old charm. Its setting is fine and there are some good walks from the town; the **Crags** (at 600 feet) are the closest vantage point. Past the golf course, north-east from the town, the **Bracklin Falls** are a favourite beauty spot in a wooded gorge of the Keltie Water. A path up Ben Ledi itself starts from the Trossachs road, a couple of miles west.

Loch Lomond

Lochearnhead · Crianlarich · Ardlui · west Loch Lomond
Drymen · Balmaha · Rowardennan
Gartmore · Aberfoyle
Callander

As much of a circuit of the loch as you can drive. 30 easy miles through the mountains to Crianlarich; the road down Loch Lomond is good but winding and often crowded. A rewarding detour up the eastern shore (24 miles) is single-track. A narrow road from Drymen 10 miles to Aberfoyle, then faster progress back to Callander. About 120 miles.

From Callander drive 13 miles north up the A84 to Lochearnhead (see next tour), and take the A85 for five miles through **Glen Ogle**, a narrow mountain defile with a place to pause beside the lochan at its highest point. The views of the heights back beyond Loch Earn are splendid, and there are more to come. The road descends to **Glen Dochart**: the A827 here leads east to Killin (see Pitlochry chapter). Turn west, and follow the river below **Ben More** (3,843 feet) – a pretty stretch of water with woods and little islands, which reaches **Loch Iubhair**, and **Loch Dochart** with a ruined castle on an island. Between the lochs, from the hamlet of Benmore, begins the steepest and shortest ascent of Breadalbane's second highest peak.

Eleven miles from the Glen Ogle junction is **Crianlarich**, a small village but an important road and rail junction in the Highlands communication network. Here the railway line from Glasgow divides, one branch heading for Oban and one for Fort William. Take the A82 south down **Glen Falloch** where the **Falls of Falloch** are the rocky rapids variety. The glen opens up as you drive south; at **Inverarnan** the Ben Glas Burn plunges down the opposite hillside and a bridge across the Falloch is the starting point of the path to the eastern bank of Loch Lomond. It's another two miles to **Ardlui** at the narrow head of the loch, with its pier and small boats. Climbers use the village as a base for **Ben Vorlich** (3,092 feet) which you won't see from the road; for the length of the loch, the visible heights are all on its opposite side.

Loch Lomond is the largest inland loch in Scotland, almost completely enclosed by mountains – yet it may well once have been a sea-loch. It's little more than a mile from salt water at Tarbet, towards its head. 24 miles long, it's wide and islanded at its southern end, with a narrow tail tapering 15 miles up into the mountains. The 'bonnie banks' are indeed beautiful, and the road very busy – it's the north-west trunk road from Glasgow, and none too wide. Coming south from Ardlui you're very close to the shore, with few places to pause until near **Inveruglas**, where there's space for car parking and picnics and admiring the view. The old castle on Inveruglas Isle belonged to the Macfarlanes; they kept stolen cattle behind Ben Vorlich, where Loch Sloy is now dammed; pipelines run down the hillside to Inveruglas power station. Half a mile south, a ferry crosses the loch to Inversnaid (see next tour). The road hugs the shore, wooded now, to **Tarbet**. This name (more often spelt Tarbert) crops up on the west coast – it means a short neck of land between waters, where portage across is possible; as at Tarbert in Kintyre, war galleys were dragged across the isthmus here from Loch Long, during King Haakon's 13th-century attempts to reassert Norwegian sovereignty. Today the railway comes this way, and the road from Rest and Be Thankful and Cowal, and Tarbet too is involved in the Loch Sloy hydro-electric scheme. But look across Loch Lomond here for the very best view of **Ben Lomond** (3,192 feet) – the mountain which dominates every lochside vista, and which gave the loch its name. Five twisting miles on at **Inverbeg** another ferry plies to Rowardennan, the starting place for climbing Ben Lomond and the most northerly point of call for the cruising loch steamer. South of here the waters become busier as the loch widens.

For **Luss**, a most picturesque village, turn off the A82; its little street of rose-covered cottages lies between the traffic and the shore, where there's a sandy bay and a pier. Offshore lie most of the wooded islands, irresistibly decorative, which add so much to Loch Lomond's appeal. The main road winds south through oak and beech and birch, with new and lovely viewpoints framed at every curve of the shore, until it swings away from the loch round the estate of **Rossdhu**, home of the Colquhouns. The present house is 18th-century with remnants of the 15th-century castle and chapel in the grounds. Your last good view from the western shore is at

Duck Bay, where the busy marina, car park and general bustle still allow you to take in the whole of the lower loch.

This area is the busiest. The **Cameron Wildlife Park** has bears and bison rather than lions and tigers in its drive-through area. There is a children's zoo, adventure playground and assault course, a giant slide, trampolines and boats. The grounds run down to the loch and Cameron House is open, too: porcelain, pictures, furniture, whisky collection, old toys and a Tobias Smollett museum. Take the A811 for the busy lochside resort of **Balloch**, where the railway ends and boat trips run from the pier. North-east, a country park has been created in the grounds of Balloch Castle, now Nature Conservancy offices; the nearest (and largest) island of Inchmurrin is a nature reserve, together with some of the smaller ones.

The route now lies along the A811 and a brief stretch of the A809 eight miles to **Drymen**, a neat and pretty village with increasing new residential development around it. From here you reach the east bank of Loch Lomond by the B837 to **Balmaha**, one of the loch's main yachting and boating centres. You can visit the near island **Inchcailloch**, full of oakwoods and wildfowl – there's a great variety of birds in the Lomond islands, and many rare species winter here.

★ The little road along the eastern shore eight miles to **Rowarden-nan** is a dead end, but a delight, not only by comparison with the traffic on the other side: it wanders up through the Pass of Balmaha, down to lochside picnic places, past forest trails and tumbling burns and isolated cottages. From Rowardennan you can continue on foot under the steep side of Ben Lomond to Inversnaid and further (see next tour); this is the route of the West Highland Way, which runs 95 miles from Milngavie, just outside Glasgow, to Fort William. It is clearly marked, with the Countryside Commission's thistle motif on posts and stones; but this walk, like the ascent of the mountain, needs stout footwear. ★

Return the 12 miles to Drymen; the unclassified and single-track road to **Gartmore** is the most attractive way back towards Callander, through the fringe of Loch Ard Forest and across the Kelty Water. It meets the A81 a couple of miles south of Aberfoyle; follow this as it swings east to the Lake of Menteith and north again to Callander, 20 miles from Drymen.

The Trossachs and east

Good roads throughout the beautiful Trossachs area except the single-track scenic detour (30 miles) to Inversnaid. No problems in the more open country to the east, with a string of attractive towns and villages, and easy driving back through the mountains. About 120 miles.

Drive north from Callander on the A84 and in a mile turn west across the river **Leny** on the A821, close to **Loch Venachar**, five miles long and popular for sailing. Here under the slopes of Ben Ledi you are already in the country of Walter Scott and Rob Roy. At **Brig o'Turk**, the **Glen Finglas** road now leads to a reservoir and dam; walkers can still skirt its eastern side. The A821 takes you past wooded little **Loch Achray**, and the right fork at its end begins the short stretch which is **The Trossachs** proper – the name originally applied only to this wild and beautiful defile between Loch Achray and Loch Katrine. Steep overhanging rocks and rugged mounds are softened by heather and moss; the pass is full of oak and birch and delicate rowan trees. You emerge at the eastern end of **Loch Katrine**; from here you can't see much of this lovely nine-mile stretch of water, but you can appreciate it at your leisure from the Victorian steamer *Sir Walter Scott*, which from mid-May to September plies between the pier and **Stronachlachar** taking 45 minutes each way. A track follows the north bank of the loch.

★ Back at the Loch Achray fork, turn south; the wonderful forest road winding up and over to **Aberfoyle** is a comparatively modern creation. When Scott set his books in this area a track had existed since time immemorial. When tourists began to follow in the footsteps of Scott's characters, the Duke of Montrose built a toll road along the line of the track. The present excellent road, opened only fifty years ago, is still known as the Duke's Road; it runs through **Queen Elizabeth Forest Park**, which extends from the east coast of Loch Lomond to Loch Venachar. Established in 1953 to celebrate the Coronation, the Park covers 65 square miles, comprising the forests of Achray, Loch Ard and Buchanan, and has 170 miles of forest roads open to walkers. A couple of miles up the Duke's Road, at a sharp bend, there is a magnificent viewpoint: the whole Trossachs area is opened up round you – mountains, lochs and forests, 'the Highlands in miniature' – and it becomes clear how Rob Roy escaped capture for years in this maze of delectable scenery. Forest walks and mountain paths lead off from a nearby car park, and in another mile is the entrance to the **Achray Forest Drive**, where motorists pay an admission fee and can then explore seven miles of forest and lochside road, with picnic places and walks. The main road's highest point is the Duke's Pass (800 feet); winding steeply down from here you come to the **David Marshall Lodge**, a pavilion with panoramic views and a Forestry Commission Visitor Centre (opens 11am). ★

In another mile you reach **Aberfoyle**; still Rob Roy territory – here he came out of hiding to meet Bailie Nichol Jarvie at the old inn – but today it's no place for a discreet bandit. Only 26 miles from Glasgow, Aberfoyle is well accustomed to day-trippers and is on every coach tour's route. Of the old 'clachan' the ruined church remains, with its mortsafes designed to thwart corpse-snatchers; all else is modern development. Its setting though is beautiful, and there are walks.

Aberfoyle is also the starting point for a wonderful scenic drive to the eastern bank of Loch Lomond. The return trip covers a distance of over 30 miles and is not to be missed. The B829 runs along the north side of **Loch Ard**, three miles long and regarded by many as the most beautifully set sheet of water in the whole Trossachs area. To the north rises **Ben Venue** (2,393 feet) and to the west in the distance **Ben Lomond** (3,129 feet); a path leads half a mile to the **Falls of Ledard**. The 'Pass of Aberfoyle' continues past wilder **Loch Chon**, then climbs through woodland on to moors and reaches a T-junction where a right turn leads to **Stronachlachar** on **Loch Katrine**, the calling place of the regular steamer. Turn left, onto a narrow single-track road past **Loch Arklet**, now a reservoir, to **Inversnaid**, a lonely outpost on the eastern shore of Loch Lomond. There is a hotel, and a landing stage where the steamer calls and a ferry runs across the loch to south of **Inveruglas**. The path along the east bank of Loch Lomond is part of the West Highland Way. Turn north, and it brings you in less than a mile to Rob Roy's Cave where not only the outlaw but also Robert the Bruce reputedly spent some time; southward, it's 10 miles to **Rowardennan** (see previous tour). By car, you must go back the way you came.

Three miles to the east of Aberfoyle lie the placid waters of the **Lake of Menteith**, Scotland's only 'lake', though no physical feature distinguishes it as such and old maps show it as a 'loch'. There are three islands; the largest, **Inchmahome**, is reached by a ferry from **Port of Menteith** half a mile off the main road. In this beautiful island setting are the romantic ruins of Inchmahome Priory, founded in 1238. There are arches and mouldings and tombs to be seen; the monastic garden is known as Queen Mary's Bower – the Queen of Scots, aged five, was hidden here for weeks.

A mile east of Menteith the A81 swings north, five miles back to Callander. But continue along the A873: there is much to see east of Callander. In another five miles just after **Thornhill** the B826 forks left towards Doune – or you can keep on towards Stirling; the A873 meets the A84, and in another mile you pass **Blair Drummond**, home of **Scotland's Safari Park**, where you can gaze from your car at lions, giraffes and other exotic animals (last admission 4.30pm). Only six miles on, great **Stirling** and its famous **Castle**, perched on a dramatic crag high above the Forth, makes a detour of distinction. Its history is Scotland's – from possible Romans and legendary King Arthur to the Battle of Bannockburn, when Robert the Bruce routed the English; the Stewart kings lived here, Mary Queen of Scots was crowned here, Bonnie Prince Charlie in 1746 took the town – but not the castle. Stirling, a splendid mixture of ancient and modern, remembers it all with museums, fine houses and an excellent Visitor Centre.

The A84 arrives at **Doune**, six miles to the north-west. **Doune Castle** (open daily) is battlemented medieval; beautifully preserved and restored, it presents in the most vivid fashion the domestic (and defensive) life here in the 14th century. Just north off the A84 are **Doune Park Gardens** and the adjacent **Doune Motor Museum**. The motors are a collection of about 40 vintage cars, most maintained in running order. From Doune turn east again, five miles along the A820 to visit the cathedral in **Dunblane**, on the site of a 6th-century church built by the Celtic St Blane. What you see today is mostly fine 13th-century Gothic: the west front is its outstanding feature. Dilapidated after the Reformation, the interior was restored in the late 19th and early 20th centuries, with some fine carving preserved. The surrounding Cathedral Close is attractive and the rest of the town, set on the River Allan, though much developed is not without character. Leave it by the A9 to the north, and after five miles fork left onto the A8220.

This was once Roman-occupied territory: just east of **Braco** are the most visible remains, the impressive earthworks making up the great Roman fort of **Ardoch**, dating from the late 1st and mid-2nd centuries. There were other camps in the area, but only stretches of Roman-straight road suggest them now – like the A822 as it approaches Crieff. If you prefer, an unclassified road to the west passes Drummond Castle (not open) and its Gardens (open every afternoon May to Aug; in Sep only Wed and Sun pm) – formal, terraced and Italianate, with an astonishingly complex sundial dated 1630.

Crieff is a thoroughly pleasant town, built on a hillside above Strathearn, a meeting place of scenic routes. It has a distillery (guided tours) and a Heritage Centre dealing largely with whisky; its historical remnants include a 17th-century tolbooth complete with stocks, and two crosses – the octagonal town cross of 1688, and a 10th-century Celtic cross of sculptured sandstone. Six miles west along the A85 and the River Earn, the charming village of **Comrie** is similarly well-sited; three rivers meet here, and the local walks include Glen Lednock, where the falls plunge through a chasm known as the Deil's Cauldron. Comrie has two other distinctions: the Museum of Scottish Tartans, and the fact that it lies on the Highland Fault – occasional earth tremors have been known to rattle the teacups.

In another five miles the A85 reaches **St Fillans**, the fishing, sailing and mountaineering centre at the east end of **Loch Earn**. You are back in Highland scenery now: this lovely seven-mile loch is surrounded by mountains over 2,000 feet high, with Ben Vorlich to the south dominating at 3,224 feet. Two roads skirt the water to **Lochearnhead**: the A85 follows the north bank, but you get better views from the narrow unclassified route to the south, winding through birch woods past Ardvorlich House (not open) and the nearby tombstone of six Macdonalds who tried to raid it in 1620. Near the head of the loch by Edinample Castle (not open) are the Falls of Edinample and a footpath up their steep glen. As the small road meets the A84, Lochearnhead itself is a short way to the right: you will probably have watched much activity on the water already, but the watersports centre here is its main base.

Turn south down the A84, and in a couple of miles at **Kingshouse** make a short detour to **Balquhidder** just west along a single-track road; here among the ruins of two ancient churches three graves are surrounded by an iron railing. Though the stones are much earlier, they are said to commemorate Rob Roy, his sons, and his wife. The little road continues for 10 miles, along Loch Voil under the wooded mountainside called the Braes of Balquhidder. The A84 follows the river south through forest to **Strathyre**, with a Forest Information Centre, trails and a mountain path; after four miles beside curving Loch Lubnaig ('the bent loch'), road and river and former railway squeeze through the tight Pass of Leny – the Falls of Leny are attractive tumbling rapids. In another mile you're back in Callander.

Accommodation

This area is well served with accommodation all types, with a number of towns where there is a wide choice of hotels, guest houses and bed and breakfast places. Even in remote areas, such as along the east side of Loch Lomond, there are isolated hotels which enjoy marvellous positions. The three hotels we recommend range from the extremely luxurious to a comparatively modest Scandinavian-style hotel where the food is reliably good and the views are excellent.

CALLANDER
Roman Camp (GFG, GHG)
Tel: Callander (0877) 30003
A pink-washed, turreted and shuttered country house, reminiscent of a small château, on the edge of this charming town. The entrance hall and library are panelled, and the dining room has a painted ceiling; antiques and paintings by contemporary Scottish artists fill the public rooms. The comfortable bedrooms have colour TV, radio and baby-listening, telephone and tea-making facilities. The grounds, which include immaculate formal gardens, lead down to the Teith, where the hotel has fishing rights.
Open Mar to mid-Nov; 11 bedrooms (including 3 suites); £££££

DUNBLANE
Cromlix House (GFG, GHG)
Tel: Dunblane (0786) 822125
Few hotels can match the excellence of this late-Victorian pile standing in a mere 5,000 acres, one of only three places in Scotland to be awarded distinctions for both food and wine in the 1984 *Good Food Guide*. The public rooms, which are littered with paintings, tapestries and antiques, are gracious, spacious and extraordinarily comfortable. Most of the bedrooms are similarly magnificent; over half are suites. All have bath or shower, telephone and baby-listening; the suites have colour TV. Tennis, fishing, riding and shooting are available.
Open all year except Feb; 14 bedrooms; £££££

ST FILLANS
Four Seasons
Tel: St Fillans (076 485) 333
An unpretentious modern Scandinavian-style hotel at the eastern end of Loch Earn. Bedrooms have large windows overlooking the loch; all have bath or shower, colour TV, telephone and baby-listening. Guests get concessions for watersports.
Open mid-Apr to Oct; 12 bedrooms (also 6 chalets); from ££

General Information

Activities
BOAT HIRE Places where possible on Loch Lomond include Ardlui
and Balmaha; see also 'sailing'. Various possiblities on the Clyde,
near Helensburgh.
BOAT TRIPS Loch Lomond: Countess Fiona from Balloch, calls at
Luss, Rowardennan and Inversnaid, Tel: 041-226 4271; for trips to
islands from Balmaha, Tel: (036 087) 214.
Loch Katrine: Sir Walter Scott, four trips daily (weekdays), two
trip daily (weekends), calling at Stronachlachar, Tel: 041-336 5333
FISHING Salmon and trout in lochs Ard, Arklet, Doine, Katrine,
Lomond, Lubnaig, Venachar and Voil and rivers Devon and Teith.
Trout in Lake of Menteith and River Lochary.
GOLF Aberfoyle, Bridge of Allan, Callander, Comrie, Crieff,
Dunblane, Drymen, Muthill, St Fillans and Stirling.
PONY-TREKKING Aberfoyle, Braco, Bridge of Allan, Dunblane,
Killearn, Kinlochard, Rowardennan and Strathyre.
SAILING Ardlui; sailing and watersports at Lochearnhead and St
Fillans.
SWIMMING Stirling
TENNIS Bridge of Allan, Callander, Doune, Dunblane and Stirling.

Entertainment
Cinema and theatre at Stirling. Pipe bands once a week at
Callander. Ceilidhs in some local hotels.

Events
JULY Highland Games at Balloch and Luss; Doune and Dunblane
Highland Show; Stirling Festival; Beating the Retreat, Stirling
Castle.
AUGUST Bridge of Allan Highland Games.
SEPTEMBER Dunblane Highland Games; Doune Hill-climb (cars);
Loch Lomond Grand Prix (power boats).

Ferries
Rowardennan to Inverbeg (passengers only),
Tel: Balmaha (036 087) 273
Inveruglas to Inversnaid, Tel: Inversnaid (087 786) 223

Tourist Information
Loch Lomond, Stirling and the Trossachs Tourist Board,
Dunbarton Road, Stirling, Tel: (0786) 70945
Stirling Information Centre, Dumbarton Road, Tel: (0786) 75019
Centres open summer only: Aberfoyle, Tel: (087 72) 352; Balloch,
Tel: Alexandria (0389) 53533; Callander, Tel: (0877) 30342;
Crieff, Tel: (0764) 2578; Dunblane, Tel: (0786) 824428;
Tarbet, Tel: (030 12) 260; Tyndrum, Tel: (083 84) 246

Cowal, Bute
and
Arran

Lamlash, Arran

The area of Argyll called Cowal lies between Loch Fyne and the Clyde, split in the south into three hilly sub-peninsulas. Projecting further south between the narrow Kyles of Bute, the Isle of Bute looks on a map almost part of Cowal. Arran is most distinctly an island – 'a great arrogant lion of an island' – its jagged cluster of mountain peaks dominating the views for miles.

Cowal is reached by only one road down the east shore of Loch Fyne; travellers from Glasgow and the south must cross between the mountains, over the windy pass of Rest and Be Thankful. It was always more accessible by sea, and the Vikings made use of all its surrounding and penetrating lochs. A century after the rise of Somerled, who gave Bute and Arran to his son, King Haakon of Norway invaded the Clyde again; he regained Bute's Rothesay Castle before the decisive Battle of Largs returned it to the Kings of Scotland. Since the second Stewart king, 'Duke of Rothesay' is the title of the heir – held by the Prince of Wales today. Arran's Brodick Castle, once itself a Viking fortress, was by the mid-16th century the peaceful home of the Hamilton family, who built on to the earlier structure. Jacobite rebellions hardly touched Arran; later during the Civil War, far from becoming 'one of the ruins Cromwell knocked about a bit', Brodick Castle was provided with a whole extra wing.

Cowal had longer troubles, largely because of the ambitious Argyll Campbells. The whole of southern Cowal belonged to Clan Lamont – whence the peninsula named Ardlamont – and their chief seat was Castle Toward, seven miles south of Dunoon. But the Campbells had been emerging from the obscurity of Loch Awe ever since they aided Robert the Bruce, and his Stewart grandson made them the hereditary keepers of Dunoon Castle. This produced a Lamont-Campbell blood feud which lasted nearly 300 years. In 1646 the 8th Earl (and first and only Marquess) of Argyll besieged Castle Toward, unsuccessfully, and a truce was declared and accepted. Argyll's brother promptly took advantage of the truce to sack the castle and take 200 prisoners to Dunoon, where they were massacred. Castle Toward was never rebuilt. Dunoon Castle stood, until in 1686 – after the 9th Earl of Argyll had backed the hapless Monmouth rebellion – James VII sent in the Marquess of Atholl and his men, with instructions to 'destroy what you can to all who joined in any manner of way of Argyll...burn all the houses except honest men's, and destroy Inveraray and all the castles'. A dozen Campbell lairds were hanged at Inveraray, and the Men of Atholl burnt the castles of Dunoon and Carrick.

Cowal is not a large area, and it doesn't offer a lot in the way of sights for holiday-makers to visit. Nor is it as dramatic as many other parts of the Highlands; but it has its scenic attraction. The introduction of the Clyde steamers brought to Cowal the prosperous citizens of Glasgow and its suburbs. They colonised huge chunks of the south-east coast, building villas for permanent or holiday use. Today, the ferries continue to provide a welcome escape for those living in the Clydeside industrial towns, and south-east Cowal gets crowded at weekends and holidays. Busiest of all is Dunoon at the end of August during the Cowal Highland Gathering: the March of a Thousand Pipers is a prestigious and spectacular event in Scotland's calendar. One of the more unusual attractions of this area is the submarines based in Holy Loch; and the waters off the south-east coast of Cowal seem permanently busy with yachts, dinghies, excursion boats and the ferries. The western peninsulas of Cowal are wilder, with fine views from the hill roads; there's hardly a community along the Loch Fyne coast, but a scattering of appealing villages up the western Kyle, including very pretty Tighnabruaich.

The popular routes to both Bute and Arran are from across the Clyde, but Bute can also be reached by car ferry from Colintraive on Cowal, and Arran from Claonaig on Kintyre. Bute is an undramatic farming island with some good beaches, a few fine remnants of early history and one large attractive holiday resort, Victorian Rothesay, where the moated castle is well worth a visit. Arran is a complete contrast. Around its rugged mountains the coastline is all accessible, with good walking and fishing. Tourism is the island's most important industry. Resorts have developed round the eastern bays; the west has a string of tiny villages, cliffs and caves, and ancient sites. There are good beaches, a range of sporting facilities, and at Brodick, the capital, an impressive castle splendidly set beneath the island's highest peak, Goat Fell.

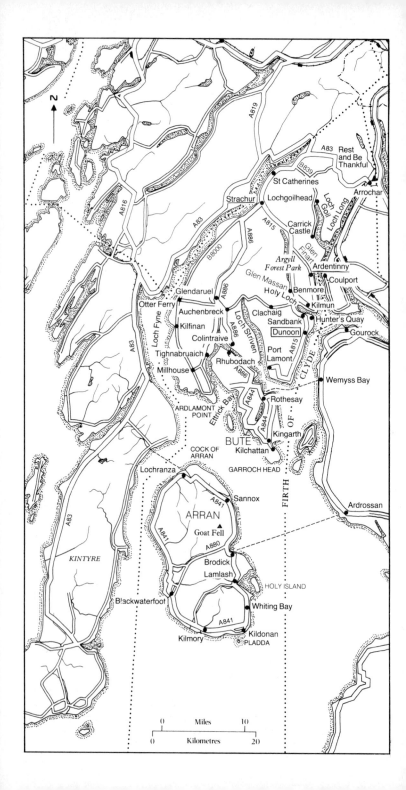

Dunoon is the largest town in Cowal and forms part of a large built-up area which extends north to beyond Hunter's Quay. Its setting on the Clyde is its main attraction, and south of the town there are good views from the coastal main road, which leads round to Port Lamont and then continues as a secondary road along part of the east side of Loch Striven.

Little remains of the 13th-century castle – just a few stones on the hillock overlooking the pier; but it was once an important stronghold. After the destruction of the castle in 1686 Dunoon lapsed into obscurity, but revived in the early 19th century when the middle classes from Glasgow began to build villas there. With the introduction of steamers it developed into a thriving resort, with Rothesay its only rival for the holiday trade from across the Clyde. Today it has all the amenities you expect from a fairly small resort but – although called the 'Clyde Riviera' – seems unremarkable but for the views. It is, however, a well-known yachting and sailing centre and makes a lovely day trip for those living across the Clyde as well as a convenient overnight stop for those touring Cowal.

Mid and North Cowal

Benmore · Strachur · Loch Fyne · Rest and Be Thankful
Lochgoilhead · Carrick Castle · Hell's Glen
Glen Finart · Kilmun
Dunoon

A tour of glen, garden, forest, sea loch and submarines. Good roads along the coast but single-track along the dramatic stretch from the summit of Rest and Be Thankful to Loch Goil. With detours and some inevitable backtracking, about 90 miles.

Leave Dunoon by the A885 heading north past little **Loch Loskin**, a haunt of wildfowl, to join the A815 at **Sandbank**. In two miles the **Glen Lean** road branches off westward (see next tour); shortly afterwards an unclassified road strikes off left for five miles along the very lovely **Glen Massan**. It first winds through a broad valley then up a green ravine where the river froths through waterfalls and rocky pools below wooded slopes.

Return to the head of Holy Loch, where the main road is joined by the A880. **Puck's Glen**, signposted here, is reached by a flight of steps. A steep climb past streams, waterfalls and rocky paths brings you out on a hillside of heather and shrubs. A mile north is the **Younger Botanic Garden** with its magnificent collections of trees and shrubs, particularly conifers. Californian redwoods, more than a 100 years old, line the main avenue. The garden is managed by the Royal Botanic Garden, Edinburgh, and the collection of rhododendrons is claimed to be the finest in the world. Beyond

Benmore Forest is the most southerly part of the **Argyll Forest Park**, the first one to be designated in Britain. The Park covers about 100 square miles, stretching from west of Loch Eck to Loch Lomond and in the north to Arrochar; and there are 165 miles of forest roads to walk. It is mainly rugged terrain: several mountains in the forest are more than 3,000 feet high.

The A815 now runs for six miles north along narrow **Loch Eck**, which lies in a picturesque glen between heavily wooded hills. At the head of the loch you enter Glenbranter Forest, the most westerly part of the Argyll Forest Park.

The centre of **Strachur** is set back from **Loch Fyne**. The nearby 18th-century Strachur House (not open) was once a home of the Campbells; it (and the Creggans Inn – see 'Accommodation') now belong to Sir Fitzroy Maclean. Follow the A815 north along the loch for five miles – it's an almost unpopulated area, where seals can often be seen near the shore. Soon after St Catherines the road leaves the lochside, passes the end of Hell's Glen (see later) and in a few miles meets the A83. At the junction turn left for a mile to see **Strone Gardens**, notable for their rhododendrons and azaleas; the pinetum contains what is claimed to be Scotland's tallest tree.

★ Return to the road junction and head east through **Glen Kinglas**, parallel to the old military road begun by General Cope in 1743. The road swings south to traverse **Rest and Be Thankful**. This pass has marvellous views of **Beinn an Lochain** (2,992 feet) to the west and **Beinn Ime** (3,318 feet) to the east – Wordsworth remarked 'who would rest and *not* be thankful?'. The modern road presents none of the difficulties which in former days justified its name. The A83 descends Glen Croe through Ardgartan Forest and past **The Cobbler** (2,891 feet) on the left to Ardgartan, and on to the resort village of Arrochar at the head of **Loch Long**. But a more exciting road leads south from the summit of Rest and Be Thankful to beautiful **Loch Goil**. This road, the single-track B828, climbs to nearly 1,000 feet and then drops steeply down **Gleann Mor** to reach the loch where a left fork brings you at once to **Lochgoilhead**, a village much enlarged by Victorian villa development. ★

The beautiful sea loch of **Goil** branches deep inland from Loch Long. Submarines are tested here, and there's a naval base at Douglas Pier. The road along the west side ends after five miles at **Carrick Castle**; the walls stand to a good height and part of the great hall survives.

Look out for herons along the shore of Loch Goil on your way back to the junction with the B839 **Hell's Glen** road, which climbs through lonely rocky scenery, ideal for ambush, and then descends to the A815. Opposite this junction, on the old road, can be seen white stones forming a heart – the 'Wedding Ring', where the tinkers of Argyll held their marriages. Follow the A815 back 15 miles through Strachur and along Loch Eck but turn left along the **Glen Finart** road, at first through forests and then more open land six miles to the attractive village of **Ardentinny**, on **Loch Long**. A mile north is a picnic place by a sandy beach on the forest edge; across the loch at Coulport are the prominent developments of the Polaris armament depot.

The drive six miles southward takes you along the A880 through the continuous residential development linking Blairmore, Strone and Kilmun, round the point on Holy Loch. In the 7th century the monastery of St Mun gave Kilmun its name, and probably made the loch 'holy'. Today **Holy Loch** is a nuclear submarine base. On its northern shore is the Forestry Commission's **Arboretum**, where many rare and exotic trees flourish. At its head, the A880 joins the A885 five miles north of Dunoon.

The Kyles of Bute

Clachaig · Auchenbreck · Glendaruel · Loch Fyne
Millhouse · Kilfinan · Ardlamont · Tighnabruaich
Glendaruel · Sandbank
Dunoon

To the lovely village of Tighnabruaich, taking in some fine coastal scenery. Mostly narrow or single-track roads; 75 miles, plus 20 miles of detours.

Follow the A885 through Sandbank and take the B836 **Glen Lean** road, wooded until **Clachaig** with its old gunpowder mills, bleak near the dam which created the reservoir of **Loch Tarsan** serving the power station at the head of **Loch Striven**. The B836 meets the A886 at **Auchenbreck**; Colintraive, the car ferry terminal for Bute, is five miles from here. The road north from Auchenbreck goes through the beechwoods and farmland of **Glendaruel**. The bridge across the Ruel – where a road branches off to Otter Ferry with superb views half-way over – was the scene of a victory in 1100 of the Scots over invading Norsemen.

After about 15 miles turn south along the B8000 through the woods of Strathlachlan and glimpse the considerable ruins of **Castle Lachlan** in green fields by **Loch Fyne**. The narrow road winds its way eight miles close by the shore to **Otter Ferry**, which owes its name to the ferry that used to ply to Lochgilphead. Here you have a second chance to climb the moorland route towards Auchenbreck and view the inlets and islands from 1,000 feet.

After Otter Ferry, outer Loch Fyne is a much broader stretch of sea. The B8000 turns inland to **Kilfinan**, then rises over moorland and drops to the crossroads at **Millhouse**, where it turns east to

Kames. The western road leads to the hamlet of **Portavadie**, interesting for the many prehistoric sites to the south but spoilt by a derelict oil-platform construction yard. South of Millhouse is the **Ardlamont Peninsula** which was used as a training ground for the Normandy landings; east is **Kames** and the beginning of a much more friendly stretch of coast.

★ **Tighnabruaich** ('House on the Hill') a mile to the north is a charming little sailing resort in a beautiful setting of trees and hills; tropical plants thrive in its sheltered gardens and gentle climate. The A8003 up **Loch Riddon**, opened in 1969, greatly improved ease of access, particularly from Dunoon, but Tighnabruaich is rarely overcrowded – though the activities of the sailing school make the waters of the Kyle very busy. Two miles to the north, the Caladh Castle Forest Trail starts high above the Kyles, descending steeply past a lily pond with a number of viewpoints on the way. Here, too, is the Forestry Commission's Wildlife Centre, where observation hides are provided for watching duck, deer and blue hares: permits may be obtained from the forest office in Tighnabruaich. There is a picnic place overlooking the Kyles on the edge of the forest. The road runs along the west side of Loch Riddon for seven miles, an extension of the Kyles; there are lovely views to the other side and the island of Eilean Dearg with its castle ruins. ★

The A8003 joins the A886 a mile north of Auchenbreck where the route again lies along the B836 through Clachaig. But instead of taking the direct road to Dunoon, turn left at Sandbank and return round Lazaretto Point on Holy Loch.

Bute

The northern half of Bute lies close to Cowal, between the narrow Kyles of Bute, and two thirds of the island is north of the Highland Boundary Fault which splits it diagonally along the Loch Fad. Yet Bute is mostly Lowland country, gentle and fertile with rich farmland. It is very much an island of the Clyde: most of its population live on the east coast, and far more of its visitors come across from Wemyss Bay than from Cowal.

Rothesay has been a coastal resort for many centuries, since the kings of Scotland regularly used it as place for recuperation. Its heyday was the mid-19th century, when fleets of paddle steamers conveyed the prosperous citizens of Glasgow across the Clyde. Now the ferries are more egalitarian as tens of thousands of holiday-makers make the crossing each year. Rothesay is generally regarded as the Clyde's leading resort. Yet even in July and August, Bute in general and Rothesay in particular have retained a certain dignity. The town's sea front is attractively Victorian, with tall colour-washed houses, gardens and a traffic-free esplanade. But its special character comes from the presence of its Castle among the narrow streets of old houses above the bay.

The first record of **Rothesay Castle** (AM) is in 1230 when it was stormed by the Norwegians; reverting to Scottish kings, it had strategic importance for the next four centuries. Cromwell's troops held it in the 1650s, and it was finally sacked by the Argyll Campbells in 1685, never again to be inhabited. In the 19th century the Marquesses of Bute restored what was still one of Scotland's finest medieval castles. Surrounded by a picturesque moat, it has a round design unique in the country: great circular walls enclose the grassy courtyard where St Michael's Chapel can still be seen, and in the entrance tower the Great Hall survives. The Castle is floodlit at night. The Mansion House nearby, built in 1687, now houses the Bute Estate Office. Opposite, the **Bute Museum** (open daily, closes 4.30pm, shut am Sep to mid-June) gives a comprehensive picture of the island's history, natural history and geology.

From Rothesay, roads lead to all but the north-western tip of Bute. The A886 up the eastern shore passes Port Bannatyne, a rather dour village on **Kames Bay** where yachts anchor. From here it is six miles north to **Rhubodach** and the Cowal ferry.

The A844 coast road south from Rothesay rounds Bogany Point to **Ascog**, with a small uninviting beach, and neat little **Kerrycroy** with a better one. From **Kingarth**, where several roads meet, the B881 goes back to the coast at **Kilchattan**, popular in summer for its fine pink sands. Return to Kingarth and take the unclassified road south towards **Garroch Head**. In a couple of miles the road ends as the hills begin, and a signpost indicates the 10-minute walk to **St Blane's Chapel** which lies in a peaceful wooded hollow. St Blane was born in Bute and founded a monastery here in the 6th century. The monastic remains date from the 12th century. Half a mile north is the Iron Age vitrified fort, **Dunagoil**.

Back on the main road turn left along the flat western side of the island. The A845 heads back to Rothesay past the deep wooded rift that holds **Loch Fad**; the A844 passes **Scalpsie Bay**, with good sands and superb views of the mountains of Arran. In a further two miles **St Ninian's Bay**, commonly called 'Cockle Shore' from the abundance of shellfish, has a large sandy beach facing south and protected by the island of **Inchmarnock**. The next beach, at **Ettrick Bay**, is the most popular on the island. It is more than a mile long, backed by a peaceful farmland; it looks across to Ardlamont Point, with Kintyre beyond. Northward up the coast a narrow road continues four miles through quiet woods, ending at Kilmichael Farm. Little remains of ancient St Michael's Chapel, but there are pleasant views. It's 10 miles back to Rothesay.

Arran

Arran, the 'high island', has dramatic northern peaks visible from many places on the mainland. It lies in the Firth of Clyde, three miles east of Kintyre, but has much in common with the Hebrides – a mild climate that in some places supports sub-tropical plants; a history of standing stones, Celtic saints, Viking raids and Highland Clearances; and a complexity of formation described as 'a complete synopsis of Scottish geology'. Much of its 20 miles by 10 is moor and mountain. Apart from sheep, some cattle farming (and famous strains of potato), Arran's livelihood is tourism: with a great variety of things to see and do, it promotes itself today as Scotland's holiday island. But development has been controlled, and only the main east-coast resorts are at all commercialised.

The great majority of Arran's annual thousands of visitors arrive by car ferry from Ardrossan to **Brodick**, the island's capital. The town is small, and extremely busy during July and August. It is dominated by its splendid castle, and by the peak of Goat Fell (2,866 feet). The old village and **Brodick Castle** (NTS; open 1-5 pm) are on the north side of the bay. This elegnt baronial building, ancient seat of the Hamiltons, dates in part from the 15th and 16th centuries but much of it is Victorian, with richly furnished rooms. Hamilton treasures include silver, porcelain and many notable paintings. The remarkably fine grounds include an extensive woodland garden with one of the finest collections of rhododendrons in the country. The gardens are part of a country park where rangers conduct guided walks for most of the year; and the popular path up Goat Fell starts near the castle. Brodick's interesting **Heritage Museum** (open daily 10.30-1pm, 2-4.30pm) at Rosaburn is a former croft and has a working smithy, a cottage, a stable block and an exhibition of agricultural tools.

Arran's road system is extremely simple. The A841 goes 50 miles round the edge of the island, generally close to the sea and flat, attracting cyclists; two roads cross the middle. From Brodick the B880, known as the **String**, goes 10 miles over to Blackwaterfoot on the west coast. Southward, the recently built main road turns inland over some high ground, giving marvellous views across to Holy Island and, beyond it, the Ayrshire coast, while behind are the mountains of northern Arran. The road regains the coast at **Lamlash**, administrative centre and cheerful holiday resort, strung along its sheltered bay. A small ferry runs to Holy Island, a rugged hump protecting the bay. It has wild goats and peregrines, and is of interest chiefly to the naturalist; on the western shore is a cave with inscriptions, once the home of a Celtic saint.

The next resort, **Whiting Bay**, has been growing since the early days of the Clyde steamers and though popular lacks charm. But from the youth hostel there is a delightful walk along Glenashdale

Burn to a 200-feet waterfall. Two miles on near **Dippin** there are fine views from the great cliffs of Dippin Head; round the south-east corner of the island a lane takes you by a slight detour to the ruined medieval keep of **Kildonan Castle**, from where you can look south past tiny Pladda to the distant mound of Ailsa Craig.

The south-west of Arran is rich in prehistoric remains. At **Kilmory** a path leads to the Torrylin Cairn (and the Torrylin Creamery produces Arran cheese); three miles north, **Carn Ban** is a bigger and better example of a neolithic burial chamber. One mile beyond the quiet inland village of **Lagg**, where palms and other exotic plants flourish, the unclassified road known as the **Ross** comes in from Lamlash down Glen Scorrodale, and in a further mile a short walk leads to the Iron Age fort of Kilpatrick Dun.

The road now runs close to the cliffs of the west coast, with wonderful sea views, and reaches **Blackwaterfoot**, once a smuggling centre, now a quiet resort with a good beach. Two miles north of Drumadoon Point at the end of the bay, the King's Cave is allegedly where Robert the Bruce received his lesson from the industrious spider. Other caves nearby are called his kitchen, stable and cellar. There are more prehistoric remains round here, the most interesting being reached by a track running two miles inland from Tormore: on **Machrie Moor**, the Standing Stones of Tormore are the most impressive visible remains of a large prehistoric site.

The road continues through a number of coastal hamlets; at **Pirnmill**, where pirns (wooden bobbins) used to be made, there is a good sandy beach. The views along here are splendid – westward to Kintyre and eastward to Arran's north-western mountains of which the highest is **Beinn Bharrain** (2,368 feet). **Catacol** has a much-photographed terrace of identical cottages, known as the 'Twelve Apostles', attractively set where a glen meets the bay.

Two miles on you reach north-facing **Lochranza**, where Arran's other car ferry docks from Claonaig on Kintyre. The village, on its sheltered sea loch, is dominated by the ruin of 16th-century Lochranza Castle on a projecting spit of land. Beyond here is wild moorland, inhabited by red deer, ending at the Cock of Arran. The road cuts inland through glorious mountain scenery, descending to the east coast at Sannox Bay. **Sannox** is an attractive village with a good beach: from here there is a fine stiff walk of about eight miles to Brodick up Glen Sannox, over The Saddle among the mountain peaks and down through Glen Rosa. The road keeps to the coast, passing **Corrie**, prettiest of all the villages, and returning through rhododendrons to Brodick.

Accommodation

With the exception of Dunoon, accommodation is spread fairly
thinly about Cowal, and good hotels are rare. On Bute, Rothesay is
the main centre for accommodation. On Arran, hotels, guest houses
and bed and breakfast places can be found all round the coast.

ARDENTINNY
Ardentinny Hotel (GPG)
Tel: Ardentinny (036 981) 209
An unpretentious, cheerful white-painted hotel which enjoys fine
views over Loch Long. The modest public rooms have a traditional
theme. Harry Lauder used to drink here and the bar contains an
ever-growing collection of Lauder memorabilia. Bedrooms are
simple but comfortable; all have bath or shower and tea-making
facilities; TV available.
Open Mar to Oct; 11 bedrooms; ££

STRACHUR
Creggans Inn (GPG)
Tel: Strachur (036 986) 279
Sir Fitzroy and Lady Maclean's comfortable inn on the shores of
Loch Fyne – though the day-to-day running is left to Mrs Huggins,
the manageress. Public rooms are tastefully furnished and
bedrooms are pretty (all have radio, telephone and baby-listening,
and black and white TV is available on request). The views are
tremendous, and there are woodland walks through the Macleans'
estate. Useful literature is provided on what there is to do and see in
the area.
Open all year; 22 bedrooms; from £££

General Information

Activities
BOAT HIRE Possible at a number of places on the mainland and on
the islands.
BOAT TRIPS Beagle Cruises, Tel: Tighnabruaich (0642) 225333;
wildlife cruises round Cowal peninsula.
A Waddell, Tel: Dunoon (0369) 6374; trips from Sandbank to see
the submarines.
The paddle steamer *Waverley* calls at Dunoon, Rothesay and
Tighnabruaich. For trips from Rothesay to the Kyles of Bute, Loch
Riddon and Loch Striven contact Rothesay Tourist Office.
FISHING Salmon in Loch Eck and rivers Cur, Eachaig, Goil and
Ruel, and River Machrie on Arran. Trout in many rivers and lochs.
GOLF Dunoon, Blairmore, Innellan and Tighnabruaich.
On Arran: Blackwaterfoot, Brodick, Corrie, Lamlash, Lochranza

Machrie Bay and Whiting Bay. On Bute: Kingarth, Port
Bannatyne and Rothesay.
PONY TREKKING Innellan, Lochgoilhead, On Arran:
Blackwaterfoot, Brodick, Sannox and Shiskine.
SAILING Yacht charter at several places; sailing and board-sailing at
Carrick Castle and Tighnabruaich.
SQUASH Dunoon. On Arran: Blackwaterfoot.
SWIMMING Dunoon. On Arran: Blackwaterfoot.
TENNIS Dunoon and Innellan. On Arran: Blackwaterfoot,
Brodick, Kildonan, Lamlash and Machrie. On Bute: Rothesay.

Entertainment
Cinema and occasional plays in Dunoon. Occasional plays and
concerts on Arran. Variety shows and other entertainment on Bute.
Scottish evenings, ceilidhs, discos etc in local hotels.

Events
MAY Goat Fell Race.
JUNE Brodick Fiddlers' Rally.
AUGUST Highland Games at Dunoon, Brodick and Rothesay; Corrie
Capers, Arran.

Ferries
Caledonian MacBrayne, Tel: Gourock (0475) 33755: Colintraive to
Rhubodach (Bute), frequent daily services, takes 5 min; Claonaig
(Kintyre) to Lochranza (Arran), 8 times daily, takes 30 min;
Gourock to Dunoon, frequent daily service, takes 20 min. Rothesay
to Wemyss Bay, frequent daily service, takes 30 min.
Western Ferries, Tel: Dunoon (0369) 4452; Gourock to Dunoon
(Hunter's Quay), leaves every half-hour, takes 20 min.

Tourist Information
Dunoon and Cowal Tourist Organisation, Pier Esplanade, Dunoon;
Tel: (0369) 3785
Brodick Tourist Information Centre, The Pier, Brodick;
Tel: (0770) 2140 or 2401
Rothesay Information Centre, The Pier, Rothesay;
Tel: (0700) 2151

Knapdale and Kintyre

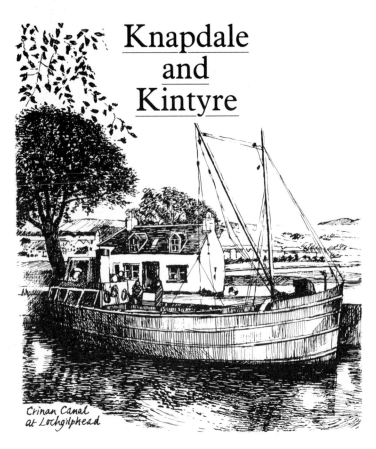

Crinan Canal at Lochgilphead

The western outpost of the Argyll mainland, the peninsula of Knapdale and Kintyre thrusts over 50 miles towards Ireland. Its early history was one of conflict: for many years lordship over it was contested – between the Scots and the Vikings, between the King of Scots and the Lords of the Isles. The Norsemen dominated the western islands and coveted Kintyre, the most desirably fertile area of Argyll. In the late 11th century King Magnus Barefoot (*Barfotr* meant 'bare leg', from his adoption of the kilt) brought his fleet up the Clyde to Tarbert and made a deal: he would accept title to every island round which his ships could sail. Preoccupied with English threats, the Scots agreed – peace in the west was cheap at the price. Magnus then sat at the helm of his galley and under full sail crossed the narrow neck of land from East Loch to West with rollers, ropes and hauling sailors. Kintyre was an island, and Norwegian.

Magnus died five years later and the (unwritten) Treaty of Tarbert was annulled at Perth in 1266, but Kintyre has to some extent never since been 'real Argyll'. It's rolling moor and farm land, except for the windswept, mountainous southern tip of the peninsula, the Mull. Knapdale, north of West Loch Tarbert, has a different character. Its lines all slant, south-west to north-east; long parallel inlets of sea loch slice into its western coast. The 'Knap' of Knapdale means a small sharp hill: the land continues in parallel folds of them to the abruptly straight shore of Loch Fyne. The only unparallel line is that of its northern boundary, the Crinan Canal, built between 1793 and 1801 as the much-needed short cut between the Clyde and the western coast and islands. Tarbert, also surveyed by James Watt in 1770, would have been a fraction of Crinan's nine miles and needed none of its 15 locks – but Crinan had the geographical advantage. The canal was and is a great convenience, but it wasn't designed for ships of the size determined by James Watt's other speciality, steam; today it's used by yachts and pleasure craft, and small fishing vessels.

Across Loch Crinan, Duntrune Castle stands ancient and intact on its rocky promontory. Along with much of Knapdale it was granted to the Argyll Campbells after the Macdonalds lost their title 'Lord of the Isles'; inevitable enemies, these clans supported opposing sides in the 17th century when the Marquess of Montrose fought his Royalist battles against the Covenanters. Duntrune never fell, but was haunted by a Macdonald piper, killed by the Campbells while acting as herald. To the south, Castle Sween was more successfully besieged – Montrose's Macdonald lieutenant burnt the Campbells out.

The peninsula as a whole is not an area of concentrated tourist interest. Its major town is a long way south; the communities dotted down the east coast are mostly small, and quiet even in summer; the beaches of the west beautiful and undeveloped. The attractions are subtle. Incentives draw you round its empty distances: Knapdale's several fingers are areas of solitude; Carradale is lush and lovely, the Mull of Kintyre unique, Castle Sween historic, Crinan delightful, and always there are views. All down the eastern shore of Kintyre the sight of Arran, with Goat Fell dominant, is quite superb. From the west the views are of gentle Islay and the rugged Paps of Jura; and on a clear day you can see across to Ireland, just 12 miles distant from the Mull.

Offshore the three islands of Gigha, Islay and Jura are quite different, each with their own appeal. Gigha is an easy day trip: pleasant strolls and a garden to visit; Jura a more strenuous excursion to a dramatic wilderness. Eric Blair, better known as George Orwell, wrote *Nineteen Eighty Four* on Jura, and died a year after leaving the island. His home there was an isolated house in the north of the island: 'It's quite an easy journey really, except you have to walk the last eight miles'. Quietly prosperous Islay has attractive scattered communities, a great deal of varied coastline and some of the finest Celtic Christian remnants. It's a haven for sportsmen, birdwatchers and lovers of scenic solitude; and it produces some very fine malt whisky.

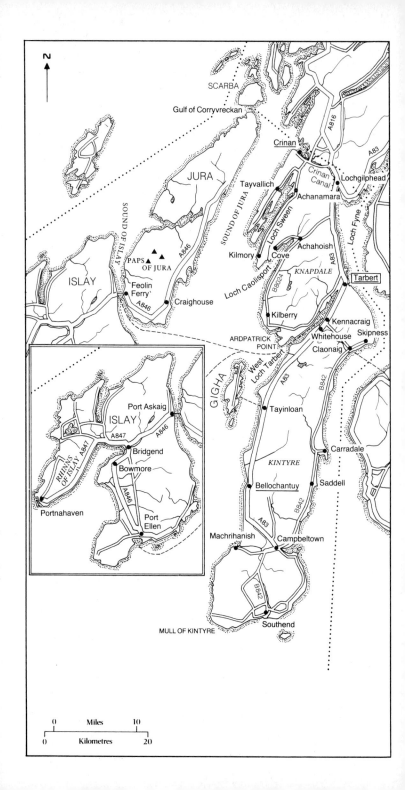

On the narrow isthmus where West Loch Tarbert almost makes an island of Kintyre, Tarbert sits on the sheltered haven of East Loch Tarbert, curving in from Loch Fyne and protected by low green hills. The town's neat stone buildings cluster round the inner harbour, where all is bright and brisk; behind them the tall church tower stands prominent. Like so many strategic places in the Western Highlands, Tarbert has a castle: the ivy-covered remains of a 16th-century keep stand on a 100-foot mound to the south, with much older remnants spread wide. Records go back to the 8th century. Robert the Bruce did a lot of building in 1326 when he was trying to dominate Kintyre – in the process dragging his galley across the isthmus like Magnus Barefoot. He made Tarbert a burgh, the first in Argyll, but the creation lapsed; the place developed as an independent fishing port. Today the fleet is much smaller than in the 19th century but the fishing is still good – Loch Fyne herring are always in demand.

The busy prosperity of Tarbert has come increasingly from holiday sailing traffic, in summer *en route* for the Crinan Canal, and today it is a popular yachting centre and is well placed for touring the lovely scenery of both Knapdale and Kintyre.

Knapdale

Lochgilphead · Crinan · Achanamara · Kilmory
Tayvallich · Achahoish · Cove
Kilberry · Ardpatrick
Tarbert

A fast modern road to Lochgilphead, then a pretty run by the Crinan Canal. A series of single-track beautiful coastal roads follow, two of them dead ends, the one to Balimore very narrow and twisting in parts. A third single-track road goes all the way round the southernmost fringe of Knapdale back to Tarbert. 130 miles in all.

The A83 runs 12 miles beside Loch Fyne, a mainly wooded road without any particular feature of interest apart from the gardens of **Stonefield Castle**, a baronial mansion now a hotel. Two miles beyond Ardrishaig, the southern terminal for the Crinan Canal, is **Lochgilphead**, an appealing market town and administrative centre. It has a wide main street and curved sea front of sturdy painted stone houses, with a long view south towards the Arran mountains.

★ Leave Lochgilphead by the A816 on the north bank of the canal and fork left along the B841. At Cairnbaan the road crosses to the southern bank and stays close to the canal, through gentle pretty scenery, with Knapdale Forest to the south. The B841 and the canal end at **Crinan**, a tiny charming village given over completely to boats, with wonderful views of Jura, Scarba and various islets. ★

The first great slanting split in the west coast of Knapdale is **Loch Sween**: roads run down each side of it; both are dead ends. The eastern road is the narrower and more difficult but is perhaps the more rewarding for the scenery and several features of interest. The B8025 turns south off the B841 two miles east of Crinan; at its junction with an unclassified road is the information centre for Knapdale Forest and the start of many fine walks.

To go down the eastern side of Loch Sween take the unclassified road. Difficult, narrow and twisting at first, after the four miles to the forestry village of **Achanamara** it is less tortuous as well as less wooded. **Castle Sween** (AM) stands on the seashore opposite the island of Danna, in a pretty setting somewhat spoiled by a caravan site. It is one of the earliest square stone castles in Scotland; much has survived including the rectangular 13th-century keep and the 14th-century Macmillan's Tower.

In two and a half miles you reach the little village of **Kilmory**, site of the Chapel of Maelrubha, the ruins of which have been given a glass roof to protect the collection of carved stones, Celtic and later. Outside is Macmillan's Cross, 12 feet high and finely carved. From Balimore a road continues three miles to **Ellary** on Loch Caolisport, but it is private.

For the western side of Loch Sween keep to the B8025, skirting Caol Scotnish, a beautiful wooded arm of Loch Sween, and in seven miles you reach the village and yachting centre of **Tayvallich**. From here you can walk less than a mile across to the grassy curve of **Carsaig Bay**, with its marvellous view of Jura. Woodland gives way to heather and broom as you travel southward to the head of **Loch na Cille**, where you can fork left to reach the tidal island of Danna by a causeway. Two miles off Danna's most southerly point lies the holy island of **Eilean Mor**. The right fork brings you to the end of the road at **Keillmore**. In the roofless but substantial 11th-century chapel of Keills is an extremely interesting collection of sculptured stone slabs; outside is a superb Celtic cross.

Having returned the 17 miles to Lochgilphead take the A83 south again, and in four miles fork right on the B8024, which climbs south-west over the hills and then drops to **Achahoish**. Here you should make a short and beautiful detour round the head of **Loch Caolisport** to St Columba's Cave at **Cove** – a small but most important site. The cave, easily seen from the road, is reputed to have been used by the saint in about 560. In it are an altar with a cross carved in the wall above, two rock basins or fonts, and other indications that mass was celebrated here. From Achahoish, the road follows the east bank of Loch Caolisport and then turns inland. After 10 miles you reach **Kilberry**; just north are the Kilberry

Stones, a collection of carved medieval gravestones.

The road now gives splendid views of the Paps of Jura to the west and the island of Gigha to the south. It descends to the head of **Loch Stornoway** and cuts across **Ardpatrick Point** to West Loch Tarbert, almost opposite the pier from which the Islay ferry sails. There is little other activity on this long quiet loch; the road takes you through peaceful woodland the 10 miles back to Tarbert.

Kintyre

Claonaig · Skipness · Carradale · Saddell · Campbeltown
Southend · Mull of Kintyre · Tayinloan · Whitehouse
Tarbert

A tour notable for the fine views of islands (and Ireland). A fast run along West Loch Tarbert followed by a much slower but scenic road 80 miles across to the east coast of Kintyre and down to the Mull. A good road back up the west coast. About 130 miles.

Head south from Tarbert on the A83 and take the B8001 across to **Claonaig** where the car ferry service to Lochranza on Arran operates in summer. Make a detour of two and a half miles, northward to **Skipness**. Skipness House is not open but more than usual remains to be seen of the square-built **castle**, dating from the 13th century. The enormously thick walls and keep retain their full height, with three projecting towers. Fragments of a chapel of St Columba are incorporated into the castle wall. It was replaced by the larger **St Brendan's Chapel** by the shore, an attractive ruin with tall pointed windows. From here you can walk past a sandy beach to Skipness Point.

The B842 from Claonaig is hilly and winding. It runs inland for most of its course but passes near the lovely bays of **Crossaig** and **Cour** and runs right by the beach at **Grogport**, eight miles south. Then a series of sharp hairpin bends take you up into Carradale Forest, and you descend quickly into the lovely wooded glen of Carradale Water, Kintyre's longest river, which flows into the fine sandy beach of Carradale Bay. **Carradale** itself is a mile or so east along the B879, its hillside houses clustered round the bay; a sheltered harbour faces north. Carradale Point ends in a tidal island bearing a circular vitrified fort. Above the south-facing sands is **Carradale House** with its renowned rhododendrons, and a Forest Centre, the starting point of several walks. To the east there are splendid views of the Arran mountains from this very Highland area. Looking west, inland across the bay, you see Kintyre's highest mountain **Beinn an Tuirc** (1,490 feet).

Four miles south is **Saddell**, a sleepy village in a deep wooded glen, possibly the burial place of Somerled, first King of the Isles.

55

Little remains of **Saddell Abbey**, the important Cistercian monastery founded in the 12th century by his son; but where the choir once stood is an outstanding collection of elaborately carved and ornamented tombstones, one of them said to be Somerled's. The road continues south with views of Arran for 15 miles, past the fine safe beach at **Peninver** on Ardnacross Bay, and through rich farmland to **Campbeltown**.

The deep inlet of Campbeltown Loch with its screening island gives a fine sheltered anchorage, the home of fishing boats and yachts. Campbeltown is a very Highland place, not pretty but with a sturdy independence, the commercial centre for dairy farming country. Its whisky distilleries have dwindled from an odoriferous 34 to two. Tourism grew with the advent of the Clyde steamers and the royal burgh became a holiday resort as well as a thriving working community. Today there is little in particular to recommend it as a holiday base or even an overnight touring stop. The island of **Davaar**, which may be reached except at high tide by a shingle bank called the Dhorlin, has a lighthouse and a more unusual tourist attraction: in a cave on the south coast is a lifesize painting of the Crucifixion, executed in 1887 by a local artist who returned to retouch it in 1934 at the age of 80.

★ At **Machrihanish**, six miles away on the west coast and separated from Campbeltown by the plain known as the Laggan, there are four miles of sand, an excellent golf course and an airfield. Southward from Campbeltown the B842 takes over from the A83 to reach **Southend**, 10 miles away close to the south coast of Kintyre. It is a small village best known for St Columba's Chapel at **Keil** a mile to the west. Outside the ruins, at the west end of the burial ground, two footprints in a rock are attributed to the saint, looking back towards Ireland on his way to Iona in 563. A narrow road runs eight miles to the **Mull of Kintyre**, ending in a precipitous descent to the coast and lighthouse. Cars are prohibited for this last mile but it is a splendid walk, with clear views of Ireland. ★

For the return along the west coast, most rewarding for the views of Islay and Jura, go back 10 miles to Campbeltown and take the A83 across to **Westport**. From here the road hugs the coast for several miles before turning inland through the pretty village of **Glenbarr** and then back to the coast at **Muasdale**, where you may well see some seals, and on to **Tayinloan**, the ferry terminus for **Gigha**.

Heading north, stop at the picnic site on **Ronachan Bay** to watch the grey seals on the inshore reef, from what is known locally as Seal View Point. After **Clachan** the road suddenly climbs steeply over wild moorland to give a marvellous panorama of West Loch Tarbert and its surrounding hills and forests; then it runs through **Whitehouse** and past the ferry terminus for Islay, to Tarbert.

Gigha

It is only a three-mile crossing from Tayinloan to this fertile island with its coastline of rocky bays and its great variety of birdlife. Just to the south of **Ardminish**, the only real community, are the ruins of the 13th-century **Kilchattan Church**; and nearby is the magnificent woodland and gardens of **Achamore House** (NTS). Gigha has a mild climate which allows many sub-tropical plants to grow.

Islay

The terrain of the 'bow-shaped isle' varies from fertile grasslands to wild peat moors, with hills and some splendid craggy coast in the south and east; dairy farming and whisky have been the island's main supports for many centuries. Today it prospers quietly with several hundred farms and eight distilleries, though the population has dwindled (from a 19th-century peak of 15,000) to 4,000. Islay has great attractions: exceptionally varied birdlife, good walking, some fine beaches, and above all, slow-paced peace and quiet.

From **Port Ellen**, an appealing place where the ferry docks, the road eastward passes the remains of **Danavaig Castle**, and after seven miles reaches **Kildalton**, where the tall **Kildalton Cross** from the late 9th century is one of the finest in Scotland. This road, narrower now, ends eight miles on at **Ardtalla**, from where you can walk to the lighthouse at McArthur's Head. The main A846 from Port Ellen runs 10 miles north to **Bowmore**, the island's administrative capital, where the 18th-century church was reputedly built circular so that the devil could find no corner to hide.

From Bowmore, the main road skirts **Loch Indaal**, with **Bridgend** at its head, charmingly set among woodland. The A847 runs 15 miles down the north-west peninsula called the **Rhinns of Islay**, through **Port Charlotte**, with a Museum of Islay Life (closed Sun am) to **Portnahaven** near the point looking across to Ireland. East from Bridgend the A846 crosses a sporting wilderness to reach pretty, isolated **Port Askaig** and the ferry to Jura.

Jura

Jura is mostly impenetrable rugged land, from the **Paps of Jura** (2,500 feet) in the south to its inaccessible northern tip, where the **Gulf of Corryvreckan's** raging tiderace can sometimes be heard for miles. The island is inhabited by red deer and shaggy sheep and about 200 people, mostly living in **Craighouse**. The eastern coast is sheltered, growing palms and fuchsias and rhododendrons; some farming and crofting is possible here, but most of the island is left to sportsmen, climbers and birdwatchers.

Accommodation

Tarbert, Lochgilphead and Campbeltown all have a reasonable amount of accommodation, and Carradale is a pretty spot with some. Elsewhere it's thin on the ground. Jura and Gigha each have one hotel, and the main communities of Islay are well enough provided with accommodation of a modest standard. The hotels we recommend on the mainland are a good balance, both in the standards they offer and as a geographical spread.

BELLOCHANTUY
Putechan Lodge Hotel (GFG)
Tel: Glenbarr (058 32) 266
This former shooting lodge enjoys a splendid position a road's width away from the rocky shore of south-west Kintyre; on a clear day you can see Ireland. The public rooms are comfortable and stylish, decorated with old agricultural implements. The individually decorated bedrooms reach the same standards of comfort; all have radio, TV, tea-making facilities and baby-listening.
There's table-tennis, and the grounds cover seven acres.
Open Mar to early Jan; 12 bedrooms (also 6 self-catering cottages); £

CRINAN
Crinan Hotel (GHG, GPG)
Tel: Crinan (054 683) 235 or 243
A thoroughly comfortable hotel which is in an outstanding position, at the head of the loch where the Crinan Canal reaches the sea. After a disastrous fire some years ago the hotel was refurbished to a very high standard and now displays some of the best of modern design. In addition to the main dining room, there is a rooftop restaurant (and bar) from which there are breathtaking views of rugged Jura and gentler Islay. The bedrooms, some of which have balconies, are as stylish as the public rooms; all have bath or shower, radio, telephone and baby-listening. The hotel has its own boat and runs trips to Seal Island and Jura.
Open mid-Mar to Oct; 22 bedrooms; from ££

TARBERT
West Loch Hotel (GFG)
Tel: Tarbert (08802) 283
Well placed for exploring both ends of the peninsula, this whitewashed old inn stands on the main road at the head of West Loch Tarbert. Though both the public rooms and the bedrooms (no private baths) offer only modest comforts, the food is of a much higher standard and the welcome is warm.
Open all year except Nov; 6 bedrooms; ££

General Information

Activities

BOAT TRIPS For trips from Tarbert, and for trips from Campbeltown to Davaar (and others to Sanda), contact the local tourist offices.

FISHING Salmon in some waters on the mainland and Islay. Trout in many lochs and rivers.

GOLF Carradale, Lochgilphead, Machrihanish, Machrie (Islay) Southend and Tarbert.

SAILING Yachts can be chartered in several places; board-sailing at Ellary.

SQUASH Carradale Hotel.

SWIMMING Campbeltown.

TENNIS Campbeltown.

Entertainment

Cinema in Campbeltown. Traditional entertainment is put on by some hotels and bars.

Events

MAY Tomatin Yacht Race, Tarbert.

JULY Campbeltown Festival; Southend Highland Games.

AUGUST Highland Games at Campbeltown and on Islay.

Ferries

Caledonian MacBrayne, Tel: Gourock (0475) 33755: Claonaig to Lochranza (Arran), 8 times daily in summer, takes 30 min; Kennacraig to Islay, 3 times daily in summer, takes about 2 hours; Tayinloan to Gigha, up to 6 times daily, takes 20 min.
Western Ferries, Tel: Port Askaig (049 684) 681: Port Askaig (Islay) to Jura, 8 to 10 times daily (4 times on Sun, takes 10 min).

Tourist information

Mid-Argyll, Kintyre and Islay Tourist Board, Campbeltown, Tel: Campbeltown (0586) 52056
Centres open summer only: Lochgilphead, Tel: (0546) 2344; Tarbert, Tel: (088 02) 429; Bowmore, Islay, Tel: (0496) 81254

Oban and Lorn

McCaig's Folly, Oban

The shattered coastline of Lorn is 40 miles of sea lochs, sounds and islands, with Oban in the middle the biggest town between Glasgow and Fort William – here and in the many small coastal communities lives the bulk of Lorn's population. Inland from Oban begin the mountain fastnesses of Argyll, Ben Cruachan massive in the centre; in Upper Lorn the empty heights of Appin and Benderloch rise between the long inlets of Lochs Leven, Creran and Etive. To the south, Nether Lorn's smaller hills and scattered lochans are bounded by the forested length of Loch Awe.

The ancient Kingdom of Lorn began in the 5th century, when according to legend Lorn the Irish Celt and his brothers took this and adjacent lands from the Picts. Later their territories together formed the great early Kingdom of Dalriada, whose kings were inaugurated on the sacred 'Stone of Destiny'. When more of Scotland was united and the centre of power shifted, the Coronation Stone was moved to Scone in Perthshire; from there in 1296 Edward I took it to London. Today it lies in Westminster – and Queen Elizabeth II is a descendant of the Dalriadic kings. No longer the hub of power, the very name of Dalriada disappeared: it became remote Argyll. But a symbol remains – the Galley of Lorn. The last Celtic King of Argyll was the mighty Somerled; part Norse himself, he defeated the Vikings at sea and exercised great power in the west of Scotland as King of the Isles. Somerled's grandson Donald is held to be the founder of Clan Donald (for many years Lords of the Isles) and his is the galley which appears on all the Macdonald coats of arms.

Galleys in Oban Bay and royal forces on Kerrera Island recur in the history of Lorn. Somerled's descendants divided his realm, and those whose position was on the mainland owed loyalties both to their Norse blood-ties and to the feudal Scottish monarchy at their back; Lorn remained unassimilated for another century or two. Alexander II of Scotland brought a fleet, but died on Kerrera before he could assert sovereignty over Dunollie, Dunstaffnage or any of a string of western castles. Haakon IV of Norway mustered his ships here, for his final attempt to restore Norse power, only to find some of the island chiefs loyal by then to the King of Scots. By the time Scotland and Norway had finally settled their differences, the Scottish crown had the co-operation of its western seaboard.

The clan history of mainland Argyll is complicated, but the rise to power of the Macdonalds' traditional enemies the Campbells began under Robert the Bruce. The rise was swift: Clan Campbell had the knack of usually backing the winning side. Their war-cry was 'Cruachan', their spiritual home Loch Awe. 'It's a far cry to Loch Awe' expressed wistful exile or defiant confidence – 'but the clan will hear us'. From their new stronghold at Inveraray on Loch Fyne they featured powerfully in later Scottish history. It wasn't just the chiefs who were canny about political cooperation: when in the early 18th century British Army engineers moved into the mountains to build roads, the resentful locals were gradually won over to good relations with the redcoats. Benefits became apparent, and appreciated: 'Had you seen these roads before they were made, You would lift both your hands and bless General Wade'. From various policing activities – checking the cattle thieves – came a sort of independent militia, which was given a new distinguishing tartan based on the Campbell plaid. The Black Watch is the oldest surviving Highland regiment.

Today this heartland of the Highlands is an area of immense contrasts: the bustle of Oban and the elegance of Inveraray; the extraordinary technology of Ben Cruachan's power station and the prehistoric sites round Dunadd Fort; the quiet inland beauty of Loch Awe and the wild and varied appeal of the coast and offshore islands. Few other Highland areas offer such beautiful views from their shores, and the good coastal road means that even the unadventurous motorist can enjoy the splendour. Although it is a fairly compact area, there are old castles to explore, lochside gardens and museums, energetic climbs and idyllic forest walks. And when you have done with the mainland, you simply take to the boats and head for the islands close offshore, across to Mull, round to wonderful Staffa or even as far as the Outer Hebrides. For a touring holiday the area has the advantage of being within easy reach of the picturesque terrain of Loch Lomond and the Trossachs, and the drama of Fort William and Lochaber. For a longer stay the visitor has his choice – activity or entertainment, stimulation or solitude.

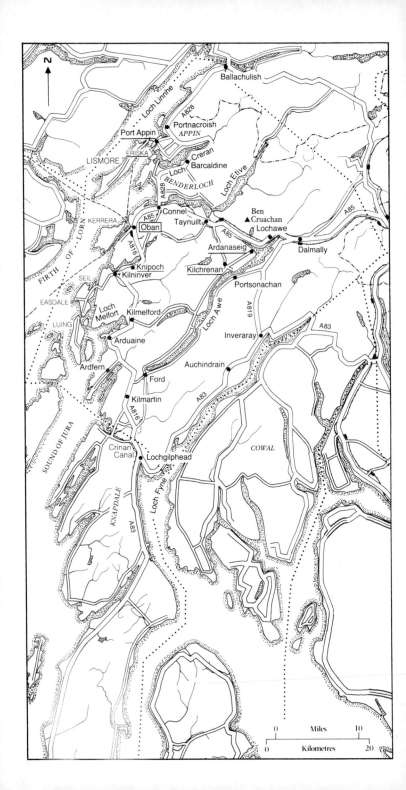

OBAN

'The Gateway to the Isles', 'The Charing Cross of the Highlands' – Oban is an ideally placed touring centre in a superb setting ringed by hills and the Firth of Lorn. To this thriving fishing port the steamboats came about 1850, the railway in 1880; in these 30 years Oban grew into a handsome Victorian town. The sweep of Oban Bay is its focus: protected by the length of Kerrera Island, this is the finest harbour on the west coast, with three piers and ample space for the fishing fleet, the excursion boats, holiday craft, and all the island ferries; from here you can get to the Outer Hebrides as well as Mull and many of the smaller Inner Hebridean islands.

> *'God rules the Scottish Highlands.*
> *And all the land contains -*
> *Except the Western Islands*
> *And they are all MacBrayne's.'*

With its trippery, commercialised air, Oban is by no means a sophisticated place; but for those who flock there by coach, train and car its vitality is the appeal. As a holiday resort, all it lacks is a bathing beach; there's a good one two miles north at **Ganavan** with plenty of facilities. There are hotels and guest houses galore and the town caters for all manner of sports and activities, indoor and out. Glassmaking can be seen at the branch of Caithness Glass, and spinning and weaving at the exhibition in the old woollen mill. There's a large modern concert hall, and a pink granite cathedral by Giles Gilbert Scott. Dominating the town high above the middle of the bay is **McCaig's Folly**, an approximation of the Colosseum; it was erected (though not completed) by an Oban banker to give work to unemployed masons in the 1890s. There's a garden inside its shell, and the views from it are splendid. Views of it are unavoidable and less admired, but it's spectacular when floodlit at night. **Pulpit Hill** above the South Pier is another fine place to stand and gaze over the panorama of town, islands and busy seas.

South of Oban, a coast road runs two miles to **Gallanach**, where a passenger ferry plies to **Kerrera**. This island of beautiful walks and views is worth visiting for the ruin of **Gylen Castle** at the south end, three miles from the ferry but an attractive walk past Horseshoe Bay. The castle was a Macdougall stronghold, impregnable from the sea in a wild cliff setting; it was burnt by Covenanting troops in 1647, and a single tower now stands on its rock pillar. Another road branches west off the A816 three miles south of Oban: it passes the 16th-century restored **Lerags Cross**, and the ruined church at **Kilbride**, ending at Ardentallan House.

The esplanade at Oban's northern end joins the little road skirting the coast to **Dunollie Castle** on its crag, once the Macdougall seat; little remains except the impressive ivy-covered keep. A fort stood on the site as early as the 7th century. South of the ruin, a rock pillar called the Dog Stone is according to legend where the mighty hero Fingal tied his dog Bran.

The Slate Islands and Loch Awe

Kilninver · Seil · Easdale · Luing · Kilmelford · Arduaine
Ford · Portsonachan · Lochawe
Taynuilt · Connel
Oban

A tour of some fine scenery – coast, loch and mountain, including a detour to three islands (one accessible by road, two only by ferry) and a variety of places of interest. Good roads for most of the tour but single-track along Loch Awe; about 120 miles.

The A816 winds its way south from Oban reaching the head of **Loch Feochan** in four miles and skirting its southern shore. At this point, make the 30-mile detour to **Seil**, **Easdale** and **Luing**, the 'Slate Islands', whose quarries are no longer worked. At the fork before **Kilninver** take the narrow B844, which in four miles crosses Seil Sound by the humpbacked Clachan Bridge, built in 1792 to Telford's design and popularly known as 'The Bridge across the Atlantic'.

Now on Seil island, you pass **Balvicar Bay** where the last slate quarries closed only a few years ago and take the right turn to **Ellanbeich**, which has become quite a tourist village with a hotel, cafés, craft shops and boat trips to cater for coach parties. **An Cala Gardens** (open only Mon and Thur pm, Apr to Sep) include rock and water gardens and flower borders. A passenger ferry runs regularly to the island of **Easdale** 150 yards away, once an important industrial area; the slate quarries there and in the adjacent islands employed several hundred workers and in the 18th and 19th centuries were extremely profitable. Easdale is now an artists' colony, very much on the day-trippers' route. From Balvicar the B8003 runs to the southern tip of Seil where another passenger ferry makes the equally short crossing to **Luing**, an island now devoted mainly to breeding cattle. From **Cullipool** there's lobster fishing (and occasional excursion boats) among the maze of islands and channels in the Sound of Luing.

Return to Kilninver and rejoin the A816 as it continues southward through the beautiful Glen Gallain to **Kilmelford**, which is popular with fishermen. It is situated near the head of **Loch Melfort** from where you can reach the old road, now a track, and walk through the spectacular **Pass of Melfort**. Eastward a narrow road climbs to Loch Avich and on to Loch Awe; the main road continues along the southern shore of Loch Melfort, turning south again by **Arduaine Gardens** (open only Sat to Wed). Attached to a baronial castle of 1856, they have been laid out on a promontory jutting between Loch Melfort and the Sound of Jura. They will appeal primarily to horticulturists, but keen amateurs should visit them for the rhododendrons and many rare trees and shrubs. There are tracks up the hillside and down to the sea, and good views over the scores of islands. Four miles on, the B8002 strikes off down the side of **Loch Craignish** through the pretty little village of **Ardfern**. On a windy day, go to the end of this road and walk to Craignish Point (an easy mile) to watch spectacular seas.

Continue south along the A816 over some dramatic high ground; visible west of the next road junction are the ruins of **Carnasserie Castle** (AM), built in the 16th century, sacked in the 17th, with enough detail remaining to give a very good idea of the original fortified house. The tower walk gives wide views along **Kilmartin Glen**, leading to Loch Awe. The route now lies this way: turn east along the B840, passing little Loch Ederline. Three miles on, from **Ford**, good roads run along both sides of **Loch Awe**; each has its special advantages (we cover the road along the western side of the loch in the next tour). For the route along the eastern shore, stay on the B840 which passes through woods of deciduous trees allowing beautiful views of one of Scotland's loveliest lochs. Loch Awe is 22 miles long, and increases in beauty from south to north.

Two miles from Ford, the ruin perched at the water's edge is **Fincharn Castle**, once a Campbell stronghold; eight miles on at the village of **Portinisherrich** a large gap in the forest allows uninterrupted views of the loch and of two islets with ruins, the southern of a chapel, the northern of another Campbell castle. The forest shortly ends and the landscape becomes more open. At **Portsonachan**, where the loch is at its narrowest, a ferry used to run across to Kilchrenan to convey drovers and their cattle and, during the troubles of 1745, soldiers to their barracks. The old drovers' inn at Kilchrenan is now a hotel – see 'Accommodation'. Now the scenery becomes more spectacular as the northern mountains come into view. At **Cladich** you meet the Inveraray road and enjoy a close view of the seven peaks of **Ben Cruachan**, the highest rising to 3,689 feet. Turn north up the A819, and in two miles you see in the middle of the loch the holy island of **Inishail** ('Isle of Rest') with its ruined 13th-century chapel; beside it are two exceptionally fine gravestones. Island burial grounds like this one were adopted partly to avoid scavenging wolves; there were many in the Highlands in the 16th century. To the north, another island, **Fraoch Eilean**, has the remains of a 12th-century castle. To explore these islands (and others in this broad northern part of the loch) enquire about boat hire on the other shore, at the village of **Lochawe**.

Turn left at the T-junction on the A85 and at the head of the loch walk the half mile to **Kilchurn Castle** (AM) set on its jutting spit of land, seeming to rise dramatically straight out of the water. It's not possible to explore the ruins fully, but they are an impressive sight; Wordsworth was inspired. The keep was originally a lone tower, built in 1440 by the founder of the Breadalbane Campbells. The walls on the south and north sides were added 250 years later.

In a couple of miles, just after Lochawe with its jetty, you pass the curious church of St Conan, first built in 1886 and tinkered with for another 20 years by its designer, an architect Campbell. The main tower is Saxon, the smaller tower from Picardy, one chapel is Decorated and another early Norman. An effigy of Robert the Bruce lies in the Bruce Chapel. A random collection of genuine ancient pieces may also be found in this jigsaw-puzzle church.

★ As the road, railway and River Awe enter the narrow **Pass of Brander**, you reach the private road, open only to walkers, which leads to the dam 1,315 feet above sea level at the south end of **Cruachan** reservoir. A Visitor Centre by the main road has displays explaining the Loch Awe hydro-electric scheme, and minibuses take visitors along the tunnel nearly a mile long leading to the underground pumped storage power station of Cruachan. Of the many hydro-electric schemes in the Highlands this is probably the most interesting for tourists to visit. The Pass itself is a formidable six miles, oppressive even today, between towering wooded crags and cliffs; here in 1308 the Macdougalls tried to ambush Robert the Bruce, but he outwitted them in a decisive rout. ★

You emerge at **Taynuilt**. Here and at neighbouring **Bonawe** there were great iron-smelting works in the 18th century, importing ore and labour from England but felling local forests for charcoal. The furnace at Bonawe has been restored and preserved. Taynuilt claims to have manufactured the cannon and shot for the Battle of Trafalgar; when the workmen heard of Nelson's death they immediately erected an ancient standing stone behind the village church, inscribed as a monument – Nelson's earliest, preceding his burial in St Paul's, let alone his column in Trafalgar Square. Cruises run daily from Taynuilt pier to **Upper Loch Etive**, which is of the utmost beauty and is otherwise inaccessible except to walkers – apart from the head of the loch which can be reached by the Glen Etive road from Kingshouse.

Seven miles on at **Connel**, Loch Etive narrows near its mouth at the **Falls of Lora**, which are more rapids than waterfall. The main road leads back to Oban via Dunstaffnage (see next tour). As a variation for the return on this route, take the unclassified road to the left under the railway line and follow a small glen up to **Barranrioch**, where you turn right for Oban.

Inveraray and inner Argyll

Dunstaffnage · Dalmally · Inveraray · Auchindrain
Lochgilphead · Kilmartin · Ford · Kilchrenan
Taynuilt · Connel
Oban

A tour which takes in several fine places of interest and a lovely town. Mostly good roads, but narrow along Loch Awe. About 125 miles in all.

Leave Oban by the A85 and three miles north at **Dunbeg** turn left to see **Dunstaffnage Castle** (AM) on a promontory overlooking Dunstaffnage Bay and the mouth of Loch Etive. Its massive and well-preserved walls and buttress towers give a good idea of the 13th-century stronghold. Robert the Bruce took it when he defeated the Macdougalls of Lorn; the Campbells of Loch Awe became its hereditary keepers, their burial place the adjacent chapel. Cromwell's troops occupied it, Atholl burned it, Flora Macdonald was briefly its prisoner. Its worst disaster was a fire in 1810, destroying the whole interior.

Drive on 20 miles through Connel and Taynuilt to Kilchurn Castle (see previous tour); a mile beyond is the village of **Dalmally**, popular with anglers and with climbers – **Ben Cruachan** and **Ben Lui** (3,700 feet) are not far away. The church on an island in the river is a fine example of a 'round' church of the 18th century. About a mile and a half to the south-west, along the old road to Inveraray, the temple-like building that serves as a monument to Duncan Ban MacIntyre (most famous of Gaelic bards) affords a wonderful view over Loch Awe. The route now lies along the modern road, the A819, which swings away southward from Loch Awe at Cladich where there are good views of the seven peaks of Ben Cruachan. The road climbs quickly to the summit of the pass (675 feet) and descends to Loch Fyne and Inveraray, through the beautifully wooded **Glen Aray**, passing the Castle Fisheries with its fish ponds, lakes, hospital and pets' corner.

★ The Royal Burgh of **Inveraray** is an excellent touring centre, but above all it's a beautifully planned and preserved Georgian town of sturdy black and white buildings with a wonderful 18th-century castle. The first castle was built in 1415 by the warring Colin Campbell (called Cailean Mor, 'the great Colin') and ever since the fortress and Inveraray and the Campbells have more or less shared the same fortunes. Chiefs became earls, earls became dukes, and 'Campbell of Argyll' became the most powerful name in Scotland. The prosperity faded, and by the mid-18th century the castle had become dilapidated; in 1745 the third duke decided to build a new home. Over the next 20 years the old town disappeared completely and the elegant layout seen today was built half a mile to the south. Well apart on the old site rose the new Gothic-revival castle. The embellishing short conical spires on its towers were added after a fire in 1877. In 1975, a more serious fire caused enormous damage to the rich interior; restoration was financed partially by an appeal sent out to Campbells everywhere. The most important treasures survived, and the State Rooms on show are as impressive as ever, with a magnificent array of weapons most appropriately dominant. There are attractive woodland walks in the grounds. (The castle is open Apr to Oct, but closed Sun am, lunch and Fri in Sep.) The town was planned by Roger Morris and completed by Robert Mylne. The **Church** was divided into two parts: one for English, one for Gaelic services. The tall separate bell-tower of pink granite, added this century, contains a full peal of ten bells; climb up past them for its panoramic view. ★

Off the A83 north of the castle, a good road goes a mile up the west side of **Glen Shira** through deciduous woodland, and then a track leads to Rob Roy's cottage on the bank of the River Shira. South of Inveraray, the A83 stays close to the shore of Loch Fyne for about three miles, passing **Argyll Wildfowl Centre**, then swings inland to reach in a further three miles the **Auchindrain Museum of Farming Life** (open daily June to Aug). In this fascinating open-air museum a joint-tenancy farm township has been restored. Buildings of the 18th and 19th centuries have been given period furnishings and all aspects of rural life are illuminated with the help of live demonstrations and audio-visual displays.

The road joins the lochside again at **Furnace**, where there is an abandoned 18th-century iron-smelting works and a granite quarry. In three miles you reach **Crarae Gardens**, a woodland paradise of flowering shrubs and rare trees, especially notable for rhododendrons and azaleas. The road continues 11 miles through Asknish Forest, past the head of lovely Loch Gair, to enter the area covered in the previous chapter. At **Lochgilphead** turn north alongside the Crinan Canal, and in two miles fork right to stay on the A816.

In less than three miles a turning to the left leads to a rocky knoll, 176 feet high, in the middle of Mhoine Mor, 'The Great Moss'. This is **Dunadd Fort**, the seat of power in western Scotland from about AD500 until Kenneth MacAlpin conquered the Picts in 843 and moved his capital – and his Coronation Stone – to Scone. Dunadd was capital of the ancient Kingdom of Dalriada, founded by Christian Celts from Ireland; St Columba probably officiated at a coronation here. On the central rock are carved the symbols of the inauguration of kings. The wide-ranging views over the hill's flat approaches show even today the natural strategic importance of this site.

North of Dunadd the area is an archaeologist's dream, scattered with innumerable remains, some not yet fully excavated – chambered cairns, stone circles, burial cists, rocks inscribed with ritual markings. The best-known concentrations are around **Nether Largie** and near **Kilmartin**.

Two miles north of Kilmartin turn east again along the B840 and, from **Ford**, take the road along the north-west side of **Loch Awe**. (The route along the opposite shore is described in the previous tour.) The road runs almost continuously through the pine and spruce of **Inverliever Forest**, with a wide choice of forest walks (details from the forest office at **Dalavich**, eight miles along). Near the foot of the loch are **Ardanaiseig Gardens**, among the finest in West Scotland, with fine views across Loch Awe to Ben Lui and Cruachan: Ardanaiseig House is now a luxury hotel (see 'Accommodation'). From **Kilchrenan**, the B845 takes you up over a watershed and down attractive **Glen Nant** to Taynuilt (see previous tour). The return to Oban via Connel is a distance of 12 miles.

Benderloch and Appin

Connel · Barcaldine · Port Appin · Lismore · Portnacroish
Barcaldine · Loch Etive
Oban

A fairly short tour which stands out for the fine coastal scenery and which includes an island detour. Easy roads throughout, but single-track for the 10 miles or so when you leave the coast to explore the heart of Benderloch. About 75 miles.

Follow the A85 to **Connel**, and take the A828 across the bridge over the **Falls of Lora** into the district of **Benderloch**, a peninsula jutting westward into the Lynn of Lorn opposite the island of Lismore. Most of the beaches of its many bays are stony, but the beach by **Ledaig** has plenty of sand. In three miles the road reaches the south shore of **Loch Creran**, and runs nine miles along its bending course to its head. Off its southern shore near **Barcaldine** is the **Sea Life Centre**: visitors walk over and round huge tanks filled with octopuses, sharks and conger eels, an encapsulated underwater world. At Barcaldine village the Forest Centre at the junction with the B845 has details of the many forest walks in the area. At the head of the loch, a road runs three miles up **Glen Creran**, merging into a track leading to Ballachulish. As you round the head of the loch you enter the district of **Appin**, famous for the Appin murder.

The victim, Colin Campbell the Red Fox, lived in a house in Glen Ure which branches off Glen Creran.

★ Soon after **Creagan** you go through the broad valley of **Strath Appin**. At **Tynribbie**, leave the A828 for a detour to **Port Appin**, a peaceful place with lovely views and coastal walks. A passenger ferry sails regularly to **Lismore** less than a mile away. The snag with this ferry is that it lands you in the remote north of the island. The car ferry (there is only one road of consequence) from Oban takes longer but lands more conveniently at **Achnacroish** in the middle of the island. Lismore is about 10 miles long and one and a half miles wide and deserves a visit if only for the magnificent views it gives of the mountainous mainland. In Gaelic its name means 'great garden', and it is indeed a green and fertile place of trees and grassy valleys. ★

Back on the A828 you come to **Portnacroish**. On a tiny island opposite and just offshore stands the romantic **Castle Stalker** (not open), supposedly built for James IV to use as a hunting lodge. It's older name is Caisteal Stalcair, meaning 'Castle of the Hunter'. The castle is picturesquely set, and has a vivid and frequently violent history – a granite stone in Portnacroish churchyard carries a graven account of 'the bloody battle of Stalc' in 1468. The massive four-storey keep with outdoor staircase, built in the 16th century, became dilapidated in the last century but has recently been restored. As you continue north close to the shore of Loch Linnhe you pass **Shuna Island**, which has its own ruined castle. The road continues to Ballachulish (see Fort William chapter) 12 miles beyond Portnacroish.

For the return journey go back along the A828 but turn left at Barcaldine onto the B845 through **Barcaldine Forest**. You climb through **Gleann Salach** to the top of the pass, with Loch Etive far below, and Ben Cruachan towering beyond. Turn west at the T-junction, to visit the remains of **Ardchattan Priory** (AM) in the grounds of an 18th-century house. The priory was founded by the Macdougalls in 1230 and here Robert the Bruce is traditionally said to have held the last Gaelic-speaking national council. Cromwell's troops burnt it in 1654. The gardens beside Loch Etive include herbaceous borders and a shrub garden. A five-mile drive along the north shore of Loch Etive returns you to Connel, five miles from Oban.

Accommodation

An area which has a surprising number of highly recommendable hotels, and where finding accommodation is not difficult. Although Oban is where you have the widest choice of accommodation, the hotels we recommend are out in the countryside. They all enjoy marvellous settings overlooking loch or sea, and range from a luxurious baronial mansion to two old ferry inns.

ERISKA
Isle of Eriska Hotel (GFG, GHG)
Tel: Ledaig (063 172) 371
A low-lying, 300-acre privately-owned island, joined to the mainland by a bridge, is the setting for this Victorian baronial mansion, run with great warmth by the Buchanan-Smiths. The public rooms are hospitably furnished. The bedrooms vary in size from spacious to cramped, and have both modern and traditional furniture; all have bath, radio, baby-listening, telephone and tea-making facilities. Dinners are six courses with a choice only at the first; and there are plenty of sports facilities for you to work off the effects of any over-eating – tennis, sea fishing, pony-trekking and croquet; there is a slipway for boats, and a yacht you can charter.
Open mid-Feb to end Nov; 17 bedrooms; £££££

KILCHRENAN
Ardanaiseig (GFG, GHG)
Tel: Kilchrenan (086 63) 333
A dignified 19th-century mansion in an exceptionally lovely situation on the shore of Loch Awe, some four miles from Kilchrenan; its gardens rank among the finest in west Scotland. It is run in an enthusiastic, efficient and friendly way by the Yeos, and everything is of the highest quality. Public rooms are stylish and extremely comfortable. Bedrooms are individually furnished; all have bath, radio, colour TV and telephone. Facilities include billiards, fishing, tennis and croquet.
Open Easter to mid-Oct; 14 bedrooms; no children under 8; from £££££

Taychreggan (GFG, GHG)
Tel: Kilchrenan (086 63) 211
Set right at the edge of Loch Awe, a lovely old inn, stable block and modern extension set round a courtyard make up this charming hotel. Public rooms are attractively furnished in modern style. Bedrooms are more varied in character; all have bath, radio and baby-listening. There are 25 acres of grounds, and hotel boats and board-sailers, as well as fishing.
Open Easter to mid-Oct; 17 bedrooms; £££

KNIPOCH
Knipoch Hotel
Tel: Kilninver (085 26) 251
Six miles south of Oban, set back across the main A816 from the
head of Loch Feochan. The original 16th-century house has been
much extended, but the additions are in keeping; all is painted
mustard. The elegant panelled reception hall and comfortable
lounge, with their hefty modern Chesterfields and reproduction
furniture, are in the country house style. Bedrooms are comfortable
and airy, with attractive fabrics and reproduction furniture; all have
bath colour TV, telephone and radio.
Open all year (not Jan); 21 bedrooms; ££££££

PORT APPIN
Airds Hotel (GFG, GHG)
Tel: Appin (063 173) 236
One of the best kinds of hotel: a splendid old ferry inn where you
can rely on comfort, good food, willing service and a warm
atmosphere. In a superb position, overlooking Loch Linnhe with
views across to the mountains of Morvern, the hotel has homely
lounges, a pleasing dining room and welcoming bedrooms.
Open end Mar to Nov; 17 bedrooms; £££

General information

Activities
BOAT HIRE Available at many places.
BOAT TRIPS From Oban to Torosay Castle, Mull, N Johnston,
Tel: Oban (0631) 63138. Caledonian MacBrayne also run trips
from Oban to: Staffa and Iona, Glen More and Iona, Tobermory,
Coll and Tiree and Colonsay, Tel: Oban (0631) 62285. For cruises
on Loch Etive, Tel: Taynuilt (086 62) 280. For cruises from
Luing, Tel: Luing (085 24) 282.

FISHING Salmon and trout in many lochs and rivers.
GLIDING Connel.
GOLF Oban.
PONY-TREKKING Appin, Ardoran, Barcaldine, Kilmelford, North Connel and Taynuilt.
SAILING Yacht charter, sailing and watersports possible at a number of places in the area.
SQUASH Oban.
SWIMMING Oban.
TENNIS Oban.

Entertainment
Cinema, variety shows and occasional plays and concerts at Oban. Scottish evenings and dancing at local hotels, with lots happening in Oban.

Events
JULY Highland Games at Inveraray and Taynuilt
AUGUST Argyllshire Gathering and Oban Highland Games; West Highland Yachting Week.

Ferries
Caledonian MacBrayne, Tel: Oban (0631) 62285, from Oban:
Craignure (Mull) several times daily, takes 45 min; Tobermory several times a week, takes nearly 3 hours (passenger only); Colonsay, several times a week, takes 2½ hours; Coll and Tiree, about 3 times a week; Barra and Lochboisdale, daily (not Tue) takes 5½ hours; Lismore, 5 times daily (not Sun).
Port Appin to Lismore, 9 times daily, takes 10 min;
Tel: Appin (063 173) 217
Oban to Kerrera, 6 times daily (not Sun), takes 5 min;
Tel: Oban (0631) 63665
Seil to Luing, frequently daily service, takes 5 min;
Tel: Balvicar (085 23) 252

Tourist information
Oban, Mull and District Tourist Board, Argyll Square, Oban,
Tel: (0631) 63122
Centre open summer only at Inveraray, Tel: (0499) 2063

Mull and Iona

Tobermory

Mull is the third largest Hebridean island; it has a claim to being the wettest, at least in its central uplands; and it is a lovely place. Thousands of visitors each summer – many making straight across to Iona – do not spoil the spacious beauty of its more remote areas. When the day-trippers have left even popular Tobermory, the island's main community, is calm and uncrowded.

The main car ferry route is from Oban to Craignure, about 20 miles south-east of Tobermory. Car ferries also make the much shorter crossing from Lochaline, on the remote Morvern peninsula (see Fort William), to Fishnish, a few miles north of Craignure. But for a day-trip, a car is an expensive luxury; two of the island's main sights are near Craignure, and there are buses to Tobermory timed to connect with arriving boats. In summer there are special daily excursions from Oban to the east-coast castles and the island's capital (as well as the ferry which calls *en route* to Coll and Tiree). You can even get to Mull from Ardnamurchan: a passenger ferry runs between Kilchoan and Tobermory.

Mull is a very unspoilt island and considerably less commercialised than Skye. It is fairly distinctly divided into two halves, the dividing line running across a narrow neck of land between Salen and Loch na Keal. The north is where most tourist development (and afforestation) has taken place, but some of the finest scenery is to be found in the south. Inland the island has large areas of soggy emptiness – 'a hilly country,' recorded Boswell, 'diversified with heath and grass, and many rivulets.' Dr Johnson thought it dreary – 'a most dolorous country'. But the north-east shore offers fine vistas of wild mainland peninsulas only a mile or two distant; and the long irregular coastline of the west and south is particularly beautiful, with magical ever-changing views out over the scattered rocks and islands, and many splendid beaches.

In the early 19th century Mull had over 10,000 inhabitants and a thriving kelp industry, but the collapse of this followed by the eviction of the crofters from their land brought an age of emigration and a massive decline in the population. Today there is some crop farming and crofting in the south, and lobster fishing off the west coast, but sheep have predominated since the Clearances; forestry, and increasingly tourism, are the main sources of employment for the present population of under 2,000.

For the holiday-maker the island is a place to relax; the pace is unhurried, and peace and quiet unlimited. Its capital is one of the most charming little towns in the Highlands; its other communities are small, often tiny. There are two castles and the occasional museum, but most of the attractions are outdoors. Roads are narrow, often single-track, but traffic is far from heavy. There is good walking, principally of a fairly gentle nature; and even the inexperienced can make it to the top of Ben More, the island's highest mountain at 3,169 feet.

One of the pleasures of a stay on Mull (and for those staying in or near Oban on the mainland) is the choice of islands to visit off the west coast. The holy island of Iona is just half a mile from the shores of the Ross of Mull. Extraordinary Staffa, whose Fingal's Cave inspired Mendelssohn and which in the words of Horace Walpole: 'proves that nature loves Gothic architecture', is only a few miles from the west coast; and boat trips also take in the Treshnish Isles.

Colonsay (and tiny Oronsay), Coll and Tiree are farther flung. Coll and Tiree are neighbours, seven miles west of Mull, and are served by ferry from Oban which calls at Tobermory. Colonsay, 10 miles south of Mull, is reached only from Oban. All three enjoy a favourable climate thanks to the gentle massaging of the Gulf Stream; and, whereas it can be hard to get away from it all on Iona, there is no difficulty finding solitude on these islands.

> *'When death's dark stream I ferry o'er*
> *A time that surely shall come;*
> *In Heaven itself I'll ask no more,*
> *Than just a Highland welcome.'*
> Robert Burns, *A verse .... on taking leave*

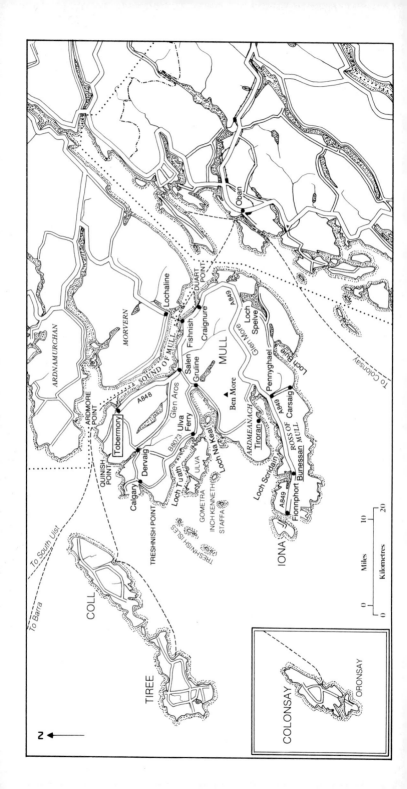

TOBERMORY

At the northern end of the Sound of Mull, the island's only town Tobermory is set round a lovely bay, sheltered by Calve Island, and one of the safest (and most popular) Hebridean anchorages. Somewhere at the bottom lies a Spanish galleon, sunk here after the Armada. Several attempts have been made to retrieve the treasure the ship was carrying; some objects have been recovered but the 30-feet layer of clay has thwarted most of the divers' efforts.

Because of the arbitrary movements of the herring shoals, Tobermory never became a fishing port; but it owes its style, like Ullapool (see West Ross chapter) to the British Fisheries Society who, in the late 18th century, developed the place and built attractive houses and shops along the harbour, at the foot of the gentle wooded slopes which surround the bay. This long curve of brightly painted stone buildings, some shabby, some immaculate, is very picturesque, and with the harbour packed full of visiting yachts in summer invites strolling in an almost Continental atmosphere.

Although right in the north of the island, Tobermory is a good base to choose on Mull because of its vivacious charm. There is plenty of accommodation and though its 'sights' do not extend beyond its appealing small folk museum there are other things to do – boating, fishing, golf; and half a mile east of the town is **Aros Park**, a drive-in forest park with cliff walk, play area and rhododendron collection.

Mull – the complete circuit

Dervaig · Calgary · Gruline · Tiroran · Bunessan
Fionnphort · Loch Buie · Duart
Craignure · Salen
Tobermory

A tour best tackled over two (or more) days. The west, from Dervaig to the Ross of Mull, is the prettiest part, but in the east there are two castles to visit. Narrow roads throughout this 150-mile tour except for the last 20 miles or so from Craignure north to Tobermory.

The northern end of Mull is windswept and deserted, but a minor road does go from Tobermory to Glengorm Castle on the **Mishnish** headland. From this impressive pile (not open) you can walk the cliffs to **Ardmore Point**. The B8073 from Tobermory climbs inland over grassy moorland, past the three Mishnish lochs, and south of the wild area of Quinish, to **Dervaig** at the head of Loch a'Chumhainn. It's a pretty little place, with white houses and a round-steepled church. The village is the home of the Little Theatre of Mull; and a mile south is the **Old Byre Heritage Centre**, a well-presented museum of crofting history with good reconstructions of old croft houses (temporarily closed).

As the B8073 continues westward a side road runs a mile north up the Mornish peninsula to **Croig**, where the pier is a reminder of the days when cattle from the outer isles were unloaded here to be driven across Mull and re-embarked for Oban. There are superb views across to Eigg and Rhum and the mountains of Skye. The main road reaches the west coast at **Calgary**, where a curving bay of pale shell-sand is backed by wooded hills. Popular belief has it that emigrants from here founded the Canadian city of Calgary. From here there are boat trips to Staffa and the Treshnish Isles. The road cuts south across the **Treshnish** headland to the northern shore of **Loch Tuath** at **Burg**, where there are yet more splendid views – the indented coast and a scatter of islands: Ulva and Gometra very close, Staffa and Iona in the far distance. At **Kilninian** the graveyard has a medieval slab carved with the figure of a Highland chieftain; at **Ballygown** the remains of a broch can be seen on the right of the road.

★ The narrow road winds down through woods to the head of Loch Tuath and the **Sound of Ulva**, where the privately-owned island of Ulva is only 200 yards distant. The drive round **Loch na Keal** is beautiful, with high wild country inland. At the head of the loch is the hamlet of **Gruline**, where at Gruline House is the mausoleum of Lachlan Macquarrie, the first governor of New South Wales, sometimes called the 'father of Australia', who was born on Ulva. From near Gruline the B8035 crosses the narrow waist of the island, two miles to **Salen** on the east coast (and 12 back to Tobermory). Along the south side of Loch na Keal the scenery is still more spectacular with **Ben More** (3,169 feet), Mull's highest mountain, prominent on the left; the easiest route to the summit starts along here from Dhiseig, and takes about two and a half hours. As you reach the sea the tilted black block that is **Staffa** comes into view, unmistakable among the islands. The road now swings south opposite another privately-owned island, **Inch Kenneth**, under the dramatic Gribun Rocks – in the hamlet of **Gribun** you can still see the massive boulder which obliterated one of the row of cottages. You can walk from here a mile down the coast to the Gribun Cliffs, where at low tide (and with a torch) you can explore **Mackinnon's Cave**, vast and deep, subject of local legends. The road cuts five miles inland across the wild headland of **Ardmeanach** to **Loch Scridain**. No cars may go further west than **Tiroran**; the intrepid take the tricky shore route round to 'The Wilderness' to see MacCulloch's tree, a fossil tree in the cliff, engulfed by lava 50 million years ago. It's a three-hour walk over National Trust land, from their office at Tiroran. ★

At the head of Loch Scridain the B8035 meets the A849; turn west down the long **Ross of Mull** which has some delightful scenery and in particular a number of lovely bays. At **Pennyghael** a narrow winding road cuts four miles across to one of the few easily accessible points on the south side of the Ross, **Carsaig**. There are some large houses among the trees here, a picturesque stone pier and good scenery. **Bunessan** at the head of a large bay, about 10 miles west of Pennyghael, is the main village of the area. Another narrow road runs south from here to a good sandy beach, the only accessible one of many along this coast. The main road ends at **Fionnphort**, the ferry terminal for Iona (see next page). South of here is a lovely beach at **Fidden**.

Return from Fionnphort the 18 miles along the Ross of Mull on the A849, and continue 11 miles through **Glen More**. This is a dramatic drive with mountains and hills close all round the winding road. Dr Johnson travelling westward through this lonely stretch found its boggy terrain depressing. He had lost his precious oak stick and was convinced it had been stolen: 'it is not to be expected that any man in Mull, who has got it, will part with it. Consider, Sir, the value of such a *piece of timber* here!'. At **Strathcoil**, take the unclassified road south through a glen and past **Loch Spelve** and **Loch Uisg** among lovely woodland and rhododendrons to **Loch Buie**. Beyond the battlemented 14th-century Moy Castle (not open) there is an excellent sheltered sandy beach, surrounded by lush greenery.

Returning to the main road and skirting the head of Loch Spelve, you come in quick succession to two castles, both of which can be reached by special boat trips from Oban. The first, **Duart Castle**, is reached by a turning on the right. The castle, ancient home of the Macleans, is splendidly set on a rocky promontory overlooking the Sound of Mull: its name means 'black height'. Built in the 13th century, it was virtually a ruin when Sir Fitzroy Maclean, 27th of his line and former Chief Scout, bought it in 1912 and fully restored it. The original keep has been preserved and rooms arranged in various styles are shown, with many relics of the Macleans (though Sir Fitzroy and Lady Maclean live in Strachur House – see Cowal chapter) and a scouting exhibition. The views from the battlements are marvellous. On the wooded inner shore of Duart Bay, the second castle is a 19th-century mansion; **Torosay Castle** has various Victorian rooms, a remarkable collection of stags' heads, family portraits and scrapbooks. It's pleasantly un-Stately. The gardens, Italian in style, include Venetian statues.

Craignure, a mile to the north, has nothing more to offer than the car ferry to Oban, a large modern hotel and an old inn. At Fishnish Bay, soon after the road branches off for the ferry to Lochaline, the road becomes double-track; but pause nevertheless at **Pennygown**, where in the ruined chapel stands the shaft of a Celtic cross with particularly lovely carvings. The road reverts to single-track after **Salen**, Mull's central point. Well placed for exploring all parts of the island, Salen's few buildings include a hotel, and there's a lane which leads down to a quiet pier. A mile north on a promontory of Salen Bay is the ruin of **Aros Castle**, built in the 13th century, part of a defensive chain along the coast of Lorn. A road runs west up **Glen Aros** over green moors to Dervaig. The main road continues north, with beautiful views over the coast, 10 miles on to Tobermory.

Iona

To the island of Iona in 563 St Columba came from Ireland, to found a monastery and spread Christianity throughout much of northern Scotland. Iona was his base for 34 years, became for a time the Christian centre of Europe, and still is a most venerated place of pilgrimage. Hundreds of thousands of visitors each year land on its three miles by one; most go no further than the eastern shore, to its famous religious buildings. Explore further and you will find small-scale charm. On the northern tip of the island there is a succession of white sand beaches; there's another beach on the western side, and there are some attractive sandy bays a short walk south from the pier. The southern part of the island is wild and pleasant, though sometimes boggy. Apart from the tiny village by the pier, there are few houses, almost none in the south.

Abbey, then cathedral, succeeded St Columba's vanished monastery. In 1899 the 8th Duke of Argyll presented the dilapidated buildings to the Church of Scotland. Over the years both the cathedral and the monastic buildings have been restored, much of the work having been carried out by the Iona Community founded in 1938. After a walk of less than half a mile from the jetty where you land, the first building you come to is the 13th-century Nunnery, a beautiful ruin composed mainly of pink granite. The oldest surviving building is the 11th-century St Oran's Chapel; in its cemetery Scottish kings, including Duncan and Macbeth, lie buried. The Cathedral Church of St Mary dates mainly from the early 16th century but there are some remains of Norman work. The former Infirmary is now a museum, containing a fine collection of Celtic crosses and various stones.

The Iona Community has about 150 resident members plus about 1,000 young people who come to stay in the course of each year. For them Iona is a place of peace and inspiration, despite the crowds of summer visitors.

Colonsay and Oronsay

Colonsay is an attractive island with pleasant countryside and beaches, a golf course, and many archaeological remains. It is eight miles long, two miles wide, and easily explored. Passengers disembark from the Oban ferry at **Scalasaig**, an uninspiring place. But the steep track behind the hotel soon brings you to the **Vale of Kiloran**, a lovely expanse of fields, woods and heather-covered hills. **Kiloran Bay** in the north-west has a good beach of yellow sand. The gardens round **Colonsay House** are open to the public and display many exotic trees and plants, including magnolias, rhododendrons and peaches, which flourish in the mild sunny climate.

Little **Oronsay**, reached across muddy sands at low tide, is well worth a visit for the ruins of the 14th-century priory; particularly beautiful are the cloisters and chapel. The impressive free-standing cross was erected about 1500.

Coll

Coll has a rocky coastline on the east, sandy bays on the west. The village of **Arinagour** a little way up the road from the ferry has rows of whitewashed cottages. Other buildings include a hotel, a few shops, two churches and some council houses. The road to the north passes near some delightful beaches and ends at **Sorisdale**, a ghost village of ruined crofts. The road southward ends at **Breachacha Castle**, a 15th-century tower house with outer fortifications, once the seat of the Macleans of Coll. When that proved uninhabitable a later Maclean built the mansion nearby in about 1750. Johnson stigmatised it as a 'tradesman's box', and Victorian additions of turrets and battlements effected no improvement. The old castle is the headquarters of the Project Trust to train young people for overseas voluntary work.

Tiree

Tiree, the furthest west of the Inner Hebrides, is remarkable mainly for its topography and climate. It is extremely flat – with just two hills of about 400 feet – and extremely windy. In compensation, it has more hours of sunshine than anywhere else in Scotland, and fertile soil. The present-day crofters raise large numbers of cattle and sheep who apparently do not mind the wind.

The main village is **Scarinish**, a little way south of the ferry pier. There is a hotel here and some self-catering accommodation. Above **Gott Bay** to the north there is a golf course, and nearby on the coast to the west of **Vaul Bay** are the remains of a broch. Along the whole of the coast there is a succession of sandy beaches.

Accommodation

There's a wide choice of hotel-type accommodation in Tobermory.
The main villages have one or two places and there are some hotels
in the countryside. The two hotels we recommend are in the
country-house style; both are extremely civilised. Accommodation
on the other islands is limited.

BUNESSAN
Ardfenaig House (GFG, GHG)
Tel: Fionnphort (068 17) 210
A peaceful place at the head of a small loch. The good taste of the
two owners, Robin Drummond-Hay and Ian Bowles, is evident
from the elegant furnishings and many antiques. Bedrooms are
most attractive and comfortable (none have private baths; all have
tea-making facilities). Food is very good, concentrating on
traditional dishes; there is no choice at dinner. The gardens are
lovely: there is fishing.
Open May to Sep; 5 bedrooms; no children under 12; £££

TIRORAN
Tiroran House (GFG, GHG)
Tel: Tiroran (068 15) 232
An old country house set in 12 acres of gardens and woodland
overlooking Loch Scridain. It has very much the feel of a
comfortable private house, and Wing Commander and Mrs Blockey
are good hosts. All the bedrooms have bath, radio and tea-making
facilities. Facilities include table tennis and croquet, and there are
sailing dinghies and canoes.
Open early May to early Oct; 9 bedrooms (and 2 self-catering
cottages); no children under 10; from £££

GFG means in the 1986 edition of *The Good Food Guide*
GHG means in the 1986 edition of *The Good Hotel Guide*
GPG means in the 1986 edition of *The Good Pub Guide*
Price categories are based on the cost for one person sharing a
double room for one night. Many hotels give reduced terms for
stays of three nights or longer.

Dinner, bed
and breakfast
£15 to £30   £
£31 to £40   ££
£41 to £50   £££
£51 to £60   ££££
over £60   £££££

General Information

Activities
BOAT HIRE Places where possible include Bunessan and Tobermory.
BOAT TRIPS Various day trips from Oban to Mull, including trips to Staffa; for details see Oban chapter. I Morrison runs trips from Calgary to Staffa and the Treshnish Isles,
Tel: Dervaig (068 84) 242
FISHING Salmon and trout in some rivers and lochs.
GOLF Craignure, Tobermory and on Colonsay and Tiree.
PONY-TREKKING Pennyghael.
SAILING Bunessan and Tobermory.
TENNIS Tobermory.

Entertainment
The Little Theatre in Dervaig is well worth a visit. Ceilidhs, dancing etc in local hotels.

Events
APRIL Mull Music Festival.
JULY Mull Highland Games.
AUGUST Salen Agricultural Show; Tobermory Regatta.

Ferries
Caledonian MacBrayne, Tel: Oban (0631) 62285 or Tobermory (0688) 2017: Craignure to Oban, several times daily, takes 45 min; Tobermory to Oban or Coll and Tiree, several times a week; Fishnish to Lochaline, several times daily, takes 5 min; the ferry doesn't take many cars and there can be queues in summer; Tobermory to Kilchoan (passenger only), 5 times daily, takes 35 min; Fionnphort to Iona (passenger only), frequent daily service, takes 10 min.

Tourist information
Oban, Mull and District Tourist Board, Argyll Square, Oban;
Tel: (0631) 63122
Centre open summer only at Tobermory, Tel: (0688) 2182

Pitlochry
and
Atholl

Blair Castle

Here in Scotland's very centre the ancient Earldom of Atholl extended from the Perthshire Highlands (later so popular with the Victorians) south to Loch Tay. From its earliest history Atholl simply assimilated the forces and influences around it: Picts and Celts, Gaels, Norsemen and Anglo-Normans merged, intermarried and ruled. Dunkeld was an important Christian centre; Blair Castle became a seat of power and magnificence, albeit at the disposal of the Scottish monarch – the Earldom tended to change hands if the incumbent grew over-mighty.

The Murrays of Tullibardine, holding the Earldom of Atholl from 1629, were loyal monarchists under Charles I and Charles II. In 1676 the second Earl was made a Marquess and sent to purge Argyll of traitorous Campbells. When James II was deposed and William of Orange sent in troops, this Marquess diplomatically retired to take the waters at Bath – while his steward seized Blair Castle for James and his son besieged it for William. The son was made a Duke, but the Atholl circumspection eluded the next generation: William the heir fought in the first Jacobite risings, and his younger brother inherited the title. When Bonnie Prince Charlie arrived in 1745 the Duke stayed loyally Hanoverian, but William landed with the Prince – and a third brother, Lord George Murray, was his brilliant military commander. After Culloden, Atholl's powers were somewhat reduced. Subsequent Dukes took an interest in forestry; the fourth ('planting') Duke laid out over 15,000 acres with larch and fir and spruce. The restored forests are today a great part of the appeal of this area at the edge of the Highlands.

Surrounded by mountains, with Schiehallion dominating at 3,554 feet, this area's scenery is relatively accessible; General Wade first constructed its great north-south artery the A9; and today Edinburgh and Inverness are less than two hours' drive away. Man has further modified the landscape while harnessing its waters for power: massive hydro-electric schemes have doubled the size of Loch Rannoch and had effects as far north as Dalwhinnie and Loch Ericht. But care and conservation have balanced the work of man and nature. The beauty that Queen Victoria admired (to the immediate and lasting benefit of the area's tourist popularity) is hardly impaired; if the Falls of Tummel were lost, the resulting new Loch Faskally is lovely. A complete circuit of the loch – 11 miles – is a favourite local walk; there are many more, from healthy mountain hikes to the gentlest of exercise. The countryside is attractively varied, much of it with a pretty pastoral softness rare in northern landscapes. Birch and beech mix with the conifers; grassy slopes rather than rocky scrambles lead to waterfalls, picnic places and delightful views. Even the weather contributes: the clear light of the Highlands is less often dimmed by rain.

Atholl's Pictish history – from the 6th century to the 9th – can be traced in parts of this southern frontier-land. There are 'ring fort' complexes, notably in Glen Lyon: small circular stone constructions, often found on farmland rather than stategic outcrops. They probably served as protection against wolves rather than human enemies – this part of Scotland had many. Local sources have it that the last Perthshire wolf was killed in 1747, by a housewife. More artistic Pictish remnants are their sculptured stones, carved with saints, symbols and animals, such as the fine example at Dunfallandy not far from Pitlochry.

There is much for the holiday-maker to do here besides finding the best viewpoints. The area is famous for its fishing, and it's excellent pony-trekking country; there are golf courses, and boating on some of the lochs. Blair Atholl has one of Scotland's grand castles (and the Duke of Atholl has Britain's only private army – a permanent privilege granted the Duke by Queen Victoria); Dunkeld, which Alexander Mackay described as 'one of the loveliest spots in all Scotland', has many fine old buildings and an ancient cathedral; and between the two – claiming to be Scotland's actual centre – is Pitlochry, the starting-point of our tours.

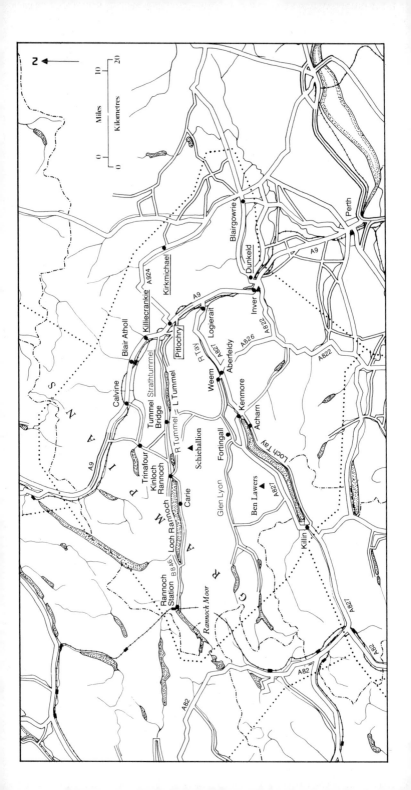

PITLOCHRY

Located in the midst of glens, lochs, hills and streams Pitlochry is one of Scotland's premier inland resorts. It became fashionable more than a hundred years ago when Queen Victoria remarked on the beautiful scenery and her physician declared that Pitlochry had 'the finest bracing mountain air in Scotland'. The town became known as a health centre. Large mansions were built, some of which have become the hotels of today. But Pitlochry was a place of some importance before the Victorian era: when the Highlands were in turmoil in the 18th century one of General Wade's military roads went from Dunkeld via Pitlochry to Blair Atholl and beyond. This became a turnpike road and Pitlochry developed into an important staging post.

The main impetus to its expansion was the opening of the Highland Railway in 1865; the influx of summer visitors began and continues, with increasing numbers from overseas. The fast A9 makes access easy but fortunately it bypasses the town. A modern sports centre and splendid opportunities for fishermen add to the attractions of its setting, and, although not by any standards the sophisticated place it was in Victorian times, the plays, concerts and exhibitions regularly held at the **Festival Theatre** add a cultural side rarely found elsewhere in the Highlands.

Ten minutes' walk from the town centre is the **Pitlochry Power Station and Dam**, one of several hydro-electric stations in the valley of the Tummel which together produce some 600 million units of electricity. There is an exhibition illustrating the work of the hydro-electric authority. But most people will probably be more interested in the 1,000-feet **Fish Ladder** which allows salmon to climb the dam on their way upstream to spawn: visitors can watch their progress from pool to pool through observation windows. There is a walkway along the dam, linking with forest paths. Its building created the reservoir of **Loch Faskally** where picnicking, boating and fishing are favourite pastimes.

About a mile north of Pitlochry on the A924 is **Moulin**, an attractive little village whose church, though only a hundred years old, occupies a most ancient site. There are some interesting tombstones, including the Crusader's Stone with a carving of a sword. Quite near the church is the ruin of **Caisteal Dubh**, the Black Castle, built by a nephew of Robert the Bruce. Above Moulin it's an easy walk up the beacon hill of **Craigower** (1,300 feet), from where you can survey in panoramic detail the area this chapter explores. Two miles north of Pitlochry is the **Linn of Tummel**, reached by the unclassified road running along the west side of Loch Faskally or by a path from Garry Bridge to the meeting of the rivers Tummel and Garry. The Linn (literally 'pool') used to be known as the Falls of Tummel and was a great attraction. But the construction of the dam forming Loch Faskally reduced the height of the fall drastically and the name was changed.

Rannoch and Tummel

Killiecrankie · Blair Atholl · Calvine · Trinafour
Loch Rannoch · Loch Tummel
Pitlochry

This tour takes you to a fabulous castle and includes some fine loch and forest scenery, as well as bleak moor. Narrow roads once you leave the A9; about 80 miles.

The A9 north from Pitlochry runs by Loch Faskally and the River Garry about three miles to the wooded gorge of the **Pass of Killiecrankie**. Here was the celebrated battle in 1689: the Jacobite Highlanders routed King William's English troops in one mad barefoot charge. But the Jacobite leader Viscount Claverhouse – best known as 'Bonnie Dundee' – was mortally wounded, and three weeks later the Highlanders were defeated. A Visitor Centre (NTS) gives the background story.

★ The road continues north-westward, with the railway between it and the River Garry, to **Blair Atholl**. The attractive village is dominated by the white baronial splendour of **Blair Castle**, at the end of its avenue of limes. This has for many centuries been the seat of the Earls and Dukes of Atholl, and the witness of many great events in Scotland's history. The oldest part, Cumming's Tower, dates from about 1270. Edward III stayed there in 1336 and Mary Queen of Scots enjoyed a hunt in the Forest of Atholl which bagged six wolves. Cromwell captured it from the royalists in 1652 but Bonnie Dundee took it and slept there before the Battle of Killiecrankie. Bonnie Prince Charlie stayed at the castle twice, but in 1746 when occupied by Cumberland it was unsuccessfully besieged by the Jacobites. Thirty-two rooms filled with fine furniture, antiques and paintings are shown, presenting a vivid picture of life in Scotland from the 16th century, in one stratum of society at least. There are collections of china and Jacobite relics, and an outstanding array of weapons including the rifles for the Atholl Highlanders, the only private army in Britain. ★

A further three miles northward along the A9, a footpath leads from the road through woods to the spectacular **Falls of Bruar**, three waterfalls formed by the Bruar Water, dropping 200 feet in total. Near the entrance to the falls is the **Clan Donnachaidh Museum**, which relates the history of five clans.

The A9 continues through wooded Glen Garry over the Pass of Drumochter to Dalwhinnie and the Spey valley. The B847, however, branches left just after **Calvine**, immediately passing through **Struan** at the confluence of the rivers Garry and Errochty. The road runs five miles through **Glen Errochty**, with Tummel Forest on the other side of the river, to **Trinafour** where it swings southward – a brief detour up the northern fork here gives you a good view back over Glen Garry to the heights beyond. Further on lie the Errochty dam and the loch it created.

Back on the B847, continue four miles to Dunalastair Reservoir, and turn right along the B846 to **Kinloch Rannoch**, set on the River Tummel as it leaves Loch Rannoch. Just outside the village on Loch Rannoch is a large time-share development which was the first to be built in Britain. Part of the Tummel valley hydro-electric scheme, **Loch Rannoch** is a beautiful stretch of water nearly 10 miles long and a mile wide. The main road runs along the north side by undulating hills; the unclassified road along the south side passes wilder scenery and higher hills. From the loch's eastern end there are classic views, west towards Glen Coe and south through birch trees to the white quartzite peak of **Schiehallion** (3,554 feet), variously described as pyramidal and conical.

To begin the 22-mile circuit of Loch Rannoch follow the B846 close to the shore, past Rannoch Power Station to Rannoch Lodge and the junction with the road along the south side. The main road continues another 10 miles to what must be the loneliest station on Britain's rail network, **Rannoch** on the Crianlarich-Fort William line, beyond which stretches Rannoch Moor. A car can go no further; turn back past **Loch Eigheach**, now the **Gaur Reservoir**, dammed and doubled in size, with its own power station.

The narrower road along the south side of Loch Rannoch runs through the fringe of the great Rannoch Forest and in particular the ancient **Black Wood of Rannoch**. Here have survived many of the pines and firs of the Caledonian Forest, which covered much of northern Scotland. There are Forestry Commission picnic places; the main one is at **Carie** from where the **Rannoch Forest Walks**, varying in length from one mile to over five, lead through birch and pine woods and along burns to reach higher ground overlooking the loch.

Back round the head of Loch Rannoch rejoin the B846 past Kinloch Rannoch and the turn to Trinafour, and continue four miles along the north bank of the River Tummel to **Tummel Bridge**, a small village almost surrounded by power stations. In all, eight power stations use the water of the River Tummel and its tributaries. From Tummel Bridge follow the B8019 along the north bank of **Loch Tummel**. One of the highlights of the tour is reached in about five miles, where the view that Queen Victoria so admired has been given the accolade of a Visitor Centre. The **Queen's View** is indeed stunning, a panorama of river, loch and mountain with Schiehallion the outstanding feature. There is a picnic place from which several forest walks begin, leading to a partly excavated ring fort and a reconstructed clachan.

At Clunie Dam the road swings northward and then eastward to join the A9 just south of Killiecrankie, where a right turn takes you back into Pitlochry.

Dunkeld and Loch Tay

Dunkeld · Inver · Aberfeldy · Kenmore · Killin
Glen Lyon · Fortingall · Weem · Logierait
Pitlochry

*To one of the most charming Highland towns and on to enjoy pretty loch
scenery and dramatic mountains. Easy roads except along the south side
of Loch Tay and through Glen Lyon; about 95 miles.*

Take the A9 south to **Dunkeld**, 12 miles from Pitlochry. This
historic little cathedral town, beautifully set on the River Tay, has
recovered much of its tranquillity since the A9 bypassed it.
Dunkeld was once the capital of ancient Caledonia and its history
can be traced back more than a thousand years. Its name means
'fort of the Caledonians'; it was the home of kings – in the 9th
century Scotland's joint capital with Scone; in 1689 it was almost
completely destroyed by the Jacobites in the battle which followed
Killiecrankie. The **Cathedral** (AM), in lovely grounds, was begun
in the early 13th century, but most of the remains are 14th- and
15th-century. During the Reformation the church became dilapidated; the Atholl family rescued it in the 1690s. In the choir,
restored in 1908, is the tomb of the Wolf of Badenoch (see Spey
Valley chapter). The nave remains a roofless but beautiful ruin. In
Cathedral Street are 20 'Little Houses' (NTS), restored to their
condition before the Battle of Dunkeld; no admission to these, but
there is a Visitor Centre (NTS). In the charming 18th-century town
square is the Museum of the Scottish Horse Regiment.

Two miles north-east of Dunkeld up the A923 is **Loch of Lowes**,
a wildlife reserve where birds including ospreys can be watched
from observation hides. South of the town is Birnam, whence
Birnam Wood came to Dunsinane to defeat Shakespeare's Macbeth.
But go the other way through **Inver**, the home of the celebrated
fiddler Neil Gow who played before Bonnie Prince Charlie, and the
start of a short walk to the delightful **Hermitage** (NTS), a rebuilt
18th-century folly above the wooded River Braan. Then fork left
along the B898, and after about eight miles turn west along the
A827. **Aberfeldy** is a popular Tayside holiday resort in a beautiful
area with a number of places of historic or archaeological interest
close by. General Wade's five-arched bridge over the river was
designed in 1733 by William Adam, father of the more famous
Robert. Beside it, a large monument commemorates the formation
of The Black Watch at Aberfeldy in 1739.

The A827 reaches **Loch Tay** six miles on at the attractive village
of **Kenmore**, grouped round a green with the church at one end and
the entrance to **Taymouth Castle** (not open) at the other. The hotel
at Kenmore has preserved a poem scratched by Robert Burns in
praise of the justly celebrated view down the loch from the bridge.
Across the bridge is **Drummond Hill**, where a network of forest
walks gives yet more spectacular views.

90

Loch Tay is one of the most beautiful of the Highland lochs, and is famous for its salmon. Its 15 miles are surrounded by mountains, the dominant peak being **Ben Lawers** (3,984 feet) to the north. Roads run along both sides of the loch but the unclassified southern road is the more picturesque; at **Acharn**, not far from Kenmore, a short track leads to another hermitage, this one a gallery of monks' cells facing the Falls of Acharn.

Amid wonderful scenery at the head of the loch, the village of **Killin** offers all manner of land and watersports in summer, and skiing in winter in the Ben Lawers range. By the loch stand the ruins of **Finlarig Castle**, once the seat of a particularly bloodthirsty Campbell chief; a large 'beheading pit' survives. There are waterfalls, picturesque rather than dramatic, on the rivers Dochart and Lochay which join to flow into Loch Tay.

★ The A827 runs round the head of the loch and along its north side. In three miles take the road to the left, past the **Ben Lawers Visitor Centre** (NTS). This area is a nature reserve famous for its alpine plants, with botany trails and hill walks. The narrow road winds eight miles north through the mountains to enter **Glen Lyon** at **Bridge of Balgie**. Glen Lyon is over 20 miles long, and towards its head (west of Balgie) much set about with hydro-electric works. Turn east through ten miles of dramatic scenery as the mountains close in. At the narrowest point of the **Pass of Lyon** is MacGregor's Leap, where a single clansman made his escape from a vicious battle with the Stewarts. In another mile you reach the attractive village of Fortingall, with thatched cottages and a vast ancient yew tree. ★

The Glen Lyon road joins the B846 at **Coshieville**, a mile north of which is the ruined keep of **Garth Castle**, built by the Wolf of Badenoch. The ruins of **Comrie Castle** stand by the bridge over the Lyon. For the return to Pitlochry take the right turn, to follow the northern side of the broad wooded valley of the Tay, here known as Strath Appin or Appin of Dull. Two miles beyond Dull is **Castle Menzies** (closed lunch and Sun am); built in the 16th century and added to in the 19th, it has been restored.

The ancient village of **Weem** stands across the Tay from Aberfeldy; its Auld Kirk, dating from the 16th century, has been used as a mausoleum by the Clan Menzies since it became disused in the 19th century. Three miles after joining the A827, a hotel at Logierait stands on the site of the court house where the lords of Atholl dealt out summary justice; criminals were hanged on the hill above the village; and Rob Roy escaped from prison in 1717. From **Logierait** an unclassified road follows the west bank of the Tummel five miles back to Pitlochry, passing at Dunfallandy the fine Pictish **Dunfallandy Stone**, elaborately carved with saints, serpents, horsemen and an ornate cross.

Accommodation

This area is well supplied with accommodation of all types; Pitlochry itself is packed with hotels. Many of the mansions and more modest houses built by the Victorians during its very fashionable days have been converted into hotels and guest houses. Unfortunately many have failed to keep pace with the times. One of the hotels we recommend is actually to the east of the ground covered in our tours, but it is near enough to use as a base for exploring the area.

KILLIECRANKIE
Killiecrankie Hotel (GFG, GHG)
Tel: Pitlochry (0796) 3220
White-painted former dower house in woodland setting off the busy A9, about four miles from Pitlochry. Far from grand, but a homely and welcoming place. Spacious lounge (with TV), friendly bar, and neat attractive bedrooms. Putting and croquet in the grounds.
Open Easter to late Oct; 12 bedrooms; from £

KIRKMICHAEL
Log Cabin Hotel (GFG, GHG)
Tel: Strathardle (025 081) 288
An unusual single-storey log cabin isolated high in the hills some 15 miles east of Pitlochry. The startling modern décor of the public rooms is in complete contrast to the bedrooms which, although small, are cosy and comfortable (all have bath or shower, radio and tea-making facilities; colour TV is available on request). Food is good, and there are log fires to warm you up after a hard day in the surrounding wilderness. There are over 300 acres of grounds; shooting and stalking is available.
Open all year (not mid-Nov to mid-Dec) 13 bedrooms; ££

STRATHTUMMEL
Port-an-Eilean
Tel: Tummel Bridge (088 24) 233
Although a bit of a hotchpotch, this austere-looking former shooting lodge on Loch Tummel, about nine miles from Pitlochry, is a welcome, relaxing and inexpensive base from which to explore the area. No recognisable theme runs through the décor but there is comfort enough, antiques here and there, and a sun lounge with tremendous views of the loch. Bedrooms are big; the ones overlooking the loch are lighter and better furnished than the others. The hotel has a boat, and there is fishing.
Open Easter to mid-Oct; 12 bedrooms; £

General Information

Activities
BOAT HIRE Loch Faskally; see also 'sailing'.
FISHING Salmon in rivers Errochty Water, Garry, Lyon, Tummel and Tay, and lochs Broom, Faskally and Tay. Trout in many lochs and rivers.
GOLF Aberfeldy, Blair Atholl, Blairgowrie, Dunkeld, Kenmore, Killin and Pitlochry.
PONY-TREKKING Blair Atholl, Blairgowrie, Dunkeld, Kenmore, Kirkmichael and Pitlochry.
SAILING Lochs Rannoch and Tay.
TENNIS Aberfeldy and Pitlochry.

Entertainment
Theatre and cinema at Pitlochry. Ceilidhs, Highland dancing, folk and jazz evenings, discos etc at many hotels in the region.

Events
MAY Atholl Highlanders Parade, Blair Castle.
JUNE Dunkeld and Birnam Arts Festival; Kenmore to Aberfeldy raft race; Rannoch Marathon.
JULY Dunkeld Gala Week.
AUGUST Birnam Highland Games.
SEPTEMBER Blairgowrie Week; Pitlochry Highland Games.

Tourist information
Pitlochry District Tourist Association, 22 Atholl Road, Pitlochry, Tel: (0796) 2215
Centres open in summer only: Aberfeldy, Tel: (0887) 20276; Blairgowrie, Tel: (0250) 2960; Dunkeld, Tel: (035 02) 688; Killin, Tel: (056 72) 254

GFG means in the 1986 edition of *The Good Food Guide*
GHG means in the 1986 edition of *The Good Hotel Guide*
GPG means in the 1986 edition of *The Good Pub Guide*

£15 to £30	£
£31 to £40	££
£41 to £50	£££
£51 to £60	££££
over £60	£££££

Fort William
and
Lochaber

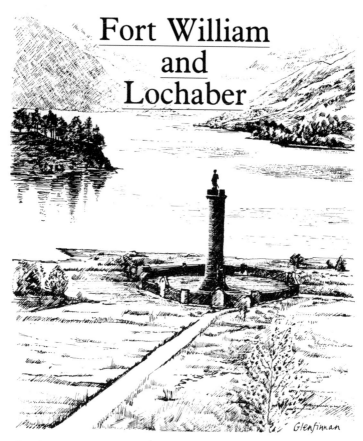

Glenfinnan

Soaring mountains, beautiful glens, sparkling rivers and streams, long serene inland lochs and wild fjord-like sea lochs – Lochaber has all these, as well as a richly evocative past. Not only is there Glen Coe, but scattered throughout are reminders of Bonnie Prince Charlie's doomed campaign; and the district suffered particularly hard during the Clearances.

Lochaber is now a large administrative district with Fort William as its capital, but old Lochaber was much smaller, bounded by Loch Arkaig in the north, Loch Treig in the east, Loch Leven in the south and Glenfinnan in the west. To its central fastnesses have been added great tracts in the north and west, giving it as much again of impenetrable mountain country, a wealth of lochs and a long wild coastline of rich variety.

The most northern peninsula, Knoydart, is one of the remotest areas in all Scotland. Apart from the lonely road to Kinloch Hourn only paths and tracks cross it, and tiny coastal communities are dependent, island-like, on boats. Dominating this secret area are mountains as sensational as you will find in Scotland – at Kinloch Hourn eight of the peaks tower over 3,000 feet. Next is Morar, split into north and south by its extraordinary loch. Loch Morar is inland – just – and over a thousand feet deep; what geological spasm created it is unknown, except perhaps to its very own monster Morag.

South of Morar, Moidart lies between Loch Shiel and the sea, its northern mountains diminishing to greener hills in the south; and Sunart has the loveliest stretch of sea loch. From here the wild Ardnamurchan peninsula juts out to the furthest westerly point on the British mainland. Lastly the lonely moors of Morvern, 'the Sea Gap', lie between Loch Sunart, Loch Linnhe and the narrow Sound of Mull.

Up Loch Linnhe, you are back in old Lochaber between the mountains of Ardgour and Ben Nevis itself. To the west runs the Road to the Isles with Glenfinnan – where Bonnie Prince Charlie raised his standard – and Loch nan Uamh, where he landed in hope and left in despair. Eastward, the region extends from Britain's highest mountain to Scotland's most famous glen: in a land full of history, Glen Coe (now one of Scotland's skiing areas) is always remembered for the Glen Coe Massacre of the Macdonalds by the Campbells. Regardless of the Massacre, Glen Coe is a memorable place; Charles Dickens wrote of 'these tremendous wilds' that 'they really are fearful in their grandeur and amazing solitude. Wales is a mere toy compared to them'.

An earlier piece of famous Highland military history was the great victory of the Marquess of Montrose in 1645. With 1,800 men, Montrose in his camp at the head of Loch Ness (the present Fort Augustus) learnt that Covenanter forces of 3,000 led by Campbell of Argyll were close by at Inverlochy Castle. Trapped, Montrose resolved to attack; but to take his men the direct route along the Great Glen would be to lose all element of surprise. Instead he marched them by a great eastward detour through the Monadhliath Mountains in midwinter: up Glen Tarff, through the Corrieyairack Pass, back across the watershed from the River Spey to the River Roy and down to Inverlochy from the foothills of Ben Nevis. It took them three days. At the Royalists' sudden appearance from an impossible direction Argyll himself fled, and his army was routed in spite of huge numerical advantage. This feat of courage and endurance was brought about by a combination of Montrose's inspired leadership, and his troops' hatred of Clan Campbell.

This is one of the best known and most visited areas in the Highlands – Sir Walter Scott's 'Land of brown heath and shaggy wood, Land of the mountain and the flood'. Whatever you seek in Lochaber – history, scenery, activity or solitude – your gateway is Fort William, so well placed that it might have been invented as a touring centre. Because it wasn't (and isn't) merely this, Fort William has its own vigour and prosperity – tourists depend on the town, not the town on the tourists.

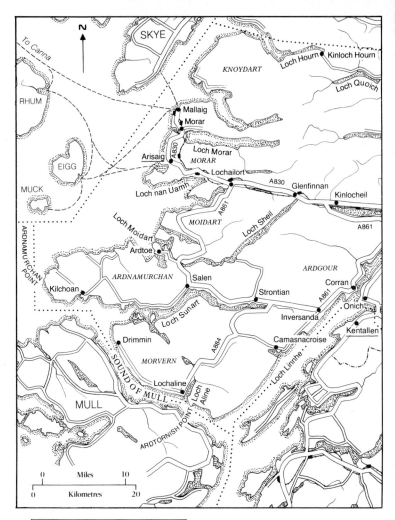

FORT WILLIAM

The original Fort, called Inverlochy, was erected on this strategic site in 1655. It was built by General Monck, whom Cromwell sent to the district after the collapse of Montrose's campaign against the Covenanters, to protect England's interests against those whom Dr Johnson described as 'savage clans and roving barbarians'. In 1690 it was rebuilt by General Mackay and called after William of Orange. In later years it went through a succession of names before reverting to the one by which the local population had long known it. Two centuries later it was pulled down to make way for the West Highland Railway. Already the terminus of the Caledonian Canal, Fort William was thus equipped to become the commercial and industrial town of today. It lacks charm, but provides most tourist

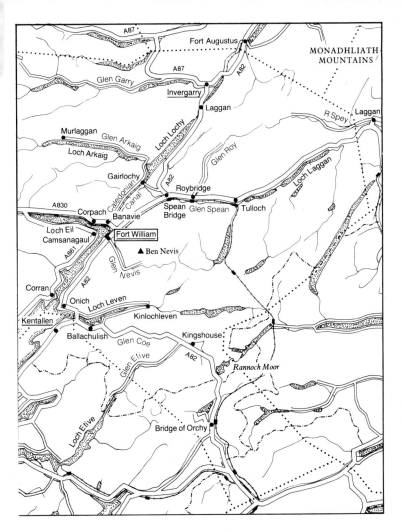

amenities. It is one of the busiest tourist centres in the Highlands, but mercifully gets less congested since the lochside bypass was completed.

Near the middle of High Street, the **West Highland Museum** (closed Sun) has the largest and most interesting collection in the Highlands of folk and historic exhibits. In a room devoted to Bonnie Prince Charlie and the Jacobites, the most famous relic is the 'secret portrait' of the Prince, a blur of paint until seen reflected in a curved mirror. Other displays cover everything from crannogs to clan tartans.

There is little else to stay for in the town, but more to see close by. If you don't want to use your car you can leave it in the car park at the south end of the High Street and take the passenger ferry across Loch Linnhe to near Camusnagaul.

Just north of the town off the A82 is the ruin of **Inverlochy Castle** – not to be confused with the luxury hotel a mile further on (see 'Accommodation'). Much of the 13th-century stronghold, a walled square with corner towers, remains overlooking the site where Montrose won a decisive battle against the Covenanters in 1645. A mile or so north-west on the A830 at Banavie is **Neptune's Staircase**, eight locks built by Telford which raise the level of the Caledonian Canal 72 feet in 500 yards.

It is **Ben Nevis**, of course, that is the supreme attraction near Fort William. It cannot be seen from the town – go to Corpach or towards Spean Bridge for the best views of its massive shape. There are several routes up its 4,406 famous feet; the intimidating north-east face is for experienced climbers only, and two others are strenuous, but the main tourist path starts about two miles from Fort William (from the north-bank road at Achintee Farm in Glen Nevis) and gets you up in four or five hours' walking. The record time for the annual race is an hour and a half – there's a small Ben Nevis Exhibition in the town, with stories of famous climbs. The relative ease of the ascent does not mean it should be tackled without due precaution and equipment, good health and good weather. From the top, near the ruins of a 19th-century observatory, the breathtaking view embraces Ben Lomond, Torridon, the Cairngorms, the Cuillin on Skye, and the Outer Hebrides.

A less energetic and very popular excursion is lovely **Glen Nevis**: you can drive 10 miles up the southern bank of the rocky river, past waterfalls and rapids to the car park and viewpoint at the end. From here a walk of a mile or so takes you through the magnificent scenery of the wooded Nevis gorge, up to the Steall waterfall.

Glen Garry, Loch Hourn and Glen Arkaig

Spean Bridge · Laggan · Invergarry · Kinloch Hourn
Invergarry · Gairlochy · Murlaggan · Banavie
Fort William

A variety of fine Highland scenery with an exceptionally marvellous trip up Glen Garry to Kinloch Hourn (a day's outing on its own). Good roads for much of the tour but not along the best bits. About 140 miles.

Take the A82 to **Spean Bridge**, named after the bridge built by Telford in 1819. If you keep right here you follow Glen Spean for Loch Laggan (see Glen Spean tour). Instead take the left fork and climb to the Gairlochy junction where the **Commando Memorial** stands. The three soldiers sculptured in bronze by Scott Sutherland look westward to their Second World War training area. The route is now up the eastern side of **Loch Lochy** by the Inverness road which passes through Letterfinlay, where wounded Highlanders, fleeing the slaughter at Culloden, were sheltered by the innkeeper; the many who died were thrown into the loch. After about 12 miles the road crosses the swingbridge at **Laggan** and runs up the west side of **Loch Oich**. On the right is the **Well of the Seven Heads**, a monument to a gruesome tale of family vengeance, inscribed in English, Gaelic, French and Latin. Here were washed the heads of the Seven Keppoch murderers (see Glen Spean tour). The well itself disappeared with the widening of the road. In a further mile, up a detour to the Invergarry Hotel, are the ruins of **Invergarry Castle**: Cumberland burnt it down because the Macdonells of Glengarry sheltered Bonnie Prince Charlie here before and after the Battle of Culloden.

At **Invergarry** the A82 continues northward to Fort Augustus (see Loch Ness chapter). The A87, part of the Road to the Isles, curves westward along the wooded valley of the River Garry, in 10 miles reaching a viewpoint from which two short walks lead to a spectacular waterfall. **Loch Garry** has been doubled in length as a result of hydro-electric developments but the shore is attractively wooded. At its east end there is a fish hatchery.

★ The recently built main road towards Kyle of Lochalsh turns northward away from the loch but the old road continues along the shore. This road, though a dead end, is well worth the detour as the views get better and better the further west you go. Upper Glen Garry and **Loch Quoich** are part of the Garry hydro-electric scheme. Its constructions include the tremendous dam at the east end of Loch Quoich, whose area has been more than doubled. One of the attractions to the planners was this area's average annual rainfall of 125 inches – it's one of the wettest places in Britain. But the landscape round Loch Quoich is marvellous, with stupendous mountains on both sides and lush vegetation by the water. The last five miles are very dramatic as the road – narrow but well surfaced – winds up over the watershed then zigzags down to **Kinloch Hourn** at the head of lonely Loch Hourn. Bring a picnic; it's a drive that deserves a rest and a reward before you turn back. ★

Return 25 miles to Invergarry and follow the A82 southward back to the Commando Memorial. Here the route turns west along the B8004 Gairlochy road. At the bridge at **Mucomir** stop to see the waterfall plunging from its man-made channel into the River Spean, part of the hydro-electric scheme completed in 1962. At **Gairlochy**, where there are two locks on the Caledonian Canal, turn right on the B8005 to **Bunarkaig**. At **Clunes** the road curves westward along the old Dark Mile of Trees, though now beeches no longer exclude the sunlight, passes two waterfalls, and then follows the wooded northern shore of **Loch Arkaig**. Bonnie Prince Charlie hid in this area after Culloden, making his escape by way of the loch's southern shore. It is a beautiful serene sheet of water untouched by the developments that have changed the character of its neighbours. The road ends at **Murlaggan**, traditionally the site of buried French treasure.

Return 17 miles to Gairlochy and head south along the B8004 beside the Caledonian Canal. A road runs up **Glen Loy** from which forest paths have been laid out. In a further two miles the ruins of **Tor Castle** stand in a loop of the River Lochy. Fort William is 13 miles by way of **Banavie**.

The north-west peninsulas

Glenfinnan · Lochailort · Arisaig · Mallaig · Lochailort
Salen · Kilchoan · Ardnamurchan Point · Salen
Strontian · Inversanda · Corran
Fort William

A long tour which would be best tackled over two or more days. The route takes you along the Road to the Isles and runs through some of the most historic and beautiful parts of the Highlands. Because the tour covers such a large area we have highlighted several sections of it. The road to Mallaig is good but, from Lochailort, winding. South from Lochailort a narrow road down the coast soon reverts to single-track. Exploratory detours – all well worth making – of 15 miles in Moidart, 56 to the far west of Ardnamurchan and 20 in Sunart increase the mileage to 210.

Leave Fort William by the Inverness road, turning left in one mile along the A830 to **Corpach**, at the meeting place of **lochs Eil** and **Linnhe** and at the entrance to the Caledonian Canal. Corpach has undergone a good deal of industrial development but the marvellous views it affords of **Ben Nevis** are ample compensation. At this point the railway line to Mallaig and the road come together for much of the route to the west coast. The single-track West Highland Railway is famous for its beautiful views: on weekdays some trains from Fort William to Mallaig and back include a saloon car with a commentary. From Corpach the first seven miles of the Road to the Isles are along the northern side of Loch Eil.

★ At the head of **Loch Shiel** you arrive at **Glenfinnan Monument** (NTS), with a statue of a Highlander on its summit. It commemorates the clansmen who rallied here to Prince Charlie's standard on

19 August 1745, and was erected in 1815 by a Macdonald descendant. The view down the length of Loch Shiel between the mountains is wonderful, even without negotiating the monument's awkward inner staircase and gazing from its height. A Visitor Centre tells the story of the Prince's campaign, and there are cruises of Loch Shiel. ★

At **Loch Eilt** the wide fast highway follows the northern side and the railway the southern; they come together again before **Lochailort**. Here a road turns south (to be followed later) but the A830 winds on westward across the head of Loch Ailort to **Loch nan Uamh** ('Loch of the Caves'). It was here that Bonnie Prince Charlie's campaign began and ended. He landed on its shores on 25 July 1745, with only seven men, to set about winning the support of the clan chiefs; on 19 September 1746, after defeat at Culloden and months of wandering, it was from here he embarked again for France. One of several 'Prince Charlie's Caves' is here, and a cairn has been built on the shore.

The road crosses a wooded peninsula to reach the coast again at **Arisaig**, a small undistinguished village on a flat rocky bay with fine views of the Hebrides, especially the mountains of Skye. It is very popular in summer when cruises run to the Small Isles.

★ After some miles of woodland the landscape becomes barer as the road turns north, over the pass at **Keppoch** and past a series of beautiful bays and coves, most of them busy in summer with campers and caravanners. **Morar** is famous for its sunsets, and for its white sands. As you cross the river before the village you can see the **Morar Falls**, once celebrated but now much diminished by the local hydro-electric scheme. A scenic road runs for three miles along the northern shore of **Loch Morar** past pretty rocky islets to **Bracora**. Loch Morar has the deepest water in Britain at over 1,000 feet and like another exceptionally deep loch claims a monster, by the name of Morag. ★

The A830 and the railway end three miles farther north at **Mallaig**, a busy ferry port and fishing town. It is not very attractive in itself but has magnificent views of Skye and the Inner Hebrides. The harbour is a fine scene of activity when the fishing boats come in: Mallaig is the main centre on the west coast for herring and shellfish catches. In addition to the ferries there are many cruises. A road runs for a mile north to **Mallaigvaig** where Bonnie Prince Charlie landed from Skye; from here, too, the views excel.

To explore the other western regions of Lochaber, return to the junction at Lochailort, 19 miles from Mallaig, and turn right along the modern A861. The road hugs the north shore of **Moidart** with views of Eigg and Muck then turns south to **Glenuig** from where cruises run to Eigg. After this, it's single-track. At **Kinlochmoidart** the Bonnie Prince stayed a week planning his campaign. The original house was burnt down by Cumberland's troops, but a little way north by the side of **Loch Moidart** are seven beech trees planted to commemorate the 'Seven Men of Moidart' who arrived with the Prince from France. One of the row fell in a gale, but has been replaced. A road goes two miles up beautiful **Glen Moidart**, but the main road continues south to **Loch Shiel**, where a left turn soon brings you to **Dalelia**. From the pier here the Prince was rowed up the loch to await the clans at Glenfinnan. St Finan's tiny island was a place of pilgrimage in the 6th century, and long the area's burial ground – coffins were carried for miles over the moors. Its church is 16th-century.

Two miles on, just before **Shiel Bridge**, a road branches off right reaching Loch Moidart at **Dorlin** where at low tide you can cross to **Castle Tioram**, seat of the Clanranalds and long coveted by the Campbells of Argyll. They never took it – Clanranald himself ordered its destruction when he left to fight for the Old Pretender in 1715. Its curtain walls and keep, dating from the 14th century, are in good condition and you can see the dungeon. After Shiel Bridge, the B8044 strikes off right to **Ardtoe**, a peaceful hamlet on Kentra Bay where there are a number of sandy coves.

★ In three more miles you reach **Salen**, on the lovely wooded shore of **Loch Sunart**, where the road forks. To explore the district of **Ardnamurchan** ('Point of the Great Ocean') take the right fork, the B8007. This is a narrow twisting road, at first rather tiresome but later extremely beautiful. There are fine views of Loch Sunart with trees down to the water's edge, rocky inlets and pebble beaches. At **Glenborrodale** the road is lined with rhododendrons. Offshore islands here are breeding grounds for oyster-catchers, eider ducks, terns and mergansers. At **Ardslignish** the road turns inland round **Ben Hiant** (1,729 feet). Here you cross high moorland with patches of bog marked by cottongrass. Beyond Loch Mudle ignore the fork north to **Kilmory** and follow the main road on to **Kilchoan**. Just before the village a track leads to the remnants of 13th-century Mingary Castle, at the water's edge. In summer a passenger ferry service runs to Tobermory from the pier at the far side of the bay. The B8007 goes on through Kilchoan, where the church has a laird's loft, four miles north-westward to **Sanna Bay**, a series of beautiful white sand bays surrounded by splendid dunes. A branch road leads off to the lighthouse at **Ardnamurchan Point**, the furthest west on the British mainland. ★

Return to Salen and drive eastward along the A861 through beautiful wooded countryside along the northern shore of Loch Sunart. After 10 miles you arrive at **Strontian**. The village, gave its name to the element strontium, which was discovered in 1787 in the lead mines to the north. A road runs up **Strontian Glen** to the five mines, which were closed at the beginning of this century. A mile up the glen a nature trail strikes off right, through oak woods to a splendid waterfall by some of the old workings. The rough road reaches some disused mineshafts, then climbs for a further mile before dropping disconcertingly steeply to **Loch Doilet**. There are some magnificent views on the way, particularly westward to **Ben Resipol** (2,774 feet). Beyond **Polloch** the road merges into the Forestry Commission track which runs along the east side of Loch Shiel right up to its head by Glenfinnan.

From Strontian the A861 widens, and runs six miles through **Glen Tarbert** between **Garbh Bheinn** (2,903 feet) to the north and **Creach Bheinn** (2,800 feet) to the south. The road swings north beside Loch Linnhe through **Inversanda** to the narrows, where you take the **Corran ferry**. Once across the loch, it's nine quick miles back to Fort William.

Morvern

Corran · Inversanda · Camasnacroise · Lochaline
Drimmin · Lochaline · Loch Sunart · Inversanda
Camusnagaul · Kinlocheil
Fort William

A tour of a lonely peninsula, desolate but for some woodland and a shore offering a few ruined castles and some fine views. Good roads to the peninsula, mostly single-track thereafter. About 130 miles.

Take the A82 from Fort William, the ferry across to Corran and the A861 to **Inversanda**. Turn south along the B8043, a very narrow road which soon reaches the western bank of Loch Linnhe and at **Camasnacroise** turns inland by Loch a'Choire into beautiful **Kingairloch** and over the moors.

In five miles the road, having skirted Loch Uisge, joins the A884 which runs southward into the heart of the wild peninsula of Morvern. After some miles of bleak moorland it is a relief to descend into wooded **Glen Geal** – the 'White Glen', perhaps so-called because of the many falls along its river. Near **Claggan** it meets the River Aline. The A884 passes through **Larachbeg**: a reminder of a humanitarian but unsuccessful attempt to keep together the inhabitants of St Kilda. They were compelled to leave their remote islands in 1930 because of the insupportable conditions there and were rehoused at Larachbeg. Unfortunately the islanders could not adapt to their life as forestry workers and gradually numbers dwindled to just one family.

Beautifully sited on a rocky crag near the old bridge at the head of **Loch Aline** stands **Kinlochaline Castle**, 15th-century seat of the Clan MacInnes – motto: 'work gives pleasure'. It was clearly a well-defended stronghold – walls nine feet thick and 40 feet high, fireplace on the battlements for heating up the boiling oil – but Cromwell's troops burnt it down. It was partly restored in 1890, and quite a lot can be explored; there are lovely views of Loch Aline and Mull. A rough road runs for five miles down the east side of Loch Aline to **Ardtornish Castle**, a complete ruin. It stands on **Ardtornish Point**, jutting out into the Sound of Mull, and is more easily reached by boat from Lochaline.

Two miles further down the A884 the Drimmin road strikes off westward; half a mile along it is Keil Churchyard. In front of the church, dedicated to St Columba, is a 15th-century Celtic cross nine feet high. There are also the ruin of a pre-Reformation church and some ancient gravestones, one of which is carved with one of the earliest known representations of the wearing of the kilt. Fork left back into **Lochaline**, in its splendid setting with views down the Sound of Mull to the coast of Lorn, past Ardtornish Point and beyond it, across the Sound, Duart Castle. The village itself, once a delight, has been taken over by the sand-mining activities which bring bustle and employment to the place but despoil its natural beauty. In the Second World War Lochaline's exceptionally pure white sandstone was Britain's only source of high-grade optical glass. It is now used in the manufacture of Caithness glass. There is a regular car ferry service from Lochaline to Mull.

The B849 runs westward from Lochaline for 11 miles along the coast. It passes through a number of deserted communities including **Fiunary**, the former home of George Macleod, founder of the Iona Community (see Mull chapter), who became Lord Macleod of Fiunary. At **Killindune** are the ruins of another fortress called Caisteal nan Con (Castle of the Dogs). The road ends at **Drimmin**, which has fine views of Tobermory, across the Sound of Mull, and a castle of which only fragments remain.

For the return journey go back on the A884 through Glen Geal to **Loch Sunart**, joining the A861 at its head. Continue through Glen Tarbert and Inversanda, but instead of taking the Corran ferry, follow the A861 ten miles up the west side of Loch Linnhe. The road skirts shallow Inverscaddle Bay and reaches **Camusnagaul** opposite Fort William (with which it is connected by a passenger ferry). Then you can take a leisurely look at Loch Eil from its south shore, and turn right at its head along the fast A830 through **Kinlocheil** and **Corpach** back to Fort William.

Glen Coe

Onich · Ballachulish · Glen Coe · Glen Etive · Kingshouse
Bridge of Orchy · Glen Coe · Kinlochleven
Fort William

A route taking you to one of the most poignant landmarks of Scottish history. Good roads, even up the steep magnificent pass itself to Rannoch Moor, with a detour along a single-track road through beautiful Glen Etive. On the return journey, 20 miles of fairly narrow scenic road round Loch Leven makes it a total of about 140 miles.

The A82 keeps close to the eastern shore of Loch Linnhe and in just under six miles reaches the car park for **Corrychurrachan**; from a picnic place here a short forest walk gives views of Loch Linnhe and the Ardgour mountains. At **Inchree**, from another picnic place, a mile's walk takes you to an impressive seven-stage waterfall. As the road turns eastward towards the mouth of Loch Leven by **Onich** the seven-foot-high standing stone known as **Clach a'Charra** keeps guard near the water's edge.

Until 1975 North Ballachulish was connected with South Ballachulish by a ferry and many made the 18-mile detour round **Loch Leven** to avoid the summer traffic jams. The road bridge has replaced the ferry but the superb views remain: across Loch Leven to the **Pap of Glencoe** and the **Three Sisters** and across Loch Linnhe to **Garbh Bheinn** dominating Ardgour, while to the south in the foreground rise the twin peaks of **Beinn Bheithir**. Cross the bridge to enter the district of **Appin**, the scene of the Appin Murder made famous by Robert Louis Stevenson in *Kidnapped*. A granite monument on the hillside near the bridge shows where James Stewart of the Glen was hanged by the Campbells, 'for a crime of which he was not guilty'. In the village of **Ballachulish**, a mile east of the bridge, is an Information Centre where displays illustrate the history of the slate quarries which were in operation from the late 17th-century until 1955; nearly 600 men worked in the quarries. The area round them was landscaped in 1979 as part of a redevelopment scheme.

★ In a further mile the village of **Glencoe** retains a few traditional croft cottages. Some of them now form the **Glencoe and North Lorn Folk Museum** (opens late May). A charming cluttered place, it has a number of fascinating exhibits, some relating to the social life and industrial developments in the area since early times and some relating particularly to the Macdonald clan and to the Jacobite risings. A lane runs by the river a short distance from the old Bridge of Coe to a hillside on which stands a slender Celtic cross 'in memory of MacIain, Chief of Glencoe, who fell with his people in the massacre of Glencoe'. The Campbells' massacre of the Macdonalds differed from other historic brutalities in two ways: the murder was deliberately planned by the government and condoned by the king, and it was carried out as a treacherous abuse of hospitality. It was 'murder under trust'.

After the Stuarts lost the throne to William of Orange, the Jacobite clans were required to sign an oath of allegiance by New Year's Day 1692. The oath of the Glencoe chief was administered five days late, for various good reasons known to the authorities. It was nevertheless decided to make an example of his entire clan; his hereditary enemies the Campbell Earls of Argyll and Breadalbane were in collusion. Some 120 Campbell soldiers were billeted in the glen, their officers giving word of honour that they came with no hostile intention but because of overcrowding at Fort William.

After two weeks of hospitality among the crofts, the massacre abruptly began before dawn on 13 February, in a raging blizzard. The soldiers butchered their hosts and the women and children. Many escaped – some to die of exposure – in the snowstorm which blocked the planned arrival of extra troops; perhaps some of the Campbells were reluctant killers; only about 40 corpses were counted. The planned annihilation failed. Revulsion swept the country and an official inquiry was held, but the perpetrators of the massacre were never punished.

The A82 runs the length of Glen Coe. In two miles is a Visitor Centre (NTS) near which is **Signal Rock**, from where the Macdonald chief could summon the clan in an emergency; the Signal Rock Trail runs through woodland and mountain scenery. As the road goes on past little **Loch Achtriochtan** the landscape becomes wilder and barer, and to the south there are superb views of the **Three Sisters** and the massive **Bidean nam Bian** (3,766 feet), Argyll's highest peak. **The Study** is a flat-topped rock at the head of the glen, to the north of the gorge in which the river drops over a waterfall and plunges to the Meeting of the Three Waters. The views from The Study are quite breathtaking. At **Altnafeadh** an old military road built by Major Caulfield in 1750 can be seen climbing the northern hillside in zigzags up the **Devil's Staircase**, eventually to reach Kinlochleven. ★

In a further two miles a road follows **Glen Etive** south for 10 miles to the head of peaceful **Loch Etive**. It is a delightful glen with a succession of pools in its twisting river, at first walled in by great bare mountainsides. At **Dalness**, half-way along, the glen becomes a placid valley with the mountains standing well back. The return drive gives you even better views of the dramatic mountains. Shortly after Glen Etive the road passes near **Kingshouse**; the hotel here is reputedly Scotland's oldest inn. A short distance south, a road leads to **White Corries**, one of Scotland's skiing areas; the chairlift operates all year, and the views from the top over mountain and moor are extensive.

The route now runs beside **Loch Ba** on the edge of **Rannoch**

Moor, one of Scotland's remotest areas. A path leads from the head of Loch Tulla to the ruins of **Achallader Castle**, a seat of the Glen Lyon Campbells, where the plans for the Glencoe Massacre are said to have been laid. **Bridge of Orchy** is dominated by **Ben Doran** (3,523 feet) with its curving sides.

For the return to Fort William you go back through Glen Coe again, but this is no hardship: the passage from east to west is generally thought to be the better way to appreciate its grandeur. From Glencoe village it's worth making the circuit of Loch Leven. This delightful trip of continually changing views is spoilt only by **Kinlochleven** at the head of the loch, dominated by the aluminium works. Nevertheless the town is a starting point for some enjoyable walks. On the north side of the loch the road keeps close to the shore giving views of the Appin mountains and eventually of the mouth of Glen Coe again. From Ballachulish to Fort William is a distance of 12 miles.

Glen Spean and Glen Roy

Spean Bridge · Roybridge · Glen Roy · Tulloch
Loch Laggan · Laggan
Fort William

To the south of the Spey Valley and back; waterfalls, mountain scenery and one remarkable natural feature. Fast roads except up Glen Roy. About 100 miles in all.

Take the fast A82 to Spean Bridge where there are good views of Ben Nevis. As well as Telford's 1819 bridge, the older High Bridge built by General Wade in 1736 may be seen two miles downstream, spanning the gorge 100 feet above the river. An arch collapsed in 1913 and it has remained a partial ruin. The first skirmish in the 1745 Rising took place here – three days *before* the Prince raised his standard at Glenfinnan – when a few Macdonells forced the surrender of a body of government troops. Fork right along the A86; in less than a mile **Tirandrish House** (not open) may be seen on the left. It stands on the site of an older house which was burnt after Culloden because the owner had led the Macdonells in the skirmish at High Bridge. He was eventually hanged for his steadfast support for Bonnie Prince Charlie.

Five miles east at **Roybridge**, history seems to move rapidly on from Spean Bridge: the last clan battle in Scotland was fought here, and Telford's bridge built in 1817 was superseded in 1966 by a new bridge. **Keppoch House** (not open), was the scene of the horrific Keppoch Murders in 1663, when rival clansmen murdered the two sons of the 12th chief. The Keppoch bard Iain Lom persuaded Macdonald of Sleat in Skye to give his help and the seven assassins, all brothers, were killed in their house at Inverlair. Iain Lom took their heads to Invergarry to show to the Macdonell chief Glengarry. On the way he washed the heads at the Well of the Seven Heads (see Glen Garry tour). To erase the stain of the murders the castle of Keppoch was pulled down by the Macdonells whose seat it was. Its successor was destroyed after Culloden. Iain Lom and many of his fellow clansmen are buried in the churchyard of **Kilchoireil**, reached by a track flanked by cairns two miles east of Roybridge.

★ An interesting trip off the main road may be taken from Roybridge. Take the narrow road running north up **Glen Roy**. As the valley opens out, four miles from the village, there is a car park and a viewpoint giving remarkable views over the **Parallel Roads**. These take the form of three grassy 'roads' running parallel along the mountains on both sides of the valley. They used to be considered the work of the mythical hero Fingal. They are in fact gravel ledges or terraces marking the levels of the lake that filled the glen during the last ice age, the water being held by a massive glacier. The lake also filled Glen Gloy and part of Glen Spean. As the water level dropped so new 'roads' formed – the top one is the oldest. The phenomenon is considered to be the most remarkable example of glacial activity to be seen in Scotland, and the area is now a nature reserve. The road up the glen ends six miles further on at **Turret Bridge**, but a track continues beside the river and eventually joins General Wade's Military Road at Melgarve near the Corrieyairack Pass. ★

About two miles east of Roybridge the Spean runs through the Achluachrach gorge forming the **Monessie Falls**. At **Tulloch** the Spean drops over the **Inverlair Falls** before being joined near the railway station by the River Treig which flows out of **Loch Treig**, one of Scotland's remotest lochs. In a further mile a car park enables you to gaze, in wonder or dismay, at the **Laggan Dam** at the west end of Loch Laggan – a concrete construction 700 feet long and 175 feet high, which is part of the remarkable scheme supplying water to the aluminium works at Fort William. From Loch Laggan water is led by a tunnel nearly three miles long to Loch Treig. Another tunnel 15 miles long takes the water from Loch Treig through the mountains to Fort William.

Loch Laggan has retained its beauty in spite of the power scheme that increased its length from seven miles to nearly twelve. Wooded mountains surround it, and an easy climb begins at **Aberarder** half-way along. A path leads through grand mountain scenery by vertical cliffs through the Window, a pass through which Bonnie Prince Charlie twice travelled after Culloden. After leaving Loch Laggan the road drops down to **Strathmashie**. Shortly after Strathmashie House a track leads left to **Dun-da-Lamh**, a well preserved hill-fort. The Mashie joins the Spey just west of **Laggan**, and the A86 continues along the popular Spey valley. It's 40 miles back to Fort William.

Accommodation

The popular heart of this region, the area surrounding Fort William, is well provided with accommodation of all sorts; so too, though to a lesser degree, is the Road to the Isles as far as Mallaig. Once you head west, however, to the lonely areas of Ardnamurchan, Moidart and Morvern the time has come for booking ahead as hotels are relatively few and far between. Of the hotels we recommend, one ranks among the best (and most expensive) in Britain.

ARISAIG
Arisaig House (GFG, GHG)
Tel: Arisaig (068 75) 622
This imposing mansion, set in 20 immaculate acres which lead down to the shore, has been largely rebuilt since the original house was burnt out in the 1930s. The thirties flavour is still evident in parts of the sumptuous interior; and from the moment you step inside there is no doubt that this is a hotel in the luxury category. The bedrooms all have bath, colour TV and telephone. There is a billiards room, croquet and a small private jetty.
Open late Mar to early Nov; 16 rooms (including 2 suites); no children under 10; ££££

FORT WILLIAM
Inverlochy Castle (GFG, GHG)
Tel: Fort William (0397) 2177
Winner of the 1984 Good Hotel Guide's award for 'incomparable grandeur', Inverlochy Castle is about as luxurious and as expensive a hotel as you can find in Britain. It is a magnificent Victorian castle which looks out over its own loch and has Ben Nevis as a backdrop. The vast entrance hall is stacked with antiques, the drawing rooms

are extremely elegant, the dining room baronial, and the billiards
room is splendid. Bedrooms are large (some vast) and airy, with
both traditional and modern furnishings; all have bath, colour TV,
telephone, baby-listening and (on request) radio. Service is
punctilious; you may well feel you ought to be, too. You can fish or
play tennis.
Open mid-Mar to mid-Nov; 16 bedrooms; £££££

INVERGARRY
Inn on the Garry
Tel: Invergarry (080 93) 206
Very well situated for touring some of the Highlands' most famous
scenery, this Victorian inn stands near the junction of the A82 and
A87, overlooking the River Garry. It's a bit shabby round the edges
but comfortable and welcoming. The main public rooms are large,
as are the bedrooms (all have bath, radio and tea-making facilities).
Open mid-Mar to mid-Oct (except for special arrangements);
10 bedrooms; £

KENTALLEN
Ardsheal House (GHG)
Tel: Duror (063 174) 227
This lovely historic house, run by an American couple, is set high
on a peninsula looking over Loch Linnhe to the mountains of
Morvern. The public rooms are comfortable in traditional country
house-style; the bedrooms are individually furnished. There is a
billiards room; and outdoors there is a tennis court as well as 900
acres of ground to enjoy.
Open Easter to late Oct; 14 bedrooms; from £££

General Information

Activities
BOAT HIRE Possible at many places in the area.
BOAT TRIPS Arisaig Marine, Tel: Arisaig (068 75) 224 or 678; the
Smill Isles from Arisaig.
Caledonian MacBrayne, Tel: Mallaig (0687) 2403; from Mallaig:
Portree (on Skye) via Kyle of Lochalsh; Armadale (on Skye);
Crowlin Islands (via Kyle of Lochalsh); Loch Duich; Canna, Eigg,
Much and Rhum (see also 'Ferries').
Cameron's Garage, Tel: Onich (085 53) 224; trips to Mull, Lismore
and Loch Leven.
Bruce Watt, Tel: Mallaig (0687) 2320; from Mallaig; Loch Skavaig
and Loch Coruisk (on Skye); Loch Nevis (via Inverie, Tarbet and
Seal Island); Loch Hourn.
Cruises also run from Fort William pier.

FISHING Sea and brown trout in many rivers and lochs.
GOLF Arisaig, Fort William and Spean Bridge.
PONY-TREKKING Places where possible include Lochailort and Torlundy (near Fort William).
SAILING Corpach and lochs Leven, Oich and Morar.
SQUASH Fort William.
SWIMMING Fort William.
TENNIS Fort William.

Entertainment
Ceilidhs, Highland dancing, piping, folk singing etc in local hotels and bars, particularly in Fort William.

Events
JULY Highland Games at Arisaig, Fort William and Invergarry.
AUGUST Agricultural shows at Fort William and Strontian; Glen Nevis river race; Highland Games at Caol, Glenfinnan and Mallaig.
SEPTEMBER Ben Nevis Race.

Ferries
Caledonian MacBrayne, Tel: Mallaig (0687) 2403; from Mallaig: Armadale on Skye, 5 times daily (not Sun), takes 30 min; Canna, Eigg, Muck and Rhum, passenger only, 5 times a week (twice a week to Muck); Fort William to Camusnagaul, passenger only, 8 times daily, not Sun; Lochaline to Fishnish (on Mull), several times daily, takes 5 min, there can be queues in summer.
Corran Ferry, Tel: (085 55) 243: frequent trips across Loch Linnhe.

Tourist Information
Fort William and Lochaber Tourist Organisation, Cameron Square, Fort William, Tel: (0397) 3581
Centres open summer only: Ballachulish, Tel: (085 52) 296; Mallaig, Tel: (0687) 2170

Spey Valley

Spey Valley near Newtonmore

If there is an area of the Highlands which has undergone greater changes than any other it must be the broad fertile valley of the Spey. It has always attracted those who appreciate the contrast between the rugged desolation of the Cairngorm and Monadhliath mountain ranges and the delightful River Spey, rich in salmon, flowing through green fields, gentle wooded slopes and small towns filled in summer by walkers, climbers and fishermen. The beauty is still there, but now the valley is busy with tourists all the year round, and the countryside is dotted with nature trails, picnic sites and forest paths. In addition, all kinds of leisure and sporting activities are provided for as nowhere else in northern Scotland. By car, access to the area is almost too easy – thanks to the fast modern A9 which runs from Perth north across the Grampians and through the valley to Inverness.

The Spey revolution occurred mainly as the result of the opening up of the Cairngorm slopes for skiing. A 'ski road' was constructed striking eastward from near Aviemore, skirting Loch Morlich, to the Coire Cas development with its two chairlifts, seven tows and the Ptarmigan restaurant which, at 3,600 feet, is the highest in Britain. Cairngorm skiing has to cope with unreliable snow and uncertain Scottish weather, but when conditions are good these mountains attract increasing crowds – the chairs and tows can cater for 10,000 skiers an hour.

To meet the needs of all the winter holiday-makers the Aviemore Centre was built – a daring decision to put a modern all-year-round tourist complex, with hotels and all manner of sporting and leisure facilities, in the middle of a previously unspoilt tract of the Highlands; or a mistaken one if you share the view of those who consider it a concrete monstrosity. This opening up of the Spey valley for winter holidays has not, however, lessened its attraction for summer holidays; quite the reverse in fact. An area which pioneered pony-trekking in Britain has widened its appeal to include facilities for gliding and watersports of all kinds. For those who don't want to spend all their time falling off board-sailers or getting pony-sore bottoms, a wildlife park and folk museum are just two of the attractions to visit in the area; or you might take a tour of a distillery and sample the malt (though the best way of doing this is to follow the Whisky Trail to the north-east of the area covered in this chapter). Once-sleepy villages have spruced themselves up and added amenities in an effort to compete with the whizz-kid resort of Aviemore up the road. But as an area for touring it is limited compared with many Highland regions; partly because of good roads, most of its places of interest can be covered in a couple of days.

Speyside history too is less rich, though Bonnie Prince Charlie did pass through, and the notorious 'Wolf of Badenoch' had 14th-century strongholds at Ruthven and Lochindorb. He was Alexander Stewart, Earl of Buchan, a 'black sheep' son of Robert II, and he terrorised the area for many years. His atrocities culminated in the burning of Elgin Cathedral in 1390.

The Spey valley remains first and foremost an area where nature has provided ample riches, and for many visitors the new attractions are essentially peripheral. The Cairngorms are the highest range of mountains in Britain with Ben Macdui at 4,296 feet their highest peak, while Cairn Gorm itself is 4,084 feet. Both peaks can be climbed from paths originating off the ski road, though Ben Macdui is much less accessible than its neighbour.

The attractions of the bird and animal life remain undiminished. But the forests of Glenmore and Abernethy are only shadows of their former selves, for as long ago as the 18th century merchants exploited them mercilessly for their timber, and a hundred years ago Glenmore was described as 'a melancholy but a terrific spectacle'. Although sadly reduced in extent the forests are now reasonably safe from exploitation. Abernethy is the haunt of ospreys and capercaillies and indeed also of tourists, though nothing can spoil the beauty of the area round Loch Garten. Glenmore too is to some extent a tourist playground, and the building of the ski road has made it and the Cairngorms accessible to many more people. But there is room for them all; and there can be few more delightful settings for picnics than the shores of Loch an Eilean, with its ruined castle on an island in the middle, or more splendid places for watersports than Loch Morlich with its backdrop of the Cairngorms.

'I am one who always think it fun to be in Scotland'

Hillaire Belloc, *Places*

113

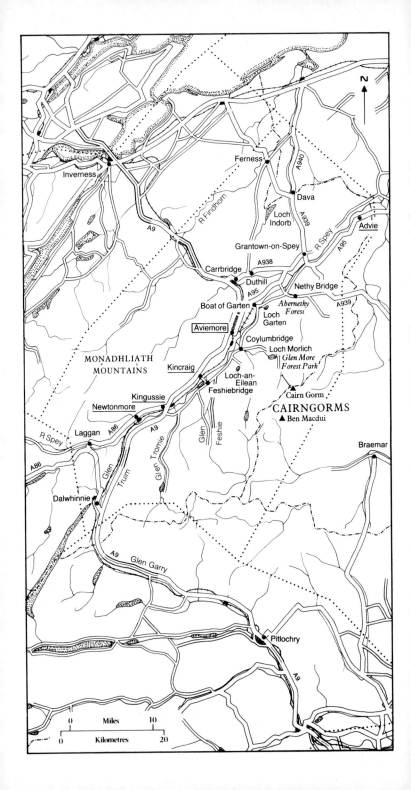

AVIEMORE

On the flat valley floor with the Cairngorms to the east and the Monadhliath Mountains to the west, Aviemore, the best known of the Spey Valley resorts, is a curious and very unHighlandlike place. A hundred years or so ago it was just a small railside community; it was then 'discovered' and developed into a quiet, rather exclusive resort. Today, since the building of the Aviemore complex in the 1960s, it is an all-the-year-round tourist resort. In winter it is Britain's best known skiing centre; in summer the holiday-makers are busy with fishing, pony-trekking, sailing and just about any other activity you care to name.

As well as transforming Aviemore, the Centre has, if to a lesser extent, changed the character of nearby village resorts who felt compelled to compete for tourist custom. By any definition its range of sporting and leisure facilities is extensive – from modern hotels and a cinema to trampolines and go karts; the latest attraction is Santa Claus Land, an outdoor children's amusement park complete with massive toy shop. But, as Aviemore never was a beautiful place, it's probably no bad thing to have all these facilities concentrated in one great concrete complex rather than distributed piecemeal over a wider area.

Aviemore Speyside station is just beyond the British Rail station, and is linked with the village by an underpass. From here the **Strathspey Railway** runs five miles to Boat of Garten, following the old Highland Railway built in 1863 and closed in 1965. The steam trains travel through the Spey valley by gentle gradients to the Summit and through woodland to the Victorian station at Boat of Garten. Services run on weekends at Easter and from mid-May; more often in high summer.

Four miles from Aviemore, along the ski road to Coire Cas, is **Glenmore Forest Park**, a huge area of mountain and forest. The watersports centre at **Loch Morlich** offers board-sailing, sailing and canoeing and a sandy beach. Each morning parties leave the **Reindeer House** to see the reindeer herd. Those who wish to ascend Cairn Gorm can take the two-stage **chairlift**, followed by about an hour's walk from the restaurant at the second stage to the summit. The views across the valley are far-reaching rather than spectacular. By Glenmore Information Office stands the **Commando Memorial** to the Norwegian company who trained in the Cairngorms in the Second World War.

One of the most beautiful spots in Scotland is just three miles from Aviemore: **Loch-an-Eilean** is reached by a turning off the B970. On an island stands a ruined castle which is claimed, quite erroneously, to have been the stronghold of the 'Wolf of Badenoch', the outlawed Alexander Stewart. The castle in fact dates from the mid-15th century. The loch is part of the Rothiemurchus Estate which also runs a Visitor Centre, from where there are guided walks and farm tours, and a trout farm at Inverdruie.

Carrbridge and Grantown-on-Spey

Carrbridge · Ferness · Dava · Grantown-on-Spey
Nethy Bridge · Boat of Garten · Coylumbridge
Aviemore

A tour along good roads through moorland and some of the lower Spey valley: from the well-organised Carrbridge Visitor Centre to the undisturbed loveliness of Loch Garten. About 55 miles.

The A9 is the direct road northward to Inverness, but the A95 and then the B9153 is the route to take for the resort village of **Carrbridge** with its **Landmark Visitor Centre**, a striking modern building pleasantly situated in a pine forest. The coach parties pack in to sample its attractions – an audio-visual triple-screen display on 'The Highland Experience', an exhibition describing the history of man in the Spey valley from the late Ice Age, nature trails and a sculpture park. There are also shops, restaurant and bar.

Take the A938 from Carrbridge to **Duthil**, formerly called Glencharnoch, the 'glen of heroes'. Members of the Grant family have been buried in the churchyard for 300 years. Half a mile west of Duthil the B9007 strikes northward over the moors to reach **Ferness**, 14 miles distant. At this point a short detour might be made to **Ardclach** on the western bank of the River Findhorn. Half a mile from the church, up a narrow lane, is its two-storey **Bell Tower** (AM), built in 1655. The bell both summoned worshippers and acted as a alarm; the tower commands a wide view above a very pretty stretch of the river.

From Ferness the A939 leads south-eastward five miles to Dava. A right turn leads to Loch Indorb ('loch of the minnows'). On an islet are the remains of **Lochindorb Castle**, originally a stronghold of the Comyns. Edward I seized and occupied it in 1303, taking the opportunity to strengthen its defences. Later it came into the possession of the Wolf of Badenoch. In 1445 James II ordered the castle to be demolished.

The road climbs Dava Moor to over 1,000 feet with fine views. About four miles towards Grantown a footpath on the left leads through a gate to **Huntly's Cave**, said to be the hiding place of Charles I's supporter Lord Huntly. In a further two miles is the entrance lodge to Castle Grant, built in 1536, now partly dilapidated (and not open). Queen Victoria was not amused by it: 'a very plain-looking house, like a factory .... we did not get out'.

Grantown-on-Spey is the most pleasant and relaxing of the Spey valley communities. It is a graceful town founded by Sir James Grant in the 18th century, with a spacious dignified square. More recent tourist developments have changed its character little.

Leave Grantown by the A95 turning right along the B970 on the eastern side of the Spey valley to **Nethy Bridge**, a small but attractive village with delightful walks in the vicinity. A pretty side road winds five miles through Abernethy Forest past **Loch Garten**

Nature Reserve. For 25 years ospreys have returned from Africa in the spring to nest here. Binoculars are provided to enable enthusiasts to watch their eyrie from a hide. Rejoin the B970 and cross the river to **Boat of Garten** by the bridge that replaced the ferry from which the village derived its name. The Strathspey Railway runs between Aviemore and here. The station is worth a visit whether or not you take a train – Victorian and fun; the waiting-rooms and office now house a museum and shop.

The B970 continues beside the Spey to **Coylumbridge**, another recently developed tourist centre, and a good starting point for walks to Rothiemurchus Forest and on to the Cairngorms, through Glen Einich and the Lairig Ghru pass. Aviemore, two miles west, is reached by way of **Inverdruie**, where the Alpine plant nursery has some attractive gardens.

The Upper Spey

Kincraig · Kingussie · Newtonmore · Laggan
Glen Truim · Glen Feshie
Aviemore

Easy driving through valley, pass and glen, with a wildlife park, an excellent folk museum and memories of Bonnie Prince Charlie. About 75 miles

Leave Aviemore by the B9153 keeping to the western side of the Spey and soon passing **Loch Alvie**. On the other side of the railway are two monuments: a pillar in memory of the fifth Duke of Gordon and a cairn to the Highlanders who were killed at the Battle of Waterloo. At the village of Kincraig there is a watersports centre on Loch Insh. **Insh Church**, overlooking the loch on a site sacred since the Druids, contains the bronze bell of St Adamnan, a simple bronze Celtic handbell.

A short way south of Kincraig is the **Highland Wildlife Park**. There are more than 50 species of mammals and birds with the emphasis on those indigenous to the Highlands, present and past. In the drive-through area the animals include red deer, Highland cattle and wild horses; the walk-round section has wilder, rarer animals from polecats to arctic foxes. There's also a children's area with domestic animals and pony rides. Entrance is charged per car.

About 10 miles upstream is **Kingussie**, a grey town and thriving summer and winter resort. The ruins of Ruthven Barracks on the other side of the Spey are visited on the return journey.

★ Actually in the village of Kingussie and well worth a visit is the **Highland Folk Museum**. This is a fascinating display of Highland life as it used to be, indoors and out. Period rooms help to show the costume, furniture, weapons and instruments of the past, with many fine example of craftsmanship. Reconstructed buildings include a Lewis black house. The farming museum has a stable, barn, dairy, carts, ploughs and other implements as well as a tinker encampment. Some machinery can be operated by visitors. The museum, a model of its kind, was founded by Dr Isabel Grant and was based first at Iona and then at Laggan. ★

Newtonmore, four miles south on the A86, is quite an attractive grey stone village which again has benefited from the development of the Cairngorm skiing area. It is no stranger to sporting enthusiasm since it has long been a stronghold of shinty (Scottish hockey). Moreover, pony-trekking, so popular now, had its origin here. A road and track along Glen Banchor enable walkers to penetrate deep into the Monadhliath Mountains. This is Macpherson country and Newtonmore is the home of the modern **Clan Museum**, its prize exhibit being a black chanter said to have been presented to the Macphersons by the 'little people', and played at a clan battle at Perth.

Beyond Newtonmore, off the A86, high in a crag of Craig Dhubh (the 'black rock') is a cave where clan chief Cluny Macpherson hid Bonnie Prince Charlie during his escape after the Battle of Culloden; a mile along the road toward Laggan is his home, Cluny Castle (not open). The original building was burnt by Cumberland's troops; the present one dates from the 19th century. Many of the Macpherson chiefs lie in the burial ground below it.

Laggan is situated in a strategic position commanding the crossing of the Spey at Laggan Bridge. This district is an important watershed: two rivers have their sources within a few miles, the Spey flowing eastward and the Spean westward. 'General Wade's Road', built in 1735, strikes off westward at Laggan, passing the Spey dam and crossing the river at Garvamore. Here the road becomes a track, winding over 20 miles to Fort Augustus through the Corrieyairack Pass at 2,500 ft. The Bonnie Prince marched his men south this way, in the hopeful early stages of the 1745 Rising, and Cluny Macpherson joined him at Garvamore.

From Laggan the A86 crosses the river and goes off westward past Loch Laggan to Spean Bridge (see previous chapter). The A889 goes south to Dalwhinnie, a hilly run of seven miles along the continuation of General Wade's Road. **Dalwhinnie** is a small and somewhat desolate village, appealing chiefly to walkers and winter-sports enthusiasts who will be glad of the presence of a distillery. The village stands at the north end of Loch Ericht, which is part of the Rannoch Hydro-Electric scheme and is surrounded by exceptionally wild country. The clans were safe here, first from Cromwell's army, later from General Cope who refused to encounter Bonnie Prince Charlie's advance. After the Battle of Culloden the Prince took refuge deep in this wilderness below Ben Alder, at the spot known variously as 'Cluny's Cave' and 'Prince Charlie's Cave'. It should, however, be noted that the line between fact and romance is sometimes unclear where the movements of the Prince are concerned. But clan history records that his supporter Macpherson spent nine years hiding here, in a strange structure known as 'Cluny's Cage', hunted by the English but never betrayed. South of Dalwhinnie the road to Blair Atholl (see Pitlochry chapter) crosses the **Pass of Drumochter** (1,484 feet), where the railway summit is the highest in Britain.

The return to the Spey valley is by way of the A9 through **Glen Truim**, a 10-mile downhill run with good views of the Monadhliath Mountains and presently, to the right, of the Cairngorms. About 14 miles from Dalwhinnie, near Kingussie, turn east onto the B970 along the south side of the valley to Ruthven. **Ruthven Barracks** (AM) stands on the site of a castle owned first by the Comyns and later by the Wolf of Badenoch. The barracks, built in 1719 to house a garrison intended to keep the rebellious Highlanders in check, was further fortified by General Wade. Nevertheless, after an abortive attempt in 1745 the Jacobites captured the barracks which became a rallying point after the Battle of Culloden. Here, to general dismay, the Prince ordered the clans to disperse and escape as best they could. The ruins are floodlit during the summer.

From nearby Tromie Bridge a rough and private road runs south along **Glen Tromie** for 13 miles through increasingly lonely scenery to Loch an t-Seilich, part of the Rannoch Hydro-Electric scheme. Four miles north of Tromie Bridge, along the B970 past Insh, a road runs southward along the west side of romantic **Glen Feshie** eight miles to Glenfeshie Lodge – the last four miles is private. A footpath leads a mile or so to a picnic place and a birdlife trail at Rock Wood Ponds, and you can continue as far as Braemar or Blair Atholl. The other side of Glen Feshie can be explored by a road beginning at **Feshiebridge**, where there is another picnic place and a viewpoint, and ending at Achlean. From Feshiebridge to Aviemore is a distance of nine miles.

Accommodation

Not surprisingly this popular area has a lot of accommodation. All the villages along the valley have the usual range of traditional hotels, guests houses and bed and breakfast places, and in the Aviemore Centre there are high-rise modern hotels. The hotels we recommend range from the modest but homely to the exclusive and luxurious.

ADVIE
Tulchan Lodge
Tel: Advie (080 75) 200
Surrounded by 22,000 acres of grounds this shooting lodge built in the early part of this century is a superb place, tailor-made for the hunting, shooting and fishing fraternity. Public rooms are dignified and sumptuously furnished. Bedrooms are slightly more modest but comfortable; some are very large; all have bath and telephone, and colour TV and baby-listening are available on request. Service is of the highest standards. There is a billiards room, and fishing, shooting and stalking on the estate.
Open Apr to early Jan; 10 bedrooms (and 1 cottage); £££££

KINCRAIG
Invereshie House
Tel: Kincraig (054 04) 332
A Georgian house, converted from a 17th-century shooting lodge, in a tranquil setting at the foot of the gentle Cairngorm slopes, near Loch Insh. Enthusiastically and informally run, the hotel is a mixture of styles. The dinning room is furnished in period; there is a comfortable modern lounge and a cosy, attractive bar. Bedrooms are simple but spacious; all have tea-making facilities. There is fishing.
Open all year except Nov; 8 bedrooms (and 5 self-catering units); £

KINGUSSIE
Osprey Hotel (GFG, GHG)
Tel: Kingussie (054 02) 510
A small family hotel just off the main road, offering a friendly atmosphere, wholesome food and comfortable, homely surroundings. Three of the rooms have private baths. You may have to share your table at dinner.
Open Jan to late Oct; 8 bedrooms; £

NEWTONMORE
Ard-Na-Coille (GHG)
Tel: Newtonmore (054 03) 214
A former Edwardian shooting lodge set 'high in the woods' among the pine trees, with commanding views of the Cairngorms. The

public rooms are comfortable. The bedrooms are more modest; all have radio and baby-listening; only one has a private bath but some have showers. There is table tennis; and games, puzzles and reading material are liberally distributed.

Open Jan to Oct; 10 bedrooms; £

General Information

Activities

BOAT HIRE Loch Morlich; see also 'sailing'.

FISHING Salmon in the Spey. Brown trout in most rivers and lochs.

GLIDING Feshiebridge.

GOLF Boat of Garten, Carrbridge, Grantown-on-Spey, Kingussie, Nethy Bridge and Newtonmore.

PONY-TREKKING Aviemore, Carrbridge, Kincraig, Kingussie, Laggan, Nethy Bridge and Newtonmore.

SAILING Watersports centres at Loch Insh and Loch Morlich; also available at Inverdruie.

SQUASH Aviemore.

SWIMMING Aviemore.

TENNIS Boat of Garten, Grantown-on-Spey, Inverdruie, Kingussie and Nethy Bridge.

Entertainment

Cinema and theatre at Aviemore. Discos, ceilidhs etc at various local hotels.

Events

AUGUST Highland Games at Abernethy, Aviemore, Dulchully and Newtonmore; Grantown Agricultural Show; Square Fayre, Grantown-on-Spey.

SEPTEMBER Carrbridge Ceilidh Week.

Tourist information

Aviemore and Spey Tourist Information Centre, Grampian Road, Aviemore, Tel: (0479) 810363

Centres open summer only: Carrbridge, Tel: (0479 84) 630; Grantown-on-Spey, Tel: (0479) 2773; Kingussie, Tel: (054 02) 297; Newtonmore, Tel: (054 03) 274; Ralia, Tel: Newtonmore (054 03) 253

Inverness
and
Loch Ness

Castle Urquhart

The dominating geographical feature of the Highlands is the Great Glen. This vast geological fault splits the country between Inverness and Fort William in a straight rift valley 60 miles long. Lochs Lochy, Oich and Ness fill two thirds of its bed; to link and complete a waterway, the 22 miles of the Caledonian Canal were constructed during the first half of the 19th century.

Begun by Thomas Telford, the route having earlier been surveyed by James Watt, the operation proved unexpectedly difficult and costly – it was necessary to raise the levels of two of the natural stretches of water as well as build 29 locks. At its initial opening in 1822 the canal proved too shallow, and though, when finally completed in 1847, it was useful for sailing and fishing boats which no longer had to negotiate the stormy north coast, the threat of French attacks on British shipping (which had been a prime reason for going ahead with the scheme) had long since disappeared. Today it is mainly used by pleasure craft.

Quite apart from the question of a monstrous existence in its depths, Loch Ness is a remarkable sheet of water – eight rivers feed it, and it is deeper than the North Sea and much of the Atlantic;

furthermore it has never been known to freeze. It is one of Scotland's longest lochs but is only three quarters of the area of Loch Lomond, Scotland's biggest loch. The first report of a beast living in these depths was in the 6th century, but since then the creature seems to have kept itself to itself until curiosity overcame it in the 20th century – perhaps as the result of the opening of the road on the north side in 1934 and the arrival of the age of radio and television. Scientific expeditions, from many countries, including Japan, have descended on the loch with echo-sounders, a submarine and even apparatus for obtaining a piece of the monster's skin or flesh. Today many eminent people are convinced of the creature's existence, and monster hunting is a full-time business; but since Loch Ness is 24 miles long, more than a mile wide and in places 900 feet deep, Nessie is probably safe for a long time to come.

This is one of the most populated areas of the Highlands but the population is concentrated in the north-east around the towns of Inverness and Nairn. Once you head south and west, villages are few and small, and there are acres of unspoilt countryside to explore – though it can take some effort to escape from all the other holiday-makers in their cars.

Much of the area east of the Great Glen is occupied by the Monadhliath ('grey mountains'), undramatic and sometimes desolate, but providing excellent opportunities for hill-walking. On the south side of Loch Ness an attractive road follows General Wade's military road partly through the mountains but also, close to the loch, through some pastoral scenery; this is the road to take to avoid the crowds. The trunk road on the north side is modern and, though running close to the loch, affords glimpses rather than prolonged vistas for most of its 35 miles.

West of Drumnadrochit, Glen Urquhart leads to the beautiful glens of Farrar, Cannich and Affric, gentle rather than wild and spectacular, and very popular. Hydro-electric schemes have caused disruption in some extremely lovely parts but, on the other hand, they have resulted in the opening up of formerly inaccessible areas for the motorist.

The coast and countryside round Inverness and Nairn are flat and without much scenic interest. But they include a splendid castle at Cawdor and a moving reminder of the Highlands' tragic past at Culloden Moor. Nairn marks the start of a seaside holiday coast; from here to Lossiemouth and beyond there are a number of lovely sandy beaches.

For those who haven't been to the Highlands before, curiosity must put Loch Ness high on their list of areas to visit. Having failed to spot the monster, there are plenty of other things to do in the way of boat trips, places of interest and generally enjoying the outdoors, but whether it's an area you would want to return to year after year is much less certain.

123

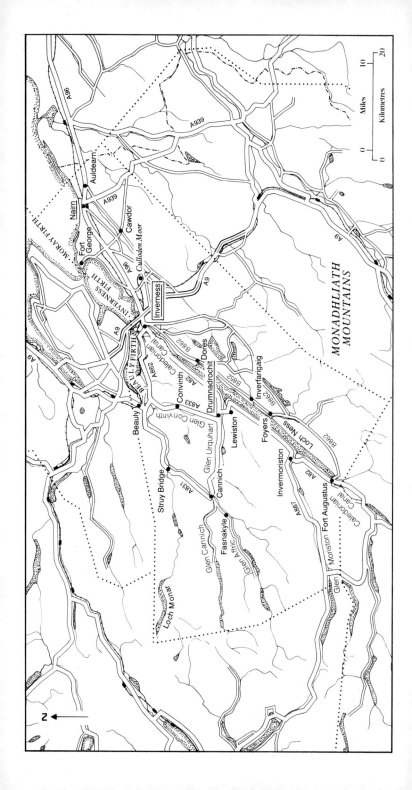

INVERNESS

Inverness has long borne the title of 'capital of the Highlands'. This is now literally true, because the reorganisation of local government in 1974 made it the administrative headquarters of both the Inverness District and the Highland Regional Council. A large and busy centre, well placed as a base for touring, it is one of the main termini for visitors coming to the Highlands by public transport from the south, and has excellent communications by road, rail, water and air with all parts of the Highland region.

Standing at the outlet of the Caledonian Canal, Inverness has easy access to both the sea and, through Loch Ness, to Fort William and beyond. Boat trips are available on the loch, coaches make excursions to all parts of the Highlands, and motorists have at their disposal the enticing network of roads that open up the remotest regions. Shops, hotels and restaurants are plentiful and there is a good cross-section of entertainment, much with a Scottish flavour. Many sporting and leisure activities are available.

For all its modern tourist facilities, Inverness, it must be admitted, lacks charm; and it is not a place to stay more than a few days, even as a base for touring. There are few buildings of aesthetic or historical interest and the old character of the town was spoilt by large-scale development in the 1960s. Its redeeming feature is its setting on the wide River Ness; and its pleasantest area is the Ness islands about a mile upstream. These leafy islands, in effect a park, are connected by bridges which cross the river.

The existing **Castle** is a mid-19th-century building now used as a courthouse and administrative offices. The previous building on the site was blown up by the Jacobites. The statue of Flora Macdonald on the esplanade looks south-west towards the countryside where Bonnie Prince Charlie hid after Culloden, and from the hill there are excellent views of the river and the town.

Nearly all the other places of interest in Inverness are within walking distance of each other, and in summer there are guided walks which start from the Tourist Office. Just down the hill from the Castle is the **Museum** and (within the same modern building) the **Art Gallery**; the former is devoted to Highland and Jacobite history, the latter largely to old Inverness. The **Town House** is 19th-century Gothic, with stained-glass windows, paintings and the council chamber which was the scene in 1921 of the first Cabinet Meeting held in Scotland. Outside is the restored Town Cross standing on a base containing the *Clach-na-Cuddain* ('stone of the tubs'). Here, long ago, the women of Inverness rested tubs of water carried from the river. **Abertarff House** (NTS), dating from 1592, is a laird's town house with a round tower staircase. It is the headquarters of the organisation devoted to the culture of the Gaels and has a small exhibition and a bookshop. Further out of the town centre is **Cromwell's Clock Tower**, all that remains of his garrison fort, pulled down by the townspeople when the English left.

The northern glens

Beauly · Struy Bridge · Cannich · Glen Cannich · Glen Affric
Glen Urquhart · Drumnadrochit · Glen Convinth
Inverness

A tour of some splendid glen scenery, including a taste of Loch Ness.
Sweeping main road to Beauly; 16 easy miles of wooded valleys to
Cannich, but slowly up and down glens Cannich and Affric (one of the
prettiest Highland glens). Major road again to Drumnadrochit, a
popular monster-watching spot. Returning not by Loch Ness but through
the gentler scenery of Glen Convinth to rejoin the route beside the Firth
back to Inverness. About 95 miles in all.

The A862 east from Inverness crosses the Caledonian Canal and
reaches the Beauly Firth at **Clachnaharry** with fine views of the
Firth until it swings away through gentle countryside, the domain
of the Frasers of Lovat. Follow the A862 to the right at Lovat
Bridge for the short trip to **Beauly**, an attractive village with a
pleasant spacious square and a ruined priory (AM) which was
founded in the 13th century. The north chapel, which contains
tombs and monuments of the Mackenzies, was restored early this
century. The monument in the square is to the Lovat Scouts, a
Highland force raised to fight in the Boer War.

Go back a mile and turn right along the A831, shortly joining the
River Beauly as it flows through woodland. At **Kilmorack** and at
Aigas, three miles farther along the river, loom hydro-electric
stations complete with dams; visitors are welcome. Each dam has a
fish pass which is opened each morning to allow fish to travel
up-river. An island in the river near Aigas was the hiding place of a
Lord Lovat on the run in 1697. The valley now becomes less rocky
and the river flows gently through fertile pastures. At **Struy Bridge**
the rivers Glass and Farrar combine to form the Beauly. An
unsurfaced road (permission needed) beside the Farrar runs for 15
miles as far as **Loch Monar**; from here a rough path continues for a
further 20 miles to Loch Carron on the west coast.

The main road turns up the **Strathglass**, close to the winding
river, past Glassburn where there is an inscribed well dedicated to
St Ignatius, to **Cannich**. This village – of little beauty or charm – is
the crossroads for exploring the four glens of Affric, Cannich,
Strathglass and Urquhart.

From Cannich's conveniently-sited modern hotel the northern
road up **Glen Cannich** runs for nine miles, at first through thick
woods backed by mountains and then through moorland to Loch
Mullardoch with its dam and power station. The road south-west
from the village goes to **Fasnakyle**, where the power station was
built in golden sandstone to help it blend into its surroundings.

★ If time is at a premium don't bother making the journey up Glen
Cannich; instead head straight up **Glen Affric**, perhaps the most

beautiful in all Scotland. Its charm is variety and pretty detail: the ferns and mossy rocks of its swift river, enclosed in all the greens of birch and beech and pine; then an islanded loch with vistas of the mountains. The first stop you should make is at **Dog Falls**, a lovely spot where there are plenty of rocks to clamber over. After that there is no shortage of places where you can stop to admire the views before the road finally ends, after 12 miles, at a well-equipped picnic site overlooking Loch Affric. From here a path heads west beside the loch passing an isolated Youth Hostel at Alltbeath, continuing another 15 miles or so right across to Loch Duich. Inevitably, Glen Affric gets crowded – in summer it is full of walkers, cyclists and cars – but there are enough passing places along the narrow road to save it from becoming unbearable. ★

From Fasnakyle another road leads to **Tomich**, at the edge of the Guisachan Estate with its marvellous forests of Scots pine. A track continues to the fine **Plodda Falls** three miles south. North from Tomich, the road joins the A831 which runs through **Glen Urquhart**. In about three miles, make a brief detour south to see the chambered **Corrimony Cairn** (AM), surrounded by a stone circle dating from about 3,000 BC. A roofed entrance passage leads to the burial chamber which was excavated in 1952.

The main road continues beside the River Enrick and past Loch Meiklie to **Drumnadrochit**, one of the few villages of any size near Loch Ness, set on the Enrick just before it flows into the loch. Behind the Drumnadrochit Hotel is the **Loch Ness Centre**. Its main attraction is the Loch Ness Monster Exhibition, which uses various media to lecture you about the sightings of the monster and the efforts made to photograph it, capture it or merely confirm its existence. What is sure is that it can never be disproved, which is very convenient for all concerned. There is also a museum with displays of kilts and weapons up to 200 years old. Not far from the village are the substantial ruins of Castle Urquhart on the shore of the loch (see following tour).

For the return to Inverness, go back almost a mile and take the A833 northward over a steep bit of unexpected moorland and down **Glen Convinth**. At Convinth village take a right turn along an unclassified road through farmland and oak trees to reach **Reelig Glen Forest Trails**, where several footpaths lead to a 19th-century bridge and grotto. From here the main A862 is only a mile to the north and Inverness a further six miles distant.

A circuit of Loch Ness

*The north shore road is the flat and busy one, your views of the loch often
impeded by bends, trees and traffic. The narrower south road, built by
General Wade, is much more varied, with better views of loch and
mountains and no great driving problems. About 70 miles in all.*

However sceptical the observer may be about monsters, there is no
doubt that this stretch of water holds a more than ordinary
fascination. Take the A82, running beside the Caledonian Canal as
it joins Loch Dochfour. At the head of Loch Ness and on the
opposite bank stands **Aldourie Castle**, the birthplace of the
historian and statesman James Mackintosh. Fifteen miles south of
Inverness the road takes a sweep inland round **Urquhart Bay** and
through Drumnadrochit (see previous tour). At **Lewiston** a trip
may be made to Glen Coiltie and the **Falls of Divach**, to which
there is a Forestry Commission walk.

★ One of the few places where you can get a leisurely view of Loch
Ness rather than a glimpse is by **Castle Urquhart** (AM), once one of
Scotland's largest castles but a ruin for more than two hundred
years. A stronghold has stood on this strategic site since the original
prehistoric vitrified fort, and the first royal castle in the 13th
century was replaced by Edward I. The present ruins, dating
mainly from 1509, are an impressive sight; they spread over a high
grassy knoll and comprise the keep, four square turrets and a
surrounding wall. The ascent is steep, but don't let that put you off
exploring them properly. On a sunny day there are few nicer places
for a picnic – if it isn't too crowded. ★

Two miles further on is the **Cobb Memorial** to the racing driver
who was killed here in an attempt on the world water speed record
in 1952. At the hamlet of **Invermoriston**, 27 miles from Inverness,
the road to Kyle of Lochalsh and the ferry to Skye strikes off
westward through **Glen Moriston**, a beautiful wooded glen now
part of a hydro-electric scheme. Just before **Ceannacroc Bridge**,
near the western end of the glen, is a roadside cairn to Roderick
Mackenzie, who in 1746 drew off the pursuers of Bonnie Prince
Charlie by pretending to be the Prince. Nearby is the cave where
Charles hid, guarded by the Seven Men of Glen Moriston.

The A82 at Invermoriston crosses the River Moriston and in
seven miles reaches the busy touring centre of **Fort Augustus**, an
undistinguished village now, but formerly of considerable importance. A garrison was stationed here after the Jacobite rising of 1715
and a barracks built, a fragment of which is in the grounds of the
Lovat Arms Hotel. The original Fort Augustus was built by
General Wade in 1730 and named after William Augustus, Duke of

128

Cumberland. During the 1745 Rising the Highlanders captured it; after Culloden, Cumberland's troops re-took it; in 1867 the fort was dismantled and sold, and on its site was built the present Benedictine Abbey and school. Part of the old fort and a model are shown to visitors, but only on guided tours. Fort Augustus stands at the extreme southern end of Loch Ness, and the Caledonian Canal runs through it to link with Loch Oich. There are six canal locks in the town and beside them is the **Great Glen Exhibition**, where exhibits and an audio-visual show give an interesting account of the history and geography of the area of the Great Glen. **Cherry Island**, close to the shore, is the site of a crannog (lake dwelling), a defensive structure built on timbers some two thousand years ago. The grave of John Anderson, Robert Burns' 'John Anderson, my jo John', is in the church graveyard. **Inchnacardoch** to the north is a recently built forestry village, and a forestry trail has been laid out.

At this point, cross the Caledonian Canal and keep left along the B862 to reach the south side of Loch Ness, following a route which is considerably less busy and on the whole more picturesque than the A82. This is one of the four roads built by General Wade that cross at Fort Augustus. In all his troops built something like 800 miles of road, much of which is now footpath. The B862 and B852 follow the line of Wade's road closely.

The road passes Loch Tarff and then climbs steadily to reach **Whitebridge View Point** at 1,162 feet, at the farthest point from Loch Ness. From here there is a surprising and splendid panorama eastward, over the Monadhliath Mountains – well worth a stop. At the next fork the main road keeps right past Loch Mhor to Dores and Inverness (22 miles). But a more attractive route is the B852 which follows Wade's road and quickly descends to the loch side at **Foyers**. Foyers was once famous for its two waterfalls, but its waters were harnessed in 1896 to provide hydro-electric power for Britain's first aluminium works. This closed in 1967, but the waters are now used for a power station and as a result the flow is only a fraction of its former volume. A steep and slippery path through gloomy conifers leads to the falls, one of 40 feet, the other of 90.

The **Farigaig Forest Trails**, at Inverfarigaig, include woodland trails and a small Visitor Centre with a well-displayed exhibition on the development of the forests of the Great Glen. The road runs very close to the shore of Loch Ness, for about 10 miles; this is the stretch (with Castle Urquhart on the opposite bank) where most of the claimed monster-sightings have taken place. Near Kinchyle, about two miles north-west is the **McBain Memorial Park**, laid out in memory of the McBain clan with views of Loch Ness and down the Great Glen. Six miles after Dores a right turn leads to the roadside **Knocknagael Boar Stone**, a Pictish stone bearing the figure of a boar; Inverness is only two miles further.

The coast, Culloden and Cawdor

A route through level country but in no other sense flat, taking you from the seaside to some vivid Scottish history, with a jewel of a castle in between. Easy roads though most are minor ones; about 50 miles.

From Inverness to Nairn is a distance of only 16 miles by the A96, but this route is dull as well as direct. Instead, branch left after about five miles along the B9039 past the airport and through **Ardersier** to **Fort George** (AM). This splendid example of Hanoverian military architecture was begun, to the design of Robert Adam, in 1748, three years after the Jacobite rising. It has six bastions and strong outer defences. It is a barracks, but sections are open to the public (closed Sun am) including the Regimental Museum of the Seaforth and Cameron Highlanders (now amalgamated as the Queen's Own Highlanders).

South-east of Ardersier, the B9092 runs eastward to join the A96 to **Nairn**, an attractive town of mellow buildings and a popular seaside resort. It has fine sandy beaches, a good sunshine record, and its wide-ranging tourist amenities include a championship golf course. It is also a place of historical interest, for it became a royal burgh in the 12th century and a castle once stood near the River Nairn. The quaint fishermen's quarter is evidence of its days as an important herring fishing port (now long past). That period is recalled in the interesting **Fishertown Museum**.

Auldearn, three miles east of Nairn, is notable as the spot where Montrose routed the forces of the Covenanters in 1645. On the motte of the now vanished castle stands the 17th-century **Boath Doocot** (NTS), or dovecote, and there's a plan of the battle on display. From Auldearn the B9101 runs south-westward, crosses the A939, and merges into the B9090 before arriving at the lovely conservation village of **Cawdor**.

★ **Cawdor Castle** was founded in the 15th-century, remodelled during the 17th and has been the family home of the Thanes of Cawdor for over 500 years. The building manages to look both impregnably fortified and very pretty, the entrance over a drawbridge and through a courtyard being particularly picturesque. The interior is well worth a visit. The rooms are finely furnished – there are impressive tapestries – and the kitchen and dungeon hold a special fascination. There are gardens, nature trails and picnic places in the well-groomed grounds. ★

Kilravock Castle, two miles west of Cawdor, has an impressive situation overlooking the River Nairn; the grounds but not the castle are open. It dates from 1460 and Bonnie Prince Charlie visited it in 1746. At Clephanton turn left and in a further mile left again onto the **B9006**. This road crosses **Culloden Moor**, where the Jacobite cause was finally destroyed with so many of its adherents. The first memorial is the roadside **Cumberland Stone**, a great boulder from which, it is said, the Duke of Cumberland directed the tactics of his army. Make a short detour here down the lane to the left to see the impressive **Clava Cairns** (AM). Set among beech trees, three great domed burial cairns with open central chambers are ringed with standing stones. At nearby Culdoich there is a similar cairn which was excavated in 1953.

The events leading up to the Battle of Culloden are outlined on page 14. Having been forced out of England and having failed to capture Stirling Castle, the Jacobite army retired to Inverness. Two days later Inverness fell and the Jacobites were scattered. In April 1746 the Jacobites attempted a surprise attack on the English force which had advanced to Nairn. When this failed the demoralised, hungry and exhausted Highlanders drew up for battle at Culloden on 16 April 1746. Cumberland's men numbered about 9,000, the Jacobites 5,000. Cumberland's overwhelming superiority in numbers and superior tactics ensured the utter rout of the Jacobites in less than an hour. Fugitives were slaughtered and in all more than a thousand men were killed, Cumberland being thenceforth known as the 'Butcher'.

The National Trust for Scotland has expended great effort on restoring this historic site since the ground and memorials were passed to it in 1944. Some would no doubt rate Culloden, not Cawdor Castle, the highlight of this tour but, although there is plenty to absorb here, there is not a great deal for the ordinary tourist to see. The 20-foot-high **Cairn** erected in 1881 to the memory of the Highlanders stands on the other side of the road from their graves, which are grouped by clans. At the **Well of the Dead** wounded Highlanders were reputedly killed as they tried to drink. Old Leanach Cottage, a farmhouse which survived the battle, is now the **Battlefield Museum** displaying various maps and mementoes. Near the museum is the Field of the English, the graves of the English dead. The excellent **Visitor Centre**, established in 1970, includes an audio-visual programme.

Culloden House, a mile north-west, occupies the site of the house where Bonnie Prince Charlie stayed on the night before the battle. Nowadays it's a luxury hotel (see next page). Not far away is the **Culloden Moor Battlefield Trail**, laid out by the Forestry Commission. Inverness is four miles from Culloden.

Accommodation

Inverness and Nairn offer a wide choice of hotels and guest houses. There's little accommodation in remoter parts, such as around the northern glens, but hotels and bed and breakfast places can be found in the villages along Loch Ness – though book ahead. The hotels we recommend in the area range from the luxurious to the highly individual.

DRUMNADROCHIT
Polmaily House (GFG, GHG)
Tel: Drumnadrochit (045 62) 343
Fairly new owners have taken over this Edwardian country house hotel and are setting high standards. Public rooms are traditional in style. Individually furnished bedrooms are comfortable and homely; all have radio, most have bath. Cuisine is both traditional – venison, lamb and salmon – and *nouvelle*. The garden covers 18 acres; facilities include tennis, croquet and a swimming pool.
Open Easter to mid-Oct; 9 bedrooms; ££

INVERNESS
Culloden House
Tel: Inverness (0463) 790461
A magnificent mansion in 40 acres of parkland, two miles east of Inverness. Bonnie Prince Charlie spent the night before the Battle of Culloden here; but the present building is essentially Georgian. The public rooms have high ceilings, Adam fireplaces and fine mouldings, though some of the new fittings seem out of keeping with the older features. Bedrooms are large, comfortable and very well-equipped; all have bath, colour TV, radio and telephone. Facilities include billiards, table tennis, tennis, sauna and solarium.
Open all year; 20 bedrooms; £££££

NAIRN
Clifton Hotel (GFG, GHG, GPG)
Tel: Nairn (0667) 53119
An attractive vine-covered house overlooking the Moray Firth, whose décor and furnishings are as flamboyant as owner, Mr MacIntyre. There are numerous paintings and prints around the walls, a mixture of Victorian and oriental furniture, and dramatic colour schemes. Bedrooms (all have bath or shower) are highly individual with personal touches such as hand-made soap and pot-pourri. Public rooms are plentiful and relaxing.
Open Mar to Nov; 16 bedrooms; £££

General Information

Activities
BOAT HIRE Fort Augustus (various types); cabin cruisers at
Dochgarroch and Inverness; see also 'sailing'.
BOAT TRIPS For cruises from Inverness to Loch Ness, through the
Caledonian Canal, Tel: Inverness (0463) 233140 or
Inverness (0463) 233999. For Loch Ness trips from Fort Augustus,
Tel: Fort Augustus (0320) 6316
FISHING Salmon in Loch Ness and rivers Beauly, Cluaire,
Findhorn, Glass, Ness and Nairn. Trout in many lochs.
GOLF Fort Augustus, Inverness and Nairn.
PONY-TREKKING Dores, Drumnadrochit and Kiltarlity.
SAILING Yacht charter at Dochgarroch and Inverness.
SQUASH Inverness and Nairn.
SWIMMING Inverness and Nairn.
TENNIS Fort Augustus, Inverness and Nairn.

Entertainment
Theatre and cinema at both Inverness and Nairn. Pipe bands and
dancing at Beauly, Inverness and Nairn. Highland entertainment,
ceilidhs, folk singing and jazz at various hotels in the area.

Events
JULY Inverness Highland Games; Great Glen Gala, Fort Augustus.
AUGUST Highland Games at Cawdor, Drumnadrochit and Nairn;
Inverness Military Tattoo; Nairn agricultural show;
Highland Field Sports Fair, near Inverness.

Tourist information
Inverness Tourist Office, 23 Church St, Inverness,
Tel: Inverness (0463) 234353
Centres open summer only: Daviot Wood, south of Inverness
(046 385) 203; Fort Augustus, Tel: (0320) 6367;
Nairn, Tel: (0667) 52753

East Ross and the Black Isle

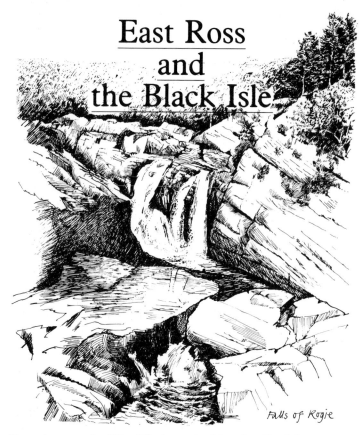

Falls of Rogie

From the summit of Ben Wyvis north of Strathpeffer, it is said, you can see both the North Sea and the Atlantic Ocean on a clear day. This may be the high spot (in both senses) of a visit to East Ross and the Black Isle; with the exception of the west in general and the roads up Straths Carron and Conon in particular, this touring area is flat. It has a great deal of coastline – miles of sandbanks and mudflats are full of seabirds but inaccessible to man. Its three great inlets were well used by the Vikings, overlords of the area for centuries: they christened Gizzen Briggs, the sandbank blocking half the entrance to the Dornoch Firth. Cromarty Firth has a sheltered narrow entrance guarded by cliffs called the North and South Sutors, and fine navigable waters. Charles II arrived here in 1650 to be crowned at Scone; the Royal Navy used it during the two World Wars.

Little Cromarty on the South Sutor was once a prosperous port but has seen many changes. By the end of the 17th century its fortunes had declined to such an extent that Daniel Defoe in 1727 could describe the Firth as 'noted for being the finest Harbour, with the least Business, of perhaps any in Britain'. A century later a new harbour and some factories helped Cromarty revive, but the building of the railway took trade north to Invergordon. Today the northern coastline from Invergordon to Nigg Bay is given over to industrial development, and the new A9 sweeps across the Black Isle towards an area transformed by oil rig construction.

There are fossils along the Moray Firth, and inland a vitrified fort that may go back to 800BC, and many Pictish stones and symbols. Throughout its later history this strategic area tucked in east of the Highlands close to Inverness was in demand, with comings and goings and changes of cast, yet the scene itself bears little record of them. The Earldom of Ross was much disputed between the monarchy and the Lords of the Isles; the Mackenzies of Seaforth were ruined by the Clearances; Munros and Mowats, McNeils and Urquharts are other local clan names – though the events in all their histories seemed to happen on stages elsewhere.

Religious remnants are more in evidence than secular ruins. The first martyr of the Scottish Reformation was burnt at St Andrews in 1528. He was among other things titular Abbot of Fearn. The abbey church there became the parish church and nothing drastic happened to it until the roof fell in, quite unprompted, in 1742. Fortrose Cathedral was simply neglected, crumbling long before Cromwell used it as a quarry. The oldest remains are at Tain: here the sanctuary at St Duthus' shrine was twice violated. Once was for arbitrary political reasons, when in 1307 the wife and daughter of Robert the Bruce were seized by the Earl of Ross for Edward I; the second time it was almost casually destroyed, when a freebooter burnt it down around his enemy. Perhaps this lack of dramatic structure or historical coherence comes from the elements of magic lingering around the Black Isle. In old Nigg Church a little 'Cholera Stone' marks the spot where the plague, in the form of a small cloud, was caught and buried; on Fortrose golf course is a stone commemorating (in competition with Dornoch) the last witch to be burned in Scotland; witches and 'little folk' haunted Hugh Miller's glens and the prophesies of the Seer of Brahan are still treated with respect – not only in the museum at Rosemarkie.

With the development of Strathpeffer as a spa resort a hundred years ago, East Ross had its fashionable side, but this faded with the people's taste for taking the waters. For southerners who want to experience the real Highlands, East Ross and the Black Isle is not the part to visit except *en route* to Sutherland and Caithness. But for others the area has its attractions. There are some pretty coastal villages with sandy beaches, and leisure activities include golf and pony-trekking. The birdlife and geology of the area are interesting; and the southern coast of the Black Isle and the area around Strathpeffer offer a pleasant range of walks. The little towns of Tain and Dingwall have their appeal, and Strathpeffer rather more. Sightseeing is limited, the scenery mostly placid, and not every aspect pleases.

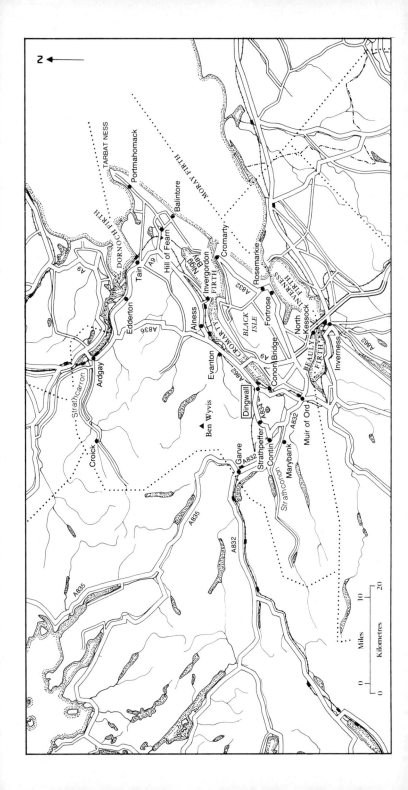

DINGWALL

Dingwall is the administrative headquarters of Ross and Cromarty and is strategically situated at the head of the Cromarty Firth. From here there is a splendid train route to Kyle of Lochalsh, and a less spectacular one to Wick; and it is well placed for exploring East Ross and the Black Isle, the large-scale reconstruction of the A9 with bridges over Beauly Firth and Cromarty Firth having left it in peace. Dingwall has a long history though few reminders of it have survived. The Norsemen, who occupied it in the 11th century, gave it the name *thingvollr*, 'place of the parliament' – its administrative function is no recent development. Of the 12th-century royal castle just a few stones remain in Castle Street. The oldest building still standing is the former school (about 1650) beside the Town House which itself dates from the 18th century. The Tolbooth Tower in the long High Street was built in 1730; in front of it is the shaft of the mercat cross. On Mitchell Hill to the south stands a square tower commemorating General Sir Hector Macdonald, whose 19th-century military career is further celebrated by a collection of memorabilia in the Town House museum. Dingwall's most famous son, however, was Macbeth, who like Sir Hector was born here, but to a less honourable career.

Strathpeffer and the Black Isle

Strathpeffer · Contin · Garve · Marybank · Muir of Ord
Fortrose · Rosemarkie · Cromarty · Conon Bridge
Dingwall

A tour of the best of the area's scenery and the Black Isle. Good roads throughout but narrow up Strathconon; about 80 to 100 miles.

Five miles west on the A834 through the pastoral Peffery valley brings you to the leisurely Victorian elegance of 'the Harrogate of the North'. The discovery in the late 18th century of iron and sulphur springs at **Strathpeffer** led rapidly to its development as a famous spa resort; for one hundred years the distinguished, the rich and the royal visited its grand hotels. Spas went out of fashion, but you can take the waters in the restored Pump Room: the town is still healthy as a tourist centre. Thick woodland and pleasant walks surround it, with **Ben Wyvis** (3,429 feet) as a Highland background to its charming setting.

There is the vitrified fort of **Knockfarrel** to the east, and to the north the 17th-century tower of Castle Leod, not open except for the annual Highland Gathering in its grounds. The **Eagle Stone**, off the main road up a lane if you can find it, commemorates a Clan Munro victory. It has another significance: a local prophet of 1600, the Seer of Brahan, said that 'ships would anchor' here if the stone fell three times. It has fallen twice, and is now protected – for the

Brahan Seer was accurate in his further predictions about Strathpeffer: 'uninviting and disagreeable as it now is, the day will come when ..... crowds of pleasure and health seekers shall be seen thronging its portals'.

Two miles on, **Contin** at the junction with the A832 is another village with pleasant walks around it. Loch Achilty, and the Torrachilty Forest Trail, are reached west and east of the bridge over the River Blackwater; two miles further north along the A832 paths lead to the **Falls of Rogie**. From a suspension bridge you get a good view of the falls and, at the right time of year, of leaping salmon. The main road continues through **Garve**, a quiet village in a magnificent riverside and mountain setting, on to **Gorstan** and the western Highlands.

Go back to Contin and follow the A832 crossing the River Conon to **Marybank** from where a narrow road runs 20 miles through **Strathconon**, a beautiful glen in which you may glimpse red deer, buzzards and even golden eagles. Much of the glen has been harnessed for hydro-electric power – there are three lochs, and only a few tiny hamlets. **Muir of Ord**, an important crossroads, was famous in the last century for its markets for cattle, horses and sheep. It lies at the base of the **Black Isle** – which is predominantly green, and a peninsula. Explanations of its name include a Gaelic linguistic confusion involving *dubh* (black) and St Duthus, and an earlier connection with peat bogs.

From Muir of Ord stay on the A832; in three miles a right turn leads to ruined **Redcastle**, originally built in 1178 by William the Lion, eventually burnt by Cromwell's army. At **Tore** there are the remains of a Knights Templar chapel and the new A9 crosses your path. **Munlochy** sits at the head of a bay by a saltmarsh, with a huge population of birds. Here, in 1400, Macdonalds besieging Inverness were massacred in their drunken sleep. After the little fishing village of **Avoch** you reach **Fortrose**, the main town in the Black Isle: a small peaceful place with a good beach and a golf course, on the edge of the Moray Firth. The red sandstone cathedral (AM) was begun in the 14th century and completed in 1485. It fell into disrepair; Cromwell is said to have used stones from it to build the fort at Inverness. Now the mellow ruins consist of the south aisle and octagonal clock tower (topped with a modern steeple), and the attractive 13th-century chapter house. A lighthouse stands at the tip of **Chanonry Point** to the south-east, just across the water from Fort George (see previous chapter). A nearby stone marks the site of the nasty death of the Seer of Brahan. He was burned in a spiked tar barrel by order of the Countess of Seaforth, for a precise and tactless answer to her question about her roving husband.

Neighbouring **Rosemarkie** owes its popularity to an excellent beach among red sandstone cliffs and coves. Beside the church is a Pictish symbol stone said to mark the grave of a local saint. The

Groam House Museum (open from June, closed lunch) presents audio-visual shows relating to the Black Isle. There are pleasant walks in the area, many well-known from the works of Hugh Miller, famous local geologist. His 'Fairy Glen' is just outside the village; the coast road south of the A832 takes you to steep cliff paths including the precipitous Eathie Burn Gorge; the foreshore is rich in fossils and the coastal path to Cromarty passes explorable caves.

At the tip of the Black Isle, **Cromarty** looks across the narrow entrance of the Cromarty Firth to the oil rig industry in Nigg Bay. It's a quiet little town with an attractive harbour area; little remains of its varied history. A prosperous port and royal burgh until the late 17th century, it had an industrial revival in the 19th until trade moved across the Firth to Invergordon with the arrival of the railway. Some interesting 18th-century buildings remain – the Court House, church and Gaelic chapel, and Hugh Miller's cottage, where he was born in 1802. It's now a museum (NTS, closed lunch and Sun am) full of fossils and mementoes. Miller's scientific discoveries enmeshed him in religious controversy; he finally shot himself on Christmas Eve 1856.

Return from Cromarty to Dingwall via **Conon Bridge**, a distance of 24 miles along the B9163, with views of the Firth, its industry and the hills behind and no incentive to stop.

Tarbat Ness and Tain

Alness · Invergordon · Fearn · Portmahomack · Tarbat Ness
Tain · Ardgay · Strathcarron
Dingwall

A tour of limited interest: the occasional pretty town or village, some good views, sandy beaches and an interesting glen. Narrow roads on the Tarbat peninsula and up Strathcarron. About 100 miles.

Leave Dingwall by the A862 and head north alongside the Cromarty Firth. After four miles, Cnoc Fyrish (1,483 feet) can be seen to the north crowned by an 18th-century folly erected by General Sir Hector Munro to provide work for the unemployed. The monument, recalling his fighting days in India, is a replica of the gateway of a captured Indian town. Even more spectacular though not as eccentric is the **Black Rock Ravine**, reached by a footpath from Evanton or by the road running westward and a short walk. A footbridge over the River Glass gives a view of the ravine which in parts is more than 200 feet deep and less than 12 feet wide.

139

Head on by the A9 through Alness then fork right on to the B817 through the industrial and residential development along the coast, rejoining the A9 about five miles after Invergordon. After three miles turn off along the B9165 into the isolated farming area of which the barely elevated village **Hill of Fearn** is the hub. The B9166 from Fearn goes to the coast at **Balintore**, which has a fine harbour and a sandy beach and is a popular sea-angling centre. The B9165 leads north-east, reaching the western coast of the low-lying Tarbat peninsula at **Portmahomack**, a picturesque village with an excellent beach. A road goes across the Ness to **Rockfield**, built under a cliff, near which are the ruins of **Ballone Castle**. Built for the Earl of Ross in the early 16th century, it is an example of a 'Z-plan' castle with two towers diagonally opposite. Another narrow road goes to **Tarbat Ness** where you can visit one of Britain's highest lighthouses, with marvellous views over the Moray Firth.

Go back through Portmahomack and in two miles fork right for **Tain**, an attractive little town built of mellow stone, set on the Dornoch Firth with wooded hills behind. It has allegedly been a royal burgh since 1066 – a Heritage Museum was opened for the ninth centenary of this strictly local date. Tain has kept traces of its long history. St Duthus, one of the great Celtic saints, was born here; long after his death his bones were brought from Ireland in 1253 to lie in his chapel by the sea, now a ruin (violated and burnt in 1427) near the golf course. The collegiate church of St Duthus, built around 1360, housed relics of the saint and many made pilgrimages here, including James IV. Fine stained glass depicts events in the town's history. The typically Scottish Tolbooth with spire and turrets was perfectly restored in the early 18th century; the town hall, mercat cross and parish church are monumentally Victorian.

The coastline east of Tain is a bombing range, closed to the public. Westward the A9 passes the Glen Morangie Distillery and Ferry Point, where the old Meikle Ferry was until 1812 the main route to Dornoch. The Morangie Forest Walk is a steep hillside tramp with views across the Firth. There are many overgrown archaeological sites in the area: the most notable (and visible) is just off the main road at **Edderton**, a Pictish stone 10 feet high with symbols commemorating a battle.

Nine miles on at **Ardgay** a road leads off 10 miles through **Strathcarron**, an area where the Clearances of the 19th century were doggedly resisted and violently enforced. Messages scratched by some of the hapless victims may be seen on the windows of the church at Croick. The A836 back towards Dingwall branches south four miles east of Ardgay; a mile from the junction, at **Struie Hill**, you can enjoy a superb view over the Kyle of Sutherland. The landscape is moorland at first but becomes wooded as you cross the River Alness on your way back to Dingwall.

Accommodation

There's no shortage of accommodation in this area, from the grandiose Victorian hotels in the spa resort of Strathpeffer to bed and breakfast in private houses. Unfortunately we were unable to find any which we are happy to recommend as offering out-of-the-ordinary standards of comfort and food.

General Information

Activities
BOAT HIRE Available at a number of places round the coast.
FISHING Brown trout in lochs Achilty, Beannacharan, Glass, Glascarnoch, Luichart, Meig and some hill lochs. Salmon and brown trout in Loch Morie and River Glass. Salmon, brown and sea trout in rivers Alness, Blackwater and Conon.
GOLF Alness, Fortrose, Invergordon, Muir of Ord, Portmahomack, Strathpeffer and Tain.
PONY-TREKKING Marybank.
SAILING Watersports centre at North Kessock.
SQUASH Alness, Dingwall, Evanton and Invergordon.
SWIMMING Alness, Dingwall and Tain.
TENNIS Avoch, Balintore, Cromarty, Dingwall, Fortrose, Invergordon, Rosemarkie and Tain.

Entertainment
Cinema in Invergordon. Discos, folk and Scottish evenings, pipe bands, ceilidhs etc in a number of villages, the main ones being Contin, Dingwall, Fortrose, Muir of Ord and Strathpeffer.

Events
JULY Highland Games at Dingwall and Strathconon.
AUGUST Highland Games at Invergordon and Strathpeffer; Black Isle Show, Muir of Ord.

Tourist Information
Ross and Cromarty Tourist Office, North Kessock,
Tel: (0463 73) 505
Centre open in summer only at Strathpeffer, Tel: (099 72) 1415

West Ross

Eilean Donan Castle

This of all Highland areas has the classic Highland scenery: Doctor Johnson described it as 'awful', and indeed it awes. Its mountains dominate, not only in single splendour but in magnificent groups and ranges; its lochs and waterfalls call for superlatives; its long complicated coastline faces the mass of western islands.

There are a few glimpses of West Ross's human history. Invaders came and went, finding more profit elsewhere and leaving little trace. In Glenelg are two fine Pictish brochs, and Applecross and Loch Maree have remnants of early Christianity; the only place of strategic importance seems to have been Eilean Donan at its sheltered meeting-place of sea lochs, where a prehistoric vitrified fort first occupied the site of Alexander II's 13th-century castle.

Even there, the Jacobite rising of 1719 – though a vivid episode – was only a small part of a much larger operation. Spain sent a second Armada towards the Jacobite west coast of England: 5,000 Spanish troops, and arms for 30,000 English sympathisers. No more successful than the first Armada, it got no further than the storms off Finistere; and when news of its failure reached Eilean Donan the clans refused to rise. The castle was destroyed and

Hanoverian troops from Inverness fought a day-long battle at Shiel Bridge. 1,100 Highlanders and 300 Spanish soldiers retreated up one of the Five Sisters, thereafter called Sgurr nan Spainteach, 'Peak of the Spaniards'. The Mackenzies of the day forfeited their lands and titles, but measures taken after this abortive rising to open up the Highlands barely touched West Ross – General Wade's network of roads and bridges did not extend so far north-west.

Communications here through history were minimal. Men and cattle trod drovers' routes to the market towns east and south: that across Glenelg from Skye was preceded by a forced swim, and that over Applecross is today one of the most challenging roads in the Highlands. At the foot of its steep descent an oil-rig construction site fills the head of Loch Kishorn: from here, the biggest-ever floating concrete structure successfully arrived at an oilfield off the Shetlands. Now the labourers are much less in demand. Attempts at industry in this part of the Highlands have never succeeded for long – 200 years ago there was iron-smelting at Loch Maree, laying waste the forests for the furnaces; in the Napoleonic wars, processing kelp brought brief prosperity at points along the coast. Fishing, the basic livelihood and trade, still thrives, despite the disappearance of the herring shoals which once filled Loch Broom.

The only grand design that has worked in West Ross is nature's own. The Forestry Commission balances commerce and conservation, repairing the ravages of the past. On the slopes of Mam Ratagan commercial timber is grown and cut; in Lael Forest Garden 150 species of tree and shrub have been planted for pleasure and preservation. Vast areas of wilderness are National Nature Reserves; vast areas are owned by the National Trust. Visitor Centres help the traveller to comprehend both the huge scale and the fine detail spread around him – naturalists and geologists, walkers and climbers and mere motorists can all appreciate the enormous variety of landscape and its wildlife.

This is the part of the Highlands where people return – to look further, to look more closely, just to look again in the ever-changing Highland light. This is the area of classic Gulf Stream climate, soft and bright along the coast where man can create sub-tropical gardens, and sunset over the islands can fill the world with glory. Inland the west winds rise and cool, bringing torrential rain to fill the lochs and waterfalls – yet in clear weather the pale peaks of Beinn Eighe look as arid as some strange landscape of the moon.

The dramatic inland distances can today be covered with little trouble, and small roads where once there were none lead round remote and beautiful stretches of coast between the strung-out communities. A land of natural wonders with only a few fine historic sites, West Ross is a place of escape – to a peaceful fishing loch, to a deserted sandy beach. Because it covers such a large area we have chosen two centres for our tours.

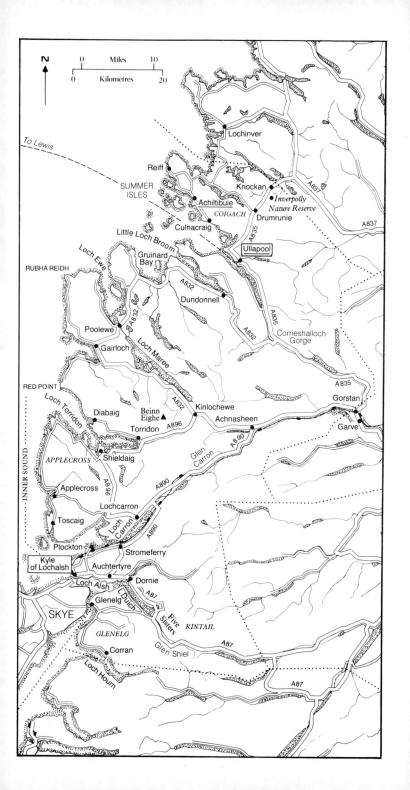

KYLE OF LOCHALSH

Here is the end of the road and of one of the most spectacular railway routes in Britain: Skye is just half a mile away by the car ferry. Though a typical fishing port, Kyle of Lochalsh owes its bustling prosperity more to its location than its character; but it makes a good enough centre for touring some of the finest scenery in Scotland. To the north is the Applecross peninsula, to the south palindromic Glenelg. Inland is magnificent mountain scenery from Beinn Eighe to the Five Sisters, and seaward from the town itself are superb views of the Cuillin Hills of Skye.

Nearly half the green Lochalsh peninsula forms the 6,400-acre **Balmacara Estate** (NTS), and at Balmacara village, three miles outside Kyle of Lochalsh, the Trust has established an Information Centre and laid out pleasant walks among woodland where many exotic varieties of plant appreciate the effect of the Gulf Stream.

Applecross and Torridon

Auchtertyre · Loch Carron · Loch Kishorn · Applecross
Shieldaig · Loch Torridon · Kinlochewe · Achnasheen
Glen Carron · Plockton
Kyle of Lochalsh

Fertile countryside up to beautiful Loch Carron soon becomes wilder as the route crosses a hair-raising pass to the Applecross peninsula. Then the magnificent mountains of Torridon and the peak of Beinn Eighe come into view. After Glen Carron, a trip to a delightful fishing village. A lot of single-track driving but new roads along Loch Carron and Upper Loch Torridon. About 135 miles.

The main A87 out of Kyle of Lochalsh follows the northern shore of Loch Alsh through Balmacara. At **Auchtertyre** take the narrower A890 running northward to **Stromeferry**. Just outside the village is the Loch Carron viewpoint, with picnic tables. **Loch Carron** is a delightfully peaceful sheet of water surrounded by fields and sheltered by mountains; the loch and the glen mark the change from the softer fertile terrain of the south to the harsher land of the north.

At **Achintee** the road rounds the head of the loch to a T-junction. Turn left along the A896 to **Lochcarron**, a long straggling village. There is a pleasant walk through the Allt Nan Carnan Nature Reserve, with a mile-long gorge and waterfalls. Four miles on, at the end of Loch Carron's north shore road, stands the small ruin of **Strome Castle** (NTS), a stronghold of some Macdonalds who were for a century at loggerheads with their neighbours the Mackenzies of Kintail. In 1602 the castle fell – the story goes that its women unfortunately emptied their pails of water into the gunpowder vat. The besieging Mackenzies blew up the castle and seized the Macdonald lands.

From Lochcarron the A896 runs west through rugged scenery to **Kishorn**, with fine views over **Loch Kishorn** (and an oil-platform construction yard), and **Tornapress** at the head of the loch. Here the main road climbs northward through Glen Kishorn, and then descends through **Glen Shieldaig** past lovely Loch Dughaill eight miles to Loch Shieldaig. But a much more thrilling 35-mile route takes in the **Applecross peninsula**, a wild lonely area of forest, mountain and lochs.

★ Turn left at Tornapress on to a narrow winding road unsuitable for caravans but ideal for the adventurous motorist, who soon finds himself on the **Pass of the Cattle** (Bealach na Ba), climbing four miles of hairpin bends, with gradients of one in four, to the rocky summit at 2,000 feet. After the pass, the moorland road, though narrow and tortuous, offers few problems and the approach to **Applecross** village is through woodland. It was once a sanctuary, with a monastery founded here in the 7th century by St Maelrubha, an Irish monk – one of the most important Christian centres in Scotland; but nothing has survived the depradations of the Vikings. The present church preserves fragments of a Celtic cross. ★

A pretty road runs south from Applecross four miles past farms and sheltered little bays to **Toscaig**; and in 1976 the peninsula was further opened up by the construction of a road north from Applecross along the coast, with views of Skye, Rona and Raasay, through tiny crofting communities to the northern tip and then south-east alongside **Loch Torridon** to **Kenmore**. The road narrows as it keeps close to Loch Shieldaig, joining the A896 just short of **Shieldaig** village. This is still a quiet community of crofters and fishermen, with a number of holiday homes.

A new fast road swings eastward on its way seven miles to Torridon, but it is worth stopping half-way at the car park to enjoy the marvellous view across **Upper Loch Torridon** to the Torridon mountains, with **Beinn Alligin** (3,231 feet) prominent. At the head of the loch at a road junction is a small **NTS Visitor Centre** (open June to Sep, closed Sun am), where there are audio-visual presentations about local wildlife; guided walks are available into the magnificent 16,000-acre **Torridon Estate.** Torridon village itself is a climbing centre; the nine miles on to **Diabaig** are strikingly scenic.

The A896 passes through **Glen Torridon**, with sensational views on both sides. To the north rise the sharp sandstone peaks of **Liathach** (3,456 feet), to the south the Ben-Damph and Coulin forests criss-crossed by stalking paths. As you pass Loch Clair you have a superb view of **Beinn Eighe** (3,188 feet).

Kinlochewe is only a mile from the **Beinn Eighe Nature Reserve** and **Loch Maree** (see Loch Maree tour); but turn right along the A832, climbing the narrow ravine of **Glen Docherty** (look back at the top) past Loch a'Chroisg to **Achnasheen**. Take the A890 which heads swiftly south-west through 20-mile **Glen Carron**, over a multitude of rivers and burns and past Lochs Gowan and Sgamhain. Five miles beyond **Achnashellach**, turn left to **Achintee** again; but after Stromeferry, rather than return to Kyle by the main road, take the longer route (12 miles) round the Lochalsh peninsula by the narrow road to lush little **Plockton**, beautifully set facing east to the wooded crags rather than west to the islands – a delightful backwater and a popular anchorage for yachts.

Kintail and Glenelg

Dornie · Loch Duich · Glen Shiel · Glenelg · Loch Hourn
Kyle of Lochalsh

A tour which takes you to one of Scotland's best known castles and the finest brochs on the mainland, and which includes some superb mountain and glen scenery. Good roads, though winding and hilly round Glenelg. About 85 miles.

Follow the A87 to **Ardelve** at the mouth of Loch Long. This is perhaps the best starting point for the hidden **Falls of Glomach** – the most spectacular waterfall in Britain, taking one of the biggest single leaps in its roaring plunge from spout to cauldron. The trip by car and on foot is long and hard: it involves driving about five miles up the northern side of Loch Long to near Killilan House, then continuing along a rough private road another five miles to a footbridge on the River Elchaig. From here there is a hard climb of about a mile to the top of the 350-feet falls, followed by some manoeuvring to get a good view from a platform further down.

★ If this excursion is not for you, drive on through Dornie to visit **Eilean Donan Castle**, the most romantic (and most photographed) place in the Highlands. It is difficult to imagine a more attractive site for a castle than this islet reached by a causeway and overlooking the confluence of three lochs – Long, Duich and Alsh. Fragments remain of the prehistoric vitrified fort that first occupied the site, but the castle proper dates from about 1230, a stronghold against the threat of the Vikings in Skye. It belonged at various times to Mackenzies and Macraes with an eventful history until in 1719 a garrison of Spanish troops aiding Jacobite rebels occupied it, whereupon three English frigates sailed up Loch Alsh and blew a

147

considerable part of the castle off its rock. Eilean Donan remained a ruin until the Macrae family began its reconstruction in 1912, a task not completed until 1932. The main rooms shown are the billeting room of the keep with its great arched roof, and the banqueting hall which recalls the great days of the Highlands. ★

The A87 continues beside **Loch Duich**, crossing Strath Croe to enter the outstandingly beautiful district of **Kintail** – with Glomach, a total of 15,000 acres of mountains, glens and rivers. The **Five Sisters** are the dominating feature, a chain of pointed peaks, four of them over 3,000 feet. Just off the main road at **Morvich** there is a NTS Visitor Centre with an audio-visual display about Kintail and its climbs and walks. From here there is also an alternative route to Glomach Falls, though this entails a walk of over three miles.

Eight miles on at **Shiel Bridge** there is an NTS information point with an account of the battle fought in 1719 between the English and the Jacobites with their Spanish allies. The excellent road through **Glen Shiel** keeps close to the river for 12 miles, then follows the north side of **Loch Cluanie** for another nine. Then the A887 heads for the Great Glen by way of Glen Moriston, while the A87 leads to Invergarry. Up and more particularly down the narrow Glen Shiel pass is an exhilarating drive, as more and more peaks come into sight in the towering mountain walls each side.

The Five Sisters are seen to better advantage from the **Glenelg** peninsula; turn west off the A87 near Shiel Bridge, take a left fork and climb the narrow winding road over the **Pass of Mam Ratagan**, where there is a car park with a view indicator to help visitors enjoy the marvellous panorama over Loch Duich and Kintail. The road descends to **Glen More** and just short of tiny Glenelg village a right fork leads to the ferry, to Kylerhea on Skye five hundred yards distant. Johnson and Boswell crossed to Skye from here in 1773 – the first of their many uncomfortable sea trips in appalling weather. The road to the ferry passes the ruins of **Bernera Barracks**. A dripping-wet Boswell recorded 'I looked at them wistfully, as soldiers have always everything in the best order'.

Two miles from Glenelg in Glen Beag stand the two **Glenelg Brochs** (AM), Dun Telve and Dun Troddan, the best-preserved Pictish brochs (circular stone towers) on the mainland. Dun Telve is 33 feet high, its courtyard 30 feet across; its double walls contain spiral galleries. Dun Troddan is similar in design. Their purpose is debated among authorities, since they pre-date enemy invasions; it seems likely that they were built by the Picts as place of safety, as lookouts and perhaps for defence, possibly against Viking pirates.

The road south from Glenelg ends after 10 miles at **Corran** on the shore of **Loch Hourn**. If you come this far you will be rewarded by a perfect view down the loch to the distant peaks of Skye, before you retrace the 35 miles to Kyle of Lochalsh.

ULLAPOOL

Ullapool, like Kyle of Lochalsh, is a fishing port and ferry terminal in a superb setting. But, unlike Kyle, Ullapool is a pretty place and a thriving holiday resort in its own right. Its streets, laid out in a grid design by the British Fisheries Society, are full of gaily-painted, clean-cut houses and busy little shops. There's a shingle beach and a good range of accommodation; and in the back room of a bookshop at the MacBrayne end of the harbour the **Loch Broom Museum** (closed Sun) is crammed full of objects natural, historical and bizarre.

Some of the best parts of both West Ross and West Sutherland are within easy reach of Ullapool, and in the immediate vicinity there's no shortage of things to do. Fishing and walking are good; pony-trekking and sailing are possible; boat trips run from the harbour; and there are the ferries, though it's not really practicable to go to the Outer Hebrides just for a day.

Loch Maree and Gruinard Bay

Corrieshalloch Gorge · Gorstan · Achnasheen · Kinlochewe
Loch Maree · Red Point · Gairloch
Poolewe · Gruinard Bay
Ullapool

*A tour of some very fine scenery – loch, mountain and intricate coast;
varied wildlife, rare arctic plants, and one of the finest sub-tropical
gardens in northern Europe. Thirty miles of good fast road; slower
driving westward, and some narrow coastal sections. About 135 miles.*

The A835 runs alongside Loch Broom, particularly beautiful when the rhododendrons are in bloom. 15 miles from Ullapool past the head of the loch are the **Lael Forest Gardens**, where 150 different species of trees and shrubs grow in the 17 acres of Forestry Commission land. A forest walk gives lovely views of the glen and loch. In a further four miles you will see the roadside car park for the spectacular and easily accessible **Corrieshalloch Gorge** (NTS). This narrow geological fault is a mile long, 50 feet wide and 200 feet deep. Woodland paths lead to a viewing platform and suspension bridge which give a vertiginous view of the gorge and of the fine **Falls of Measach**, which plunge 150 feet into the depths.

The route climbs through moorland for much of the 20-mile run towards Garve, passing **Loch Glascarnoch** which was created in

1950 as part of a hydro-electric scheme. At **Gorstan** turn west along the single-track A832 beside the railway line to **Loch Luichart**, the first Highland loch whose waters were used to generate electricity, and its power station. The road continues 15 miles through bleak **Strath Bran** to **Achnasheen** where the right fork leads more scenically to **Kinlochewe** (see Applecross tour).

★ The route north from Kinlochewe is through some of the finest of all Highland scenery and beside the loch that many regard as the loveliest in Scotland. But the first attraction is the **Beinn Eighe Nature Reserve**: 10,000 acres of pine forest and high moorland dominated by the white quartzite peaks of Beinn Eighe, a paradise for naturalists because of its varied wildlife and rare arctic plants. Beinn Eighe was the first National Nature Reserve, so designated in 1951. A mile west of Kinlochewe is the Aultroy Visitor Centre; two nature trails start from the car park a mile or so further along the road. There is a field station at Anancaun.

Wooded **Loch Maree** is more than 12 miles long and at its broadest more than two miles wide. Beautiful in itself, it has a perfect setting of distinguished mountains. On the northern side **Slioch** (3,217 feet) is the dominating presence attended by Beinn Lair (2,817 feet) and Beinn Airigh Charr (2,593 feet). On the southern side looms Beinn Eighe (3,188 feet). At first the road hugs the bank; it turns briefly inland to the **Bridge of Grudie** where there is a small nature reserve. **Isle Maree**, one of many islets off **Talladale**, has an ancient graveyard and the remains of a chapel. Two miles farther along the loch is **Slattadale Forest**. Here there is a picnic place with superb views over the broad islanded water, a forest walk and the start of the old footpath to Poolewe called the Tollie Path. The **Victoria Falls** nearby are reached by a slippery log footpath through pine forest. ★

At this point the road swings west away from Loch Maree past **Loch Bad an Sgalaig** and beside the River Kerry. After five miles, just before Loch Gairloch, the narrow B8056 winds through a charming little stretch to the sea, with distant views of the Hebrides on the way to **Red Point's** dune-backed beach. Any or all of its eight miles are worth a detour.

The shore of Loch Gairloch is reached at Charlestown beyond which is the busy fishing port of **Gairloch**. Though not a particularly prepossessing place, Gairloch has a good beach, plenty of accommodation and a number of tourist amenities, all of which combine to make it one of the main resorts of the north-west. The **Gairloch Heritage Museum** (closes at 5pm, shut Sun) houses a small but excellent and imaginatively displayed collection of domestic, farming and fishing items.

At the exit from Gairloch the B8021 branches west through

Strath, which is virtually a continuation of Gairloch, to **Melvaig** (nine miles). A private road continues to the lighthouse at Rubha Reidh. The main road, single-track after Gairloch, crosses five miles of moorland offering wonderful views; the best is the panorama revealed at the turn-off to Tollie Bay, where the whole of Loch Maree lies before you framed by mountain peaks. In a further mile **Poolewe** sits where the river flows into **Loch Ewe**. A narrow road runs up the western side of Loch Ewe for eight miles past two sandy beaches. Facing Poolewe across the head of the loch is **Inverewe Gardens** (NTS). When Osgood Mackenzie took over the estate in 1862 it was virtually bare of vegetation; he (and after him his daughter) created one of the finest sub-tropical gardens in northern Europe. It was handed over to the Trust in 1952. It is essentially a wild woodland garden yet has become the home of many exotic trees, shrubs and flowers with an emphasis on Asian species; its magnolias, hydrangeas and rhododendrons are particularly famous. Many paths thread their way through the 2,000 acres of woodland and there are fine views over Loch Ewe.

The road climbs from Poolewe on to the moor and then descends to **Loch Thuirnaig**. As it rises to the next hilltop there is a viewpoint giving a wonderful mountain vista to the south and east; there is another viewpoint two miles farther on. The main road swings north-eastward reaching **Gruinard Bay** at **Laide**, where a road turns off to reach in three miles the pretty cove of **Mellon Udrigle**. The main road continues round the bay to a viewpoint from Gruinard Hill over three perfect beaches of pinkish sand, formed of red sandstone.

Out in the bay **Gruinard Island** is prominent: it was the site of an experiment in germ warfare during the Second World War. The experiment involved the dissemination of anthrax. As the notice boards warn, the island is still infected; regular checks are made, but no other landing is permitted.

In five miles the road reaches the shore of Little Loch Broom, and turns south-eastward passing **Ardessie**, where there is a fish farm and a waterfall. From Dundonnell at the foot of the loch the route is through wooded Strath Beag and Dundonnell Forest, below the chain of mountain tops called **An Teallach**. After nearly 30 miles from Poolewe, the A832 joins the A835 at Corrieshalloch, and it's a rapid 12 miles back to Ullapool.

Coigach and Achiltibuie

Drumrunie · Knockan · Drumrunie · Reiff
Achiltibuie · Drumrunie
Ullapool

*A fairly short tour which takes you to a National Nature Reserve then up
through superb mountain scenery and down to a beautiful stretch of
coast, all the best parts on difficult or narrow roads. About 65 miles.*

The A835 north from Ullapool, after reaching Loch Kanaird at
Ardmair, strikes inland and traverses the wild district known as
Coigach. The main road continues north into Sutherland, skirting
the **Inverpolly Forest**, since 1962 a National Nature Reserve. This
remote area of more than 26,000 acres combines mountains,
moorland, woodland and aquatic habitats for the wide variety of
wildlife. There is a Visitor Centre and a nature trail at **Knockan
Cliff**, 15 miles from Ullapool; there is also a geological trail
connected with the fault known as the Moine Thrust. The road
descends to Elphin and joins the A837 at Ledmore; for the route
north to Inchnadamph and the pretty village of Lochinver see West
Sutherland chapter.

★ Even wilder than the main road, and more thrilling, is the
unclassified single-track road running westward from **Drumrunie**
(about half-way between Ullapool and Ledmore) with branches
north to Lochinver and south to Achiltibuie. This road enables
motorists to enjoy the marvellous mountain scenery of Coigach
with, on the left, **Ben More Coigach** (2,438 feet) and on the right
Cul Beag (2,523 feet) and **Stac Polly** (2,009 feet). The road now
runs past two of the many lochs of Coigach, **Lurgain** and **Bad
a'Ghaill**, and then divides. A sharp right turn and many twists and
turns along a hilly road with fine views take you across the River
Polly. The route zigzags inland and then makes for the coast by way
of Glen Strathain, entering Sutherland at the bridge over the River
Kirkaig, three miles south of Lochinver. ★

The road to Achiltibuie keeps straight on after Loch Bad a'Ghaill
and passes **Loch Osgaig**. After a right fork (where a side road leads
to the extensive dunes of Achnahaird Bay), **Altandhu** is a delightful
crofting village, with a pretty cluster of cottages. **Isle Ristol** can be
reached by a causeway at low tide. North of Altandhu the road ends
at **Reiff**, which has cliffs and a sandy beach. Return through
Altandhu to **Achiltibuie**. The village is strung out along the coast
with the pier in the north, the church, hotel, school and shops in the
middle and crofts in the south. Along this shore the land is flat and
gentle, with wide views out across the bay to the many **Summer
Isles**; they are all uninhabited except **Tanera More**. This is the
largest of the islands with an area of 804 acres and is only two miles
from Achiltibuie with which it is linked by ferry. There are also

regular cruises from Ullapool to the Summer Isles, some of which land at Tanera. At one time more than a hundred people lived on the island, most working in the fish-curing industry established in 1783. Later it was the home of the naturalist Fraser Darling – all the islands in the group are interesting, especially to birdwatchers. In recent years old crofts have been modernised and are used as holiday cottages. Tanera has a post office, and issues its own postage stamps.

East of Achiltibuie the road ends at Culnacraig; walkers can complete the trip round the peninsula, covering six miles to Strath Kanaird and the A835, but motorists must go back to Ullapool the way they came – 24 miles.

Accommodation

Finding accommodation in West Ross is generally not the problem it can be further north. Ullapool and Gairloch offer quite a wide choice and are good bases to choose for a overnight stop or a longer stay. And throughout most of the rest of the region there is a fairly liberal distribution of hotels, guest houses and bed and breakfast places. The three hotels we recommend in this area must rank among the most original we include in this book.

ACHILTIBUIE
Summer Isles (GFG, GHG)
Tel: Achiltibuie (085 482) 282
A comfortable hotel in a marvellously tranquil setting with rugged mountains around and fine views of the Summer Isles. Bedrooms in the main building are simple and their furnishings a bit of a hotchpotch (though there is talk of refurbishment). Better are the rooms in the wooden annexe, which are individually furnished to the same high standard as the public rooms. Beside each bed is a list of tried and tested local walks. Dinner is served promptly at 7.30pm; there is no choice, but the food is expertly prepared and almost entirely (including the meat) home produced. There is a well-stocked cellar, though the owner, Robert Irvine who makes this hotel so original prefers to direct your choice of wine rather than allow you the benefit of a wine list.
Open Easter to Oct; 13 bedrooms (including one suite and nine annexe rooms), all with bath; no children under 8; £££

153

ALTNAHARRIE
Altnaharrie Inn (GFG, GHG)
Tel: Dundonnell; (085 483) 230
A gem of an isolated inn reached only by a two-mile track from
Dundonnell or by the inn's boat from Ullapool. The hotel is run by
Fred Brown and his Norwegian partner, Gunn Eriksen. She, no
doubt, is responsible for the Scandinavian theme which runs from
the décor and the furnishings through to the food – Nordic
tapestries, red pine floor, wood-burning stoves and smørrebrød
lunches. Fred Brown also runs a yacht charter business.
Open Easter to Oct; 4 bedrooms (1 in annexe), all with bath;
children discouraged; £££

ULLAPOOL
Ceilidh Place (GHG)
Tel: Ullapool (0854) 2103
An unusual hotel which started life as a coffee shop in one old
cottage and has grown to include another two, much revamped –
not to mention another series of old buildings across the road which
have been converted into a 'clubhouse', with gallery, auditorium
and extra rooms. The furnishings are modern – dark-stained pine
and tweedy fabrics; the lounge is comfortable, so are the bedrooms,
though some overlook a caravan site and others the gardens of local
residents; all have baby-listening. The rooms in the clubhouse are
much simpler, with bunk beds. The hotel is run in a highly
individual fashion and the atmosphere is totally informal. In
summer there are special folk and jazz evenings, and a special
interest programme. The hotel has fishing rights.
Open Apr to Oct; 15 bedrooms (plus 11 in clubhouse annexe); ££

GFG means in the 1986 *Good Food Guide*
GHG means in the 1986 *Good Hotel Guide*

Price categories are based on the cost for one person sharing a
double room for one night, inclusive of tax and service. Many hotels
give reduced terms for stays of three nights or longer.

Dinner, bed
and breakfast
£15 to £30   £
£31 to £40   ££
£41 to £50   £££
£51 to £60   ££££
over £60   £££££

154

General Information

Activities
BOAT HIRE Available at a number of places in the area.
BOAT TRIPS Trips to Summer Isles from: I Macleod,
Tel: Achiltibuie: (085 482) 200; Mackenzie Marine, Tel:
Ullapool (0854) 2008; and Sunrise, Tel: Ullapool (0854) 2264
FISHING Salmon and trout in many lochs and rivers.
GOLF Gairloch and Lochcarron.
PONY-TREKKING Strathcarron and Ullapool.
SAILING Yacht charter at several places on the coast.
TENNIS Ullapool.

Entertainment
Hotels and inns provide entertainment with a local flavour. Folk
and jazz evenings are held regularly in summer in Ullapool.

Events
JULY Highland Games at Lochcarron; Ullapool Regatta Week.

Ferries
Badluarach across Little Loch Broom to Scoraig: once daily
passenger ferry run by A Beavitt of Carnoch.
Ullapool to Altnaharrie: four times daily passenger ferry in
summer, not Sun, run by Fred Brown of the Altnaharrie Inn (see
'Accommodation'); takes 10 min.
Caledonian MacBrayne, Tel: Kyle of Lochalsh (0599) 4218 or
Ullapool (0854) 2358; frequent services daily from Kyle to Skye;
Ullapool to Stornoway, daily (not Sun).

Tourist information
Ross and Cromarty Tourist Office, North Kessock,
Tel: (0463) 73505
South-west Ross and Isle of Skye Tourist Information Office,
Portree, Tel: (0478) 2137
Gairloch Tourist Information Office, Tel: (0445) 2210
Centres open summer only: Kyle of Lochalsh, Tel: (0599) 2371;
Ullapool, Tel: (0854) 2135.

Skye, Raasay
and
the Small Isles

The Cuillin from Elgol

Sometimes called the 'Winged Isle' because of its shape – so irregular and indented that no point of it is more than five miles from the sea – and also known as the 'Misty Isle' because of the cloud which habitually shrouds its mountain peaks, Skye is the best known and one of the largest of the islands of Scotland. It was hit very hard by the Clearances: in the latter half of the 19th century over 30,000 of the population left, and in 1882 first policemen and then gunboats were sent from the mainland to put down riots caused by the evictions. It was also in the 19th century that the teachings of an austere church took firm hold over the island people. Calvinist attitudes are still prevalent – at least in parts of the island; it's not long since there was uproar over the start of Sunday ferry services to the island, and for many the Sabbath is still strictly kept. Although farming, fishing and forestry play a part, tourism is the backbone of the island's present-day economy.

Skye is the most visited of the Scottish islands and although its popularity has led to a great variety in what there is for tourists to do, it has also led to a good deal of commercialism – a rash of craft and souvenir shops, for example. Skye, perhaps more than any other of the Hebrides, has attracted migrants from the south in search of a peaceful life style; but this island, 50 miles long and up to 25 miles wide, manages both to accommodate them and the summer influx of tourists and retain an aura of remote magic. It is a marvellous combination of moor, mountain, loch and sea, illuminated by a long romantic history (in which Bonnie Prince Charlie plays an almost inevitable role).

There are three ferry routes to Skye; all take cars. The longest and most expensive is from Mallaig, at the end of the 'Road to the Isles', to Armadale in the extreme south. The most popular and most frequent service is the five-minute crossing from Kyle of Lochalsh to Kyleakin; and there is another route across the narrow strait between Glenelg and Kylerhea. These two quick and frequent crossings mean that it is possible to make a day trip to Skye and see quite a lot of the island, while the ferries from Uig, in the north, to Harris and North Uist enable you to use Skye as a stepping stone on your way to explore the Outer Hebrides.

It is the northern half of Skye, across the A863, which attracts most visitors. Here are the island's attractive capital, Portree, and its most celebrated sight, Dunvegan Castle. In this part too is the lonely Trotternish peninsula, notable for its interesting rock formations and its associations with Flora Macdonald, and remarkable for the absence of trees. Less bleak are the peninsulas of Waternish and Duirinish.

The southern half of the island has two very distinct areas. One, the Sleat peninsula, is a peaceful area with pretty villages, extensive woodland and some lovely scenic spots; it is a part where the Gaelic culture is still much in evidence. The other, the Cuillin Hills, is desolate and spectacular. 'Hills' is inappropriate: the Cuillin are categorically mountains, with some of the best climbing in Britain for both experts and learners, and walks to satisfy both the keen and the casual. Unfortunately they are often obscured by the cloud for which Skye is famous, but on a clear day they provide a breathtaking panorama – which can be enjoyed from the mainland as well as all parts of Skye – of sheer mountains and, in the north-east, paler red hills. The spectacle of Loch Coruisk surrounded by the dramatic horseshoe of the Black Cuillin is unforgettable in its majesty, and the boat trip from Elgol that conveys visitors to the loch is not to be missed. Climbers approach these most difficult mountains from Glen Brittle, the base for Sgurr Alasdair, the highest peak. Sligachan is one of the most popular starting places for walkers.

If you really want to get off the beaten track, indeed to where there are few tracks of any kind, visit the island of Raasay, east of Skye, or one of the group to the south called 'The Small Isles' – Eigg, Rhum, Muck and Canna. They are all quite different from each other in character, but have at least one thing in common: there is nothing much to do except enjoy their various natural features. There is little accommodation, and access to some is limited. In summer the Small Isles can be reached from Skye itself and services run from Mallaig and from the peninsulas of Morar and Moidart; for most people a day trip will probably be enough. Boswell found even Skye too isolated, but Dr Johnson had the right attitude. 'Sir, when a man retires into an island, he is to turn his thoughts entirely to another world. He has done with this'.

157

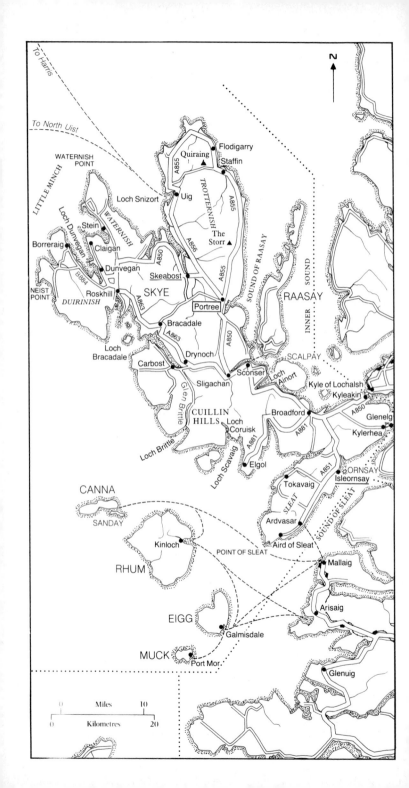

PORTREE

Portree is the administrative capital of Skye and, with its population of around 1,500, easily the largest community on the island. Its name, originally Port an Righ, means king's harbour, and derives from a visit of James V in an attempt to settle a feud between the Macleod and Macdonald clans.

While those devotees of Skye who come for serious walking and solitude might decry Portree on account of its somewhat trippery air, there's no denying that it is an attractive and cheerful place. The harbour nestles at the foot of the wooded hills that encircle the picturesque bay; whitewashed houses line its pier, and above the harbour are narrow streets and the town's large main square. There is little of historical interest – the Tourist Office is housed in the old jail and courthouse building, and preserved in the Royal Hotel is the room where Bonnie Prince Charlie bade Flora Macdonald farewell before leaving for Raasay. But Portree is an excellent centre from which to tour the island: there is plenty of accommodation and a good range of shops from supermarkets to craft boutiques; coach trips leave from the square and boat trips from the harbour, and there are boats for hire. Just to the south on the A850 is the Glen Varragill Forest, with steep walks through larch and spruce and fine views over Portree.

Northern Skye

Staffin · Uig · Skeabost · Waternish · Dunvegan
Duirinish · Bracadale · Drynoch · Sligachan
Portree

A long tour of the three main peninsulas; it takes in some extraordinary rock formations, Scotland's oldest continuously inhabited castle and a taste of the Cuillin. Single-track roads at first, but south of Dunvegan mainly fast modern roads. About 175 miles, including detours.

To the north of Portree stretches the **Trotternish Peninsula**, some 20 miles long and eight miles wide, and almost treeless. A road runs right round it, generally keeping close to the coast which is quite well populated with crofts. Leave Portree by the A855 which soon becomes single-track and passes **Loch Fada** and **Loch Leathan** (since 1952 joined to form one reservoir). In clear view are **The Storr** (2,350 feet) and to its right directly ahead the **Old Man of Storr**, a precarious black monolith 150 feet high among several similar pinnacles. It is easily reached from the road from the northern end of Loch Leathan.

The road now runs along the top of high sea cliffs. There are several waterfalls including one by the northern end of **Loch Mealt**. A short distance beyond it is the **Kilt Rock**, a cliff stratified with alternate horizontal and vertical bands giving the effect of tartan folds. After **Staffin** a road strikes off westward six miles through hills to Uig; this gives a close view of **Quiraing**, with its prominent Needle (120 feet) and its hidden Table, a high-walled grassy plateau on a crag fairly easily reached from the road. The coast road (15 miles round) passes **Flodigarry** where Flora Macdonald lived. In a further mile there is a good viewpoint out to sea before the road swings westward across the head of the peninsula, past **Duntulm** and its ruined castle perched on a sheer cliff.

The road down the western side soon reaches **Kilmuir**, Here you can visit the **Skye Cottage Museum** and look across to Uist, Flora Macdonald's birthplace, from beside her monument. Flora's part in Bonnie Prince Charlie's escape was to disguise him as her maid ('Betty Burke') and bring him back to Skye from Benbecula – 30 miles through storm and patrolling warships. They landed at Prince Charles' Point on **Kilbride Bay** three miles south of Kilmuir. Flora took the Prince to Monkstadt House (now a ruin) but, finding militia quartered there, went 12 miles on to Kingsburgh for the night. The next day the Prince left Portree for Raasay. Flora was arrested, and imprisoned in the Tower of London for two years.

South is **Uig**, an attractively-set fishing port and ferry terminal; and several miles further on is **Kingsburgh** where Prince Charlie found refuge (the actual house is gone); Flora Macdonald subsequently entertained Dr Johnson there, who was allowed to nurse his cold for a night in the very bed the Prince had occupied but reported 'no ambitious thoughts in it'.

The countryside is gentle and pleasant alongside **Loch Snizort Beag**. Soon after leaving the loch take the B8036 to join the Portree-Dunvegan road (A850) west through **Skeabost**; it becomes single-track for about five miles, from the western side of the loch to beyond **Loch Greshornish**. After five miles the B886 turns up the **Waternish Peninsula**, offering pleasant scenery and views of a number of islets. **Stein** is a pretty village of terraced houses, with a lovely old inn. The road ends at **Trumpan**, with the remnant of its church; in 1578, during a bloodthirsty feud with the Macleods, some Macdonalds burnt it complete with congregation. Near the junction with the main road is the **Fairy Bridge**, where the fairy wife of the 4th chief of the Macleods left him having given him the Fairy Flag of Dunvegan.

★ The A850 heads south for two miles and then forks right for **Dunvegan** at the head of its loch. The **Castle** (open daily Apr to Oct, not am Apr to May) has been the seat of the Macleods for more than 700 years and is the oldest continuously inhabited castle in Scotland. It is entered by a bridge crossing the former moat; this approach is slightly disappointing since this side of the castle is fairly undistinguished architecturally, dating from the early 19th century. Originally the castle was accessible only from the sea and from there it is much more imposing, towering on its crag with narrow gateway and portcullis. The interior is of several different periods from the 15th century onward. The keep with its nine-feet-thick walls has been modernised and the great hall is now the drawing room. The dungeon has a pit 16 feet deep. Many items of clan history are on show, from the ancient Dunvegan Cup to a commemorative portrait of Dr Johnson, and more mementoes of the Bonnie Prince. But the prize treasure is the **Fairy Flag**, which has the power to save the Macleods from disaster three times – it has twice been used successfully. The grounds make for pleasant strolls, and boat trips run to see seals in the loch. ★

The attractive road running north from the village up the east side of the loch ends after three miles at **Claigan**, but there are two splendid coral beaches 15 and 45 minutes' walk beyond. A mile south from Dunvegan down the A863, turn right along the single-track B884 to explore the **Duirinish Peninsula**, which has fine wild mountain scenery dominated by the two flat hills known as Macleod's Tables. At **Colbost** is the Black House Folk Museum. A right fork leads a mile northward to **Borreraig**, the home of the MacCrimmons, hereditary pipers to the Macleod chiefs. A **Piping Centre** including a museum has been established here; courses are also held. Back on the B884, continue west along a narrow road to **Glendale**, a pretty village with a water mill. There are marvellous views from the lighthouse at **Neist Point** three miles on.

Return to the A863 and head for **Roskhill** where detours can be made to the peaceful hamlets of **Orbost** and **Harlosh**, on the lovely sea loch of Bracadale. At Bracadale village the B885 runs directly back to Portree. The main road continues to the head of **Loch Harport** at **Drynoch**, with a fine viewpoint over the loch to the mountains beyond. A sharp right turn along the B8009 leads round the loch to **Carbost** and the Talisker distillery.

A mile before Carbost a narrow road runs south through **Glen Brittle** to **Loch Brittle**. The glen is the main centre for climbing among the Cuillin, with a Youth Hostel and a mountain rescue post. The highest peak Sgurr Alasdair (3,257 feet) can be scaled without rock-climbing – though with considerable exertion.

The main road sweeps eastward five miles through **Glen Drynoch** to **Sligachan**. The mountain views are magnificent and it's a centre for walks; a path runs through **Glen Sligachan** to **Loch Coruisk** in the heart of the Cuillin, and to tiny **Camasunary** on Loch Scavaig. From Sligachan it's under 10 miles to Portree.

Southern Skye

Broadford · Elgol · Kyleakin · Aird of Sleat
Tokavaig · Broadford
Portree

A tour best tackled over two days, one for each of the main areas it explores: the Cuillin (via boat from Elgol), and the Sleat Peninsula. The road along the coast from Portree to Broadford (and on to Kyleakin) is fast; other roads are not. Roughly 185 miles in all excluding the detour to Kyleakin.

Take the A850 to Sligachan (see previous tour) and fork left on the Broadford road alongside Loch Sligachan. After **Sconser** where there is a car ferry to Raasay (see later) the coast road swings southward and affords superb views of the Cuillin – weather permitting. Then it skirts the south side of **Loch Ainort** and stays close to the coast opposite the island of Scalpay before reaching **Broadford**, 27 miles from Portree. Broadford is a somewhat straggling and dull village but it's centrally placed for touring.

★ The most attractive trip from here is the 14-mile drive to **Elgol** followed by the boat trip to **Loch Coruisk** – the heart of the Cuillin. In the early stages of the single-track A881 there are views of the rounded Red Hills to the north, with **Ben na Cailleach** (2,400 feet) prominent. At **Torrin** is the contrasting view across Loch Slapin of **Blaven** (3,042 feet), the first ridge of the Black Cuillin. The road keeps close to the western end of the loch to the hamlet of **Kilmarie**, soon after which a path strikes westward for little **Camasunary** and remote but much admired Loch Coruisk.

The easiest way to reach Loch Coruisk is the spectacular boat trip from Elgol across Loch Scavaig. Carried deep into the Cuillin you are landed (for about 20 minutes) near the River Scavaig, and by footbridge and track you walk to their very heart, to the cauldron loch so romanticised by Victorian painters and writers. They liked it dark and brooding, shadowed and stern; at the whim of the weather it can instead be blue and green and sunlit.

From Elgol you can also walk the five miles round the shore of Loch Scavaig but it isn't easy: the notorious Bad Step across a rock face keeps this mountaineers' terrain. You can instead drive to Glasnakille and (at low tide) visit Spar Cave to see its stalagmites; or just enjoy the splendid views from the beach and remember Bonnie Prince Charlie again – he escaped to the mainland from here. The A850 east from Broadford goes straight to **Kyleakin** and the Kyle ferry. The village is quite pretty and has good views. Castle Moil was built as a lookout and a defensive stronghold against the Norsemen. According to tradition it was built by a Norwegian princess called 'Saucy Mary', who stretched a chain across the Kyle from here and extorted payment from all who wished to pass. From

Lusa (about half-way between Broadford and Kyleakin) a narrow hilly road forks right to **Kylerhea** and the ferry to Glenelg.

From Broadford the A851 leads you to **Sleat**. This peninsula is less developed generally than northern Skye and has less dramatic scenery. Nevertheless there are some appealing spots, particularly off the main road. The Gaelic culture holds more sway here than elsewhere in the island and the language is often heard. The single-track A851 runs along the coast giving impressive views across to the mainland mountains, and then a short road leads to **Isleornsay**, a very attractive village facing the small island of Ornsay on which stand a lighthouse and the ruins of a church.

Two miles farther on the road passes Loch nan Dubhrachan, said to be inhabited by a monster, and then nears the sea again by the scanty remains of **Knock Castle**. A mile farther on, **Kilmore** is traditionally the place where St Columba first landed in Skye. The chapel there is dilapidated, as is Ostaig House, half a mile to the south, where Johnson and Boswell were entertained. By its ruins is the Gaelic College. **Armadale Castle**, dating from the early 19th century, was the seat of Lord Macdonald. Today it is a ruin, part of which has been restored and houses the **Clan Donald Centre** (open Easter to Oct, not Sun in Apr, May, Oct) with a museum and an audio-visual display on the clan's history. The grounds run down to the Sound of Sleat and have an arboretum and pleasant woodland walks, some guided. Just half a mile south of the castle is the pier for the ferry to Mallaig, and then the pretty village of **Ardvasar**. The road ends in four miles at **Aird of Sleat**, but a path continues to the **Point of Sleat**, opposite Rhum and Eigg.

The return journey from Ardvasar to Broadford can be varied by a 12-mile detour. Take the narrow twisting road that runs westward from **Ostaig House** over wild moorland past Loch Dhughaill to **Tarskavaig Bay**, where there is a sandy beach. The road goes up the coast through the large crofting village of Tarskavaig to another bay near **Tokavaig**, where on the northern rocky point stands **Dunscaith Castle**. This was a fortress of the Macdonalds in the 15th and 16th centuries, but it is claimed to be the oldest castle in Skye, having belonged previously to the Norse kings and even, according to legend, the mythical Irish hero Cuchulainn. The grassy battlements give marvellous views of the Cuillin; and just as striking are the views from **Ord** a mile to the north. Here the road swings away from the coast along the River Ord, then over moorland to the A851: it's 12 miles back to Broadford.

On the way north to Portree, leave the A850 at the head of **Loch Ainort** a mile beyond **Luib** and its folk museum: a narrow road to the right hugs the coast, rejoining the main road just before it reaches Loch Sligachan. It's slower but hardly longer, and much more interesting, with views out past Scalpay and Raasay towards Applecross on the mainland.

163

Raasay

The island of Raasay stretches northward between Skye and Applecross. It is reached by ferry from Sconser, three miles from Sligachan. In the 18th century the whole island was devastated: the English army burned all the houses and boats because the laird supported the Jacobites in the 1745 rebellion and sheltered Bonnie Prince Charlie after Culloden for two nights. However, when Johnson and Boswell visited the island in 1773 they were comfortably housed and recorded no mention of violent history. The houses in **Inverarish** were built for the workers in an iron-ore mine, developed for a while in the early 19th century but discontinued after the First World War; some remains of mine buildings and railway can still be seen. A little road runs north up the island to the ruins of **Brochel Castle**, the ancient home of the Macleods of Skye; before the days of the car ferry – as indeed today – the walk to here along the central ridge was the point of a visit. Boswell 'had a Highland dance on the top of Dun Can' (1,456 feet) and was proud to have walked 24 miles and still have the energy for an evening's entertainment back at Raasay House.

Canna

Canna, five miles by one with a population of under 30, is green and fertile and relatively flat, with an extremely mild climate. The pier is at the east end below **Compass Hill** (458 feet) whose rich iron deposits are liable to distort ships' compasses. The ruined tower near the harbour was reputedly the prison of the wife of a Macdonald chieftain who had taken a Macleod as her lover. Canna is a single farm, and there are crofts on the island of **Sanday**, across a small bridge. There is a post office but no shop or holiday accommodation. Permission is given for camping.

Eigg

Eigg is privately owned and managed in an energetic fashion. It is the most developed of the Small Isles – though that is not saying much. There is an emphasis on community spirit and self-sufficiency, yet a warm welcome to tourists who have only started to come here in any number in the last couple of years. The local population is about 80, most of them engaged in crofting with a finger or two in the tourist pie. Accommodation is mainly self-catering.

The dominating feature of the island is **An Sgurr** (1,289 feet), a volcanic outcrop composed of black pitchstone dropping away into sheer cliffs. It's immensely dramatic from the sea, easily climbable from inland, and from its peak the view is vast. The lowest land with fields and woods is on the east side round **Galmisdale**, where the ferries call and where the estate office and a couple of shops are located. The longest road on the island leads from Galmisdale three miles or so north to the crofting village of **Cleadale**; west of here is **Laig Bay**, a beautiful though rather exposed stretch of white sand. A mile north are the Singing Sands, so called because the white quartz sand squeaks underfoot.

The most dramatic bit of the island's history concerns the **Massacre Cave**, about half a mile from Galmisdale. In 1577 a raiding party of Macleods from Skye landed on Eigg. The Macdonalds of Eigg took refuge in the cave for three days. Then the Macleods spotted the footprints of a returning scout; unable to storm the cave, they lit a fire at its mouth and suffocated 400 Macdonalds, the entire population. A short distance to the west is the **Cathedral Cave**, where for years the islanders secretly celebrated mass.

Muck

Muck is the smallest Small Isle, only two miles long. Its unfortunate name comes from the Gaelic for 'pig', perhaps after the sea pigs, or porpoises, that have been seen round its shores. Most of its people – like those of Eigg – were forced to emigrate to Nova Scotia in 1826. Now sheep and cattle are reared here: though almost treeless and very exposed, it is surprisingly fertile. The only road is just over a mile long; it leads from **Port Mor**, where passengers are landed, to **Gallanach** on the north side with its attractive beach.

Rhum

The island is owned by the Nature Conservancy Council and managed as a National Nature Reserve. About eight miles square, it's the largest of the Small Isles and extremely rugged, particularly in the south where peaks rise more than 2,500 feet; only a few acres around Kilmory, Kinloch and Harris can be crofted. After an impoverished period culminating in the islanders' emigration *en bloc* to Canada in 1826 (to make room for sheep) red deer virtually took over the island which became a sporting domain; now it is the scene of intense research into the habits and habitats of the deer. Geological and botanical work is also in progress. As a result some restrictions on access have to be imposed on visitors.

Kinloch, where the ferry docks, is the only settlement, with a shop and Edwardian **Kinloch Castle**, now the NCC headquarters. There are two nature trails, one along Kinloch Glen, the other on the south side of Loch Scresort. There is little accommodation, and if you want to stay on the island you should contact the Nature Conservancy Council first.

Accommodation

There's no shortage of accommodation on Skye – from hotels to bed and breakfast places to youth hostels. Its distributed fairly evenly throughout the island, with a wide range of hotels in Portree. Accommodation is extremely limited on the other islands; Eigg has the most.

ISLEORNSAY
Kinloch Lodge
Tel: Isleornsay (047 13) 214
Lord and Lady Macdonald's rambling white-washed house set in acres of open moorland at the head of a small loch. The lounge is comfortable and welcoming, the dining room elegant. The bedrooms, though on the small side, are prettily decorated; there are books and flowers, and all have tea-making facilities.
The food, under the care of Claire Macdonald, is prepared from fresh ingredients and generously served; breakfasts are particularly noteworthy. A place to relax in an informal atmosphere and enjoy the good things of life.
Open all year (not Jan); 10 bedrooms; from £££

SKEABOST BRIDGE
Skeabost House (GFG)
Tel: Skeabost Bridge (047 032) 202
A Victorian mansion set in 12 acres of grounds overlooking Loch Snizort. Public rooms are mainly traditional in style, with wood panelling and velvet curtains, though their elegance is somewhat faded. Bedrooms in the main house are spacious and comfortable, those in the annexe small and rather plain; all have tea-making facilities, most have radio and baby listening. With fishing rights on the River Snizort, and a resident angling coach, the hotel is particularly popular with fishermen. Small golf course.
Open Easter to mid-Oct; 27 bedrooms (including some in annexe); from £

General Information

Activities
BOAT HIRE At several places. Various types of boats can be hired from Strollamus Boat Centre, near Broadford.
BOAT TRIPS Caledonian MacBrayne run cruises as well as ferries; Tel: Portree (0478) 2075.
For details of the Elgol to Loch Coruisk trip (not Sun) Tel: Loch Skavaig (047 16) 213 or 235.

W Kennedy runs trips from Portree to the Sound of Raasay or Loch Ainort, Tel: Kyle (0599) 4435.
Macdonald Marine also run trips, Tel: Duntulm (047 052) 217
FISHING Brown trout in the Storr lochs. Salmon in rivers Hinnisdal, Lealt, Sligachan, Snizort and Staffin.
GOLF Sconser and Skeabost House Hotel.
PONY-TREKKING Strollamus and Ullinish.
SAILING Armadale, Duisdale Hotel and Strollamus Boat Centre (also watersports).
SQUASH Portree.
SWIMMING Portree.
TENNIS Portree.

Events
JUNE Skye Round Table Week.
AUGUST Skye Highland Games; Skye Folk Festival.

Entertainment
Ceilidhs, dances and discos are held at hotels and halls. Pipe band performances in the square at Portree.

Ferries
Caledonian MacBrayne, Tel: Kyle of Lochalsh (0599) 4218 or Mallaig (0687) 2403: Armadale to Mallaig, 5 times daily (not Sun), takes 30 min; Kyleakin to Kyle of Lochalsh, frequent services daily, takes 5 min; Uig to Outer Hebrides daily (not Sun), takes from 1½ hours; Mallaig to Small Isles (no cars), 5 times a week (also services once a week from Armadale); Sconser to Raasay, 6 times daily (not Sun), takes 15 min.
M A Mackenzie, Tel: Glenelg (059 982) 224: Kylerhea to Glenelg, frequent services daily (not Sun), takes 4 min.
Arisaig Marine, Tel: Arisaig (068 75) 224: Arisaig to various combinations of the Small Isles.

Tourist information
South-west Ross and Isle of Skye Tourist Information Office, Portree, Tel: (0478) 2137
Centre open summer only at Broadford, Tel: (047 12) 361

West Sutherland

Ben Loyal

The Vikings who dominated northern Scotland for nearly two hundred years should have felt much at home in this area. The great coastal indentations of Lochs Inchard, Cairnbawn, Glencoul and Glendhu are reminiscent of the Norwegian fjords; similarly Loch Eriboll and the Kyles of Durness and Tongue cut deep into the northern coastline. In contrast are the many sandy beaches, such as those at Sandwood Bay, Balnakeil and Clachtoll.

It is a wild and rugged country, with a sensational coastline and some fine mountain scenery – arguably the best of the Highland areas for getting away from it all. In the words of Matthew Arnold 'there is a sense of vastness; and then the desolation .... miles and miles of mere heather and peat and rocks, and not a soul. And then the sea comes up from the land on the west coast, and the mountain forms there are quite magnificent'.

There are few roads and no towns in West Sutherland, and the weather is bad even by Highland standards. Being so far north it enjoys some of the longest summer days in Britain (not quite the land of the midnight sun but a definite twilight zone) but one of the shortest holiday seasons. In parts you have as much chance of coming across a golden eagle as you do a petrol station; except for the occasional museum and ruined castle, the attractions are provided by nature. Fishermen delight in the well-stocked rivers and lochs and the teeming seas. Wildlife abounds in the largely undisturbed tracts of heather and peat bog, and there are bird sanctuaries and nature reserves to visit. West Sutherland boasts the highest waterfall in Britain and some of the highest cliffs; the vistas of mountain and moor, sea and loch are exhilarating for walkers, spectacular even from a car. Only the central moorland route from Lairg to Tongue and the journey along Loch Shin become monotonous.

Although a wet and windy area today, at the time of the Roman incursions into northern Scotland under Agricola, West Sutherland's climate was much milder; it is thought that vines were grown even in the extreme north. The Roman Empire declined, the weather changed; and areas where trees had flourished became the vast tracts of open peat-based moorland you see today.

The depopulation of so much of the area is not due solely to the inhospitable terrain. It also stems from the ruthless evictions or Clearances carried out in the early 19th century. The initiators of this upheaval were the Countess of Sutherland and her husband the Marquess of Stafford, and other landowners, who found their vast estates unprofitable. They wanted large and regular rents which the crofting tenants, near subsistence level, could not afford; those who could were the big sheep farmers from the Lowlands and beyond the Border who were eager for more land. Between 1809 and 1819, 15,000 crofters were cleared from nearly half a million acres to make room for sheep. Many families emigrated to the Canadian provinces of Nova Scotia or Newfoundland, while some moved south to Glasgow or Dundee. Those who stayed were shifted to coastal areas, and left to extract some sort of living from the alien sea. Attempts to start new industries and improve communications did little to erase the bitterness.

Most people pass through West Sutherland on a tour along the the road which follows the coast for most of its way from Dornoch in south-east Sutherland right round to West Ross. East Sutherland and Caithness have several sizeable towns, but there is no major tourist centre in West Sutherland; inland, there is very little habitation at all, though every little lochside village seems to have its fishing hotel. But hospitality is to be found along the coast, in the scattered handful of fishing and crofting communities, from lively Lochinver in the west to pretty Tongue in the windswept north. Closest to the north-west corner of Britain is Durness, from where we start our tours.

*'It's grand, and ye canna expect
to be baith grand and comfortable'*   J M Barrie

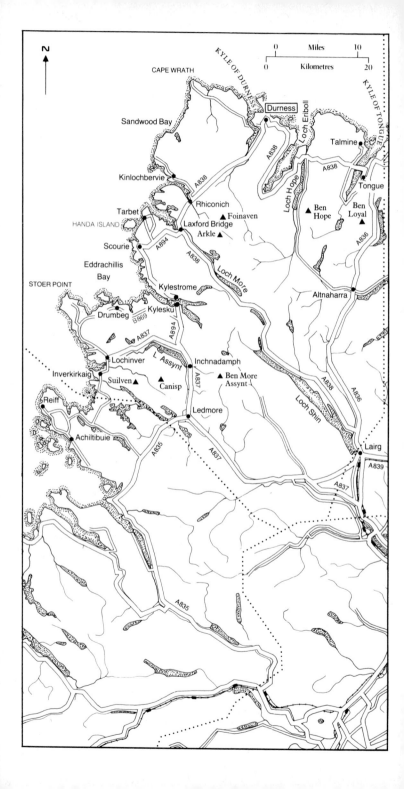

DURNESS

Durness is just one of several small villages where you might stay in this area, but it is close to a number of interesting places. To the west, the excellent white sands at **Balnakeil Bay** are overlooked by the ruins of the 17th-century **Old Church**; and near here the stark concrete buildings of the former radar station at Balnakeil have been converted into a **Craft Village** (closed Sun).

To the east by another sandy beach at Sango Bay is **Smoo Cave**, a huge limestone cavern easily accessible by a path from the car park. Two of the three chambers are negotiable only by boat or with diving equipment. There are views from the cliffs here across to **Loch Eriboll**, a remarkable and beautiful deep inlet where fishing boats shelter from the worst Atlantic weather, and grey seals come to breed.

Durness is the nearest place of any size to the wild and stormy headland of **Cape Wrath**. It is accessible – weather permitting – by the passenger ferry from Keoldale, south-west of Durness. A connecting minibus service covers the 11 miles to the Cape's lighthouse; a mile or so north and reached only by foot are the **Clo-Mor cliffs**, among the highest in Britain, the haunt of colonies of puffins, kittiwakes, guillemots and razorbills.

Loch Shin and the extreme north-west

Loch Eriboll · Loch Hope · Altnaharra · Loch Shin
Laxford Bridge · Handa Island · Kinlochbervie
Durness

Forty miles of narrow road through moorland scenery; forty more between increasingly dramatic mountains past lochs and down the River Laxford. The distractingly pretty detours on the west coast are shorter, but deserve and require to be taken slowly. About 120 miles in all.

The road eastward from Durness skirts **Loch Eriboll** for 12 miles, passing delightful sandy bays and coves. Shortly after turning inland from the eastern shore a narrow unclassified road strikes southward; this is a lonely run over wild moorland. Beyond tranquil Loch Hope is **Alltnacaillich**, the site of a spectacular waterfall. Beside the River Hope in Strathmore is the **Broch of Dornadilla**, an unusually well-preserved Pictish defence tower in a lovely setting below towering Ben Hope (3,042 feet).

From the main road – still narrow – 20 miles south of tiny **Altnaharra** through Strath Vagastie, there are views of Ben Klibreck on the left, and Strath Tirry. Shortly before reaching Lairg (see East Sutherland chapter), turn right along the A838 beside **Loch Shin** (17 miles long). The scenery becomes impressive as the mountains and woods close in around Loch Merkland and Loch More. The road reaches the coast at **Laxford Bridge**, where there are marvellous views east towards the peaks of Arkle, Ben Stack and Foinaven.

★ The A894 goes to Scourie (see next tour), but a short and pretty detour may be taken to **Tarbet**, a tiny fishing community from which **Handa Island Bird Sanctuary** is just a 10-minute boat trip. You will see few birds after early August. May and June are the months when the cliffs are thick with auks, puffins, fulmars, kittiwakes and many other sea birds. Sea trips round the island give splendid views of the cliffs, which rise to 400 feet. ★

From Rhiconich the detour to Kinlochbervie is of great interest. Turn off the main road through the rugged beauty of Loch Inchard, bordered by crofts amid fertile hollows and bare hilltops. **Kinlochbervie** is an important fishing port, with a harbour on each side of the isthmus projecting into Loch Inchard.

The road continues five miles to Oldshore More (above a lovely sandy bay), Blairmore and Sheigra. After that, it's worth the four-mile walk to **Sandwood Bay**, one of the loveliest and loneliest in Scotland, wide and backed by dunes (though strong tides make bathing unsafe). Legend tells that mermaids haunt the area – not to mention the ghost of a 'Bearded Sailor'. Rejoin the main road at Rhiconich for the return to Durness through the gentler, more fertile terrain of Strath Dionard.

Assynt, Lochinver and the central uplands

Laxford Bridge · Scourie · Kylestrome · Drumbeg
Lochinver · Inchnadamph · Ledmore · Lairg
Altnaharra · Tongue
Durness

An easy enough drive to Kylestrome. Not so the tremendous 23-mile coastal route to Lochinver. Another easy 20 through Assynt before the road narrows on the route east among the peaks, 30 miles across to Lairg. On the return nothing but moorland until you reach the coast (after 40 miles) at Tongue. About 145 miles in all.

The road from Durness to Laxford Bridge was described in the previous tour. A further seven miles south-west is **Scourie**, a fishing and crofting village, with a sandy beach and flourishing palm trees. As the A894 leaves Scourie the views become better: on the right is Eddrachillis Bay, a lovely seascape of islands and bays; on the left superb mountain scenery. A climax is reached at **Kylestrome** with views of Lochs Glencoul and Glendhu and the peaks of Quinag, Glas Bheinn and Beinn Leoid. There used to be a ferry to Kylesku across Loch Cairnbawn but the new bridge has greatly reduced the delays that sometimes used to be experienced in summer.

Beyond the head of Loch Glencoul is **Eas Coul Aulin**, at 658 feet Britain's highest waterfall. The easiest approach is by boat, followed by a tramp of about a mile. Alternatively there is a three-mile route from the main road by Loch na Gainmhich – or an even longer path from Inchnadamph.

The vast rocky wilderness of **Assynt**, an area of myriad tiny lochs, is dominated by the great rugged mountains of Canisp, Quinag, Suilven and Ben More Assynt. The main centre of Assynt, Lochinver, is reached directly by following the main road to Skiag Bridge and then the A837 westward to the coast. But more varied and spectacular (though considerably more tortuous) is the route by way of Drumbeg and Clashnessie. A couple of miles south of Kylesku, turn right along the B869 and prepare for 23 miles of difficult driving: you will be rewarded.

★ A steep descent to Loch Nedd is followed by an equally steep ascent to the first fine viewpoint and to **Drumbeg**. For the next few miles there are enthralling glimpses of **Eddrachillis Bay** and its islands, particularly the largest, Oldany. The road reaches the coast again at **Clashnessie** with its beautiful sandy bay. Shortly, a side road to the right leads to Culkein on the bleak Stoer Peninsula; another branch of this ends at the lighthouse. Two miles beyond on **Stoer Point** is the rock pillar known as **The Old Man of Stoer**. The B869 passes through Stoer village and Clachtoll, whose sandy beach is protected against erosion by a peat wall, then winds on past Achmelvich Bay. The right turn to Achmelvich leads to another sandy beach. After the many ups and downs and twists and turns, the final reward is one of the most attractive villages in the Highlands. **Lochinver** is a busy fishing port and the main centre for a large area. Backed by dark mountains, the long lochside street is bright as new paint, and in the evening the pier is a scene of intense activity as fishing boats unload their catch. In view of the beautiful coastline and the attractive walks available inland, it is not surprising that Lochinver can be extremely busy in the season. Boat trips run regularly to view the coast, the colonies of seals and the bird-haunted islands. ★

A favourite walk from Lochinver is to the summit of **Suilven**, the Sugar Loaf (2,399 feet). Though not visible from the village it is only four miles or so as the crow flies, and dominates the immediate area. The view from the summit over loch and moor is sensational. An excursion better begun by car is south to **Inverkirkaig**; from here there is a beautiful walk by the River Kirkaig to the Falls of Kirkaig and Fionn Loch. This walk may be used as the start of another route to the summit of Suilven.

The unclassified road from Lochinver continues southward to join eventually the Achiltibuie-Reiff road (see West Ross chapter) while the main A837 runs north of the River Inver to lonely Loch Assynt. At first wooded, the terrain becomes open and bleak; the gaunt ruin of **Ardvreck Castle** is a solitary feature at the water's edge. This 16th-century stronghold of the Macleods of Assynt had a dungeon where in 1650 a Covenanter Macleod imprisoned the Marquess of Montrose, defeated in his attempted support of the exiled Charles II. Montrose was taken from Ardvreck to Edinburgh and hanged.

The A837 is joined by the A894 and shortly reaches **Inchnadamph**; a mile or so south, above the Allt nan Uamh burn, are limestone caves where prehistoric – including human – bones have been found. At Ledmore, the A835 heads southward to the Inverpolly Nature Reserve and Ullapool, the main town in West Ross. But the A837 swings south-east, to link Assynt with Bonar Bridge and eastern Scotland. Near **Altnacealgach**, which stands on the northern shore of Loch Borralan, a number of chambered cairns are more evidence that prehistoric man inhabited this area.

Five or six miles from Altnacealgach – just before you reach woodland – stop and look back at the wonderful mountain panorama, including Cul Mor, Breabag, Suilven and Canisp – all except Suilven over 2,500 feet. Then continue through the mountains to Oykel Bridge and down Strath Oykel. At Invercassley a road strikes left up Glen Cassley. A few yards up, after Auchness House, an iron gate on the left marks the start of a footpath to the attractive **Cassley Waterfall**. Back on the main road, take the narrower left fork, the A839, to Lairg (see next chapter).

From Lairg, follow the A836 for 20 moorland miles to Altnaharra, and on to skirt the western shore of **Loch Loyal** with Ben Loyal's four splintered peaks rising above the surrounding hills. A narrow tongue of land separates Loch Loyal from Loch Craggie. After so long a passage through deserted uplands, arrival at **Tongue** is comforting. It's a pretty place set on the magnificent Kyle of Tongue, with romantic **Castle Varrich** dominating the fine view – a stronghold once Norse, later Mackay. 17th-century Tongue House was the clan seat.

The main road westward crosses the Kyle by a causeway on which there is a view indicator, but more attractive though 10 miles longer is the old road round the Kyle which offers good views from its most southerly point. A short road strikes off north from the west side of the Kyle to **Melness** and **Talmine**, crofting communities established after the Clearances. At low tide you can walk across the sands from Talmine to **Rabbit Islands**. As you return to the main road, enjoy the view of the Kyle backed by Ben Loyal. The drive back to Durness passes the head of Loch Hope and skirts Loch Eriboll (see previous tour).

Accommodation

Hotel accommodation is thin on the ground in West Sutherland. To have a choice, though not a particularly large one, head for the villages of Durness, Kinlochbervie, Lochinver, Tongue or Scourie. Though it's not an area of outstanding hotels, there are a number which enjoy fine situations in an area which does excel for its scenery.

General Information

Activities
BOAT HIRE Row boats and fishing boats at Lochinver.
BOAT TRIPS Laxford Cruises, Tel: Scourie (0971) 2151; trips to Loch Laxford and the seal islands.
N A MacAskill; various trips from Lochinver.
Trips to Handa Island from Tarbet, Tel: Scourie (0971) 2156
John Ridgeway School of Adventure run longer cruises – to St Kilda and Faroes, Tel: Kinlochbervie (097 182) 229
FISHING Trout in many lochs and rivers; salmon in lochs Shin and Naver and River Oykel.
PONY-TREKKING Durness and Tongue.
SAILING Durness, waterskiing at Lochinver.

Entertainment
Some local hotels and halls put on ceilidhs.

Events
JULY Durness Highland Games.
AUGUST Lochinver Highland Games.

Ferries
Cape Wrath, Tel: Durness (097 181) 244

Tourist information
Sutherland Tourist Office, Dornoch, Tel: (0862) 810400
Centres open summer only: Durness, Tel: (097 181) 259;
Lochinver, Tel: (057 14) 330

East Sutherland
and
Caithness

Girnigoe Castle

Too far north to be anything but 'the Highlands', this corner of Scotland yet has none of the typically Highland scenery – no dramatic peaks and ranges, no deep forested lochs, no intricate coastline. It's drier than the north-west (no mountains) but colder (no Gulf Stream). Inland the moors roll on for ever, damp but not fertile, empty and bleak, crossed by a handful of narrow roads. Round the coastline there's an occasional stretch of sand, but more generally cliffs and small harbours; north of Lairg, the coast is where the people live. There are two obvious reasons for the lack of settlements inland – poverty of soil, and of communications; the second of these problems was tackled at least for the eastern fishing villages when in 1803 a Commission was established 'for making Roads and building Bridges in the Highlands of Scotland'. Thomas Telford's far-reaching results included roads across the Dornoch Firth and Loch Fleet, previously negotiated lower down by ferries; expansion and improvement of many little harbours; and a whole new town at Wick. The fishing industry expanded, and here and there others were introduced. But all dwindled again and many failed, not surviving accident, distance, competition from more convenient or more profitable sources.

The north-east was never an area of small kingdoms and clan territory. The Norsemen with their early freedom of the seas (extending to Normandy and beyond) as a matter of course exercised easy dominance here. It was the first landfall after their Shetland and Orkney strongholds: Orkney and Caithness was a single earldom. Of all the coalescing peoples of ancient Scotland the Picts held out longest against Christianity; their brochs and stones are found everywhere in the region, the language of their symbols undeciphered. For centuries, ownership of the land changed through intermarriage and adoptive heirs, treaty and political overlordship, rather than by physical conquest. The Earls of Sutherland eventually owned vast areas, and in the far north, from the 16th century, the Sinclairs had most of Caithness. There were some crofting Mackays in Strathnaver, ruthlessly driven out in the Clearances of the 19th century; and there is a 17th-century Campbell story, even up here. The 6th Earl of Caithness sold his estates to Campbell of Glenorchy, but another Sinclair objected to the deal. Campbell laid siege to the Castle of Girnigoe. The outcome was apparently unsatisfactory for all parties – five years later Girnigoe was deserted – but this was the occasion of the song 'The Campbells are coming'.

Today's visitors need a little more determination here than elsewhere in the Highlands. North of the attractions near the Dornoch Firth – Dornoch itself, splendid Dunrobin Castle, rivers and forests and gardens inland – it's a long haul round the coastline and a lonely one across the middle. There are seascapes and viewpoints and brochs, but they do have a certain monotony. Among the eastern fishing villages and the scattered communities of the north, Wick and Thurso are the only towns – 'no beauty', wrote Robert Louis Stevenson of Wick; 'bare, grey shores, grim grey houses, grim grey sea: not even the gleam of red tiles; not even the greenness of a tree'. The 'atrocious quality of the climate' in September 1868 clearly had much to do with the gloom of his letter. As D H Lawrence remarked 50 years later, 'It is rather nice, but dampish and Northern and one shrinks a little inside one's skin .... one should be amphibian'. Failing that, one should travel equipped with warm and waterproof clothing.

The north coast has some fine beaches, the east is well supplied with golf courses, the fishing and birdwatching are famous. There are ruined castles and churches and notable archaeological sites, museums of local history and the contrast of Dounreay's futuristic fascination. But the real lure of the area must be to travel its length to the northernmost headlands, the ultimate cliffs, the fiercest seas. All that you find along the way is of curious interest, on the way to the end of the world. To cover this large area we have used two centres for our tours.

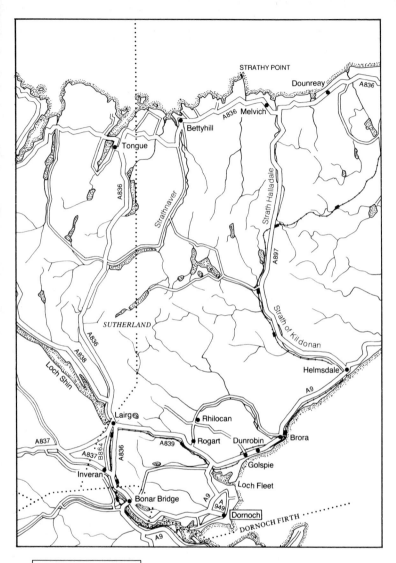

DORNOCH

A royal burgh since 1628, Dornoch is a small but spacious town of considerable dignity. It is no longer an administrative centre and its cathedral is now a parish church, but its atmosphere is tranquil and historic. The small cathedral was begun by Bishop Gilbert de Moravia of Caithness in 1224: a fire in 1570 destroyed all but the tower. After long neglect the nave was rebuilt in the 19th century, and extensive restoration in 1924 revealed some of the original stonework. The 1570 fire also destroyed most of the Bishops' Castle nearby: a medieval tower remains, now part of a hotel.

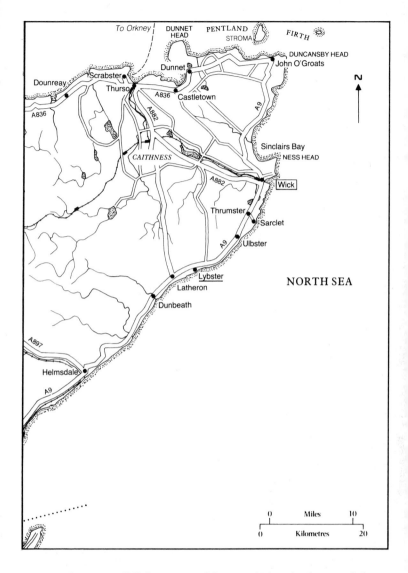

The famous golf links are rated in superlatives by lovers of the game. Dornoch also has miles of fine sandy beach and ample accommodation – the latter includes two large caravan sites, near the town and north at **Embo**, but much of the holiday shore is peaceful and undeveloped.

Besides its tourist amenities, Embo has a well-preserved prehistoric site – there are several in the neighbourhood of Dornoch. **Loch Fleet**, four miles north, is a beautiful inlet with much birdlife; on its southern shore are the 14th-century keep and walls of ruined Skelbo Castle.

179

Lairg and Helmsdale

Bonar Bridge · Inveran · Lairg · Rhilochan
Brora · Helmsdale · Golspie
Dornoch

*Coast and moor, rivers and waterfalls, archaeological remains and a
splendid castle. Easy driving along the coast, narrower but rarely
difficult roads inland. About 85 miles.*

A mile or so out of Dornoch, the A949 meets the A9; turn left to
Clashmore and the wooded Skibo Estate. Skibo Castle (not open)
was built by Andrew Carnegie in 1898, on the site of a much older
stronghold. A minor road branches south from **Ospisdale** a mile to
Newton Point, with splendid views down Dornoch Firth. Back on
the main road, **Spinningdale** is a sad remnant of industrial history;
a cotton mill and workers' cottages were built here in 1790 by the
local laird, but a fire in 1808 ended the experiment.

At **Bonar Bridge**, a quite attractive village, 13 miles from
Dornoch at the head of the Firth, rivers meet and roads disperse in
all directions – one tempting detour winds and climbs up past **Loch
Buidhe**, to reach the coast after 15 miles at Loch Fleet. Continue
north along the A836; in a mile there is a car park from which a
forest walk leads through birch woods with fine views of the sea
loch called **Kyle of Sutherland**. From **Invershin** your eye is drawn
to towered and turreted **Carbisdale Castle**, high up across the
river: it's Scotland's only 20th-century castle, built for the Countess
of Sutherland around 1910 and now a youth hostel.

Fork left on the A837 and at **Inveran** with its power station turn
right along the B864 up the west bank of the River Shin. At the
Falls of Shin a platform allows you to watch the salmon leap the
tumbling rapids, and a forest walk starts from the car park. This
road continues through the wooded countryside of Glen Achany to
join the A839 a mile south of **Lairg**. This busy and attractive village
makes a good touring base; here the roads arrive from the
north-west Highlands to meet the eastern routes. It is famous for its
salmon and trout fishing, and for the great sheep sales held in
August. Head east from Lairg by the A839, still in pleasant
countryside through **Strath Fleet** past **Rovie Lodge**, where
beautiful gardens are open in the summer. Ten miles from Lairg,
leave the main road and turn left along an unclassified moorland
road to **Rhilochan**, where a road to the right traverses pretty
Dunrobin Glen on the way to Golspie. Keep straight on however
along **Strath Brora** 10 miles to **Balnacoil** at the confluence of the
rivers **Blackwater** and **Brora**. There follows a delightful drive
beside tranquil **Loch Brora**; half-way along, on the far side, is the
imposing crag of **Carrol Rock** (684 feet); farther on above the road
is the slightly higher **Killin Rock**.

This peaceful road reaches the river mouth, the railway and the
A9 at **Brora**. A rather dull town but with a sandy beach, golf course

and good fishing, it has been called the 'industrial capital of Sutherland'. Coal was discovered and mined here in the 16th century, and in the 19th an industrially enterprising Duke of Sutherland sank a fresh shaft; he also developed brick-making, extended the railway and even built a locomotive works, which was soon turned into a woollen mill. Shetland wool is still a local industry, but though there's plenty of coal left the miners have migrated to oil rigs. You can visit the mill and also (by appointment) the town's distillery, and there are many archaeological remains in the vicinity. One of these is the ruined broch just seaward of the A9 three miles north, near **Kintradwell**. This and a similar broch at **Crakaig** lie on the far side of the railway which runs close to the coast. Between the two is **Lothbeg**, where a stone marks the spot where the last wolf in Sutherland was killed in about 1700. A little road goes off north from Lothbeg, among high peaks to Glen Loth. At this point the A9 runs nearly a mile inland and does not approach the coast again until south of Helmsdale.

Little grey **Helmsdale** huddles round its river mouth and harbour, reached by a bridge built in 1972 not far from the graceful Telford bridge of 1812. Helmsdale offers a sandy beach, good fishing and a golf course; and the shore holds riches in the form of amethyst, jasper and other semi-precious stones. It is still principally a working port: while not as prosperous perhaps as during the great herring boom of the last century, its fishermen keep the harbour busy as they bring in their catches.

★ Ignore the roads to the north and east and return 12 miles to Brora: stay on the A9 another five miles and you come to the entrance of **Dunrobin Castle** (closed Sun am), deep in woodland beside the sea. The seat of the Earls and later Dukes of Sutherland is one of Scotland's most impressive fortresses. To the original core of the castle, a square keep with turrets built in the late 13th century, much was added over the years. The most radical alterations and additions were made in the 19th century; the castle now is magnificently Scottish baronial, designed by Sir Charles Barry. There is much worth seeing, including the ornate ceiling of the dining room, the library lined with sycamore wood and the elegant drawing room furnished in Louis Quinze style and containing Mortlake tapestries and two Canalettos. The rooms were designed about 1920 by Robert Lorimer who restored Barry's work after a serious fire. No less impressive are the lovely gardens, overlooking the sea and laid out formally in imitation of Versailles. A museum in the grounds contains Pictish stones, fossils, agricultural implements and mementoes of Queen Victoria. ★

Golspie, the administrative headquarters of Sutherland, is a peaceful small resort with a long sandy beach and a golf course. It lies beneath Ben Vraggie (1,293 feet) which is surmounted by an enormous statue of the first Duke of Sutherland, responsible for the Clearances in the early 19th century as well as less unpopular economic measures. This is an area of woods and hills and there are many delightful walks – the most popular is to the Big Burn waterfall in **Dunrobin Glen**. Golspie has always been the Sutherland family 'capital'; on the old Mill Brae bridge is an inscribed 'rallying stone' for the clan, and in its 17th-century church is the finely carved and panelled Sutherland Loft, complete with retiring room, installed for the Earl in 1739.

Loch Fleet, four miles south of Golspie, used to have a ferry across its narrow mouth: a small road leads from Golspie down to its site at Littleferry. Now the A9 crosses Loch Fleet by The Mound, half a mile of causeway built over the sands at its head by Telford in 1815. From The Mound's southern end the Loch Buidhe road to Bonar Bridge passes the Torboll Falls, with an old fish ladder. Five miles south, take the B9168 to Dornoch.

WICK

Though a well-placed touring centre with ample accommodation and leisure facilities Wick is not a tourist town. Set round the bay named by the Vikings, its spread of sober grey makes no picturesque compromises. The original settlement and royal burgh was on the north bank of the river – now the shopping centre for miles around. On the south bank is Pulteneytown, called after a president of the British Fisheries Society which commissioned Telford's new harbour, bridge and burgh. Wick became county town of Caithness in the heyday of the herring industry when over 1,000 boats were based here; unlike other ports, it weathered the industry's decline. Pulteney has a distillery and a cheese factory; fishing still thrives, though not the herring; and by canny coincidence Wick's biggest industry is also its major tourist attraction. Thousands of people each year visit **Caithness Glass** to watch the glassblowing (closed lunch, Sat pm and Sun).

Some of Telford's harbour buildings, restored in the 1970s, constitute the excellent **Wick Heritage Centre** (limited opening hours). There are fine cliff walks along the dramatic coastline: south to the tall gaunt ruin of the **Castle of Old Wick** (AM), north (by road too) to the lighthouse on Noss Head, and from there to the romantic remnants of **Castles Sinclair and Girnigoe**, close together on their rocky promontory.

The Caithness Coast

John O'Groats · Duncansby Head · Dunnet Head · Thurso
Dounreay · Melvich · Bettyhill · Melvich
Helmsdale · Latheron · Sarclet
Wick

A circular tour which takes in the most northerly point of the British mainland (which is not John O'Groats), some pretty villages, remarkable prehistoric remains and a taste of nuclear power. Roads are mainly narrow, some are single-track. About 160 miles.

Head north on the A9 which passes two golf courses with a splendid stretch of sandy beach beyond. At **Keiss**, the main centre in Caithness for crab fishing, there are remains of two brochs. The ruins of **Keiss Castle**, dating from the late 16th century, stand close to its Victorian successor. At **Auckengill** three follies by the little pier were built by the Victorian painter John Nicolson. South of **Noss Head** Bucholie Castle, unsignposted but visible on its promontory, was the 12th-century seat of the Norse pirate Sweyn. The harbour of **Freswick** is used by a few of the traditional clinker-built yawls which are particularly suitable for the strong currents experienced in the Pentland Firth.

The road climbs inland over Warth Hill – only 412 feet, but sufficient for a splendid view across the Pentland Firth as you approach **John O'Groats**. This not-the-northernmost point of the mainland takes its name from Jan de Grot, a 16th-century Dutch immigrant. Here ends the A9; here arrive the hopeful record-breakers after 874 miles from Land's End – cyclists have made the trip in two days, and it has been done in a wheelchair. There is a signpost for you to be photographed in front of and souvenir shops abound – indeed there's not much else to see. A mound with a flagstaff marks the site of de Grot's fabled eight-sided house with eight doors, built to avoid disputes among his eight descendants. Another version of this story is that de Grot ran a ferry, and constructed a shelter for his waiting customers with a protected corner against the wind from any direction. Today boat trips run to the Orkneys, Duncansby Head and the seal-colonised cliffs of **Stroma Island**, deserted now except by its lighthouse keepers. **Duncansby Head** can also be reached by road. There are marvellous views from the lighthouse with its square tower, and the waves and wind have produced remarkable rock formations. Walk along the cliffs to the south, where the great pinnacles of the **Duncansby Stacks** are the home of myriad sea birds.

Continue along the north coast by the A836 to attractive Canisbay Church, probably built in the 15th century; the aisles were added in the 17th, the present tower in the 18th. As you pass **Gills Bay** look out for seals: here is one of Britain's largest colonies. In a further four miles a side road leads seawards to the **Castle of Mey**, which was built in the late 16th century for the Earls of Caithness. The

183

Queen Mother bought it in 1952 and carefully restored it. The gardens are open a few days in summer.

★ The road now runs through flat, windy, featureless country five miles to the pretty hamlet of Dunnet. At **Dunnet Bay** two miles of golden sand is backed by great wind-sculptured dunes, fine turf and flowering plants. The B855 runs five miles to **Dunnet Head**, the true northernmost point of the British mainland. The view from the lighthouse on the 300-feet-high promontory across the Pentland Firth to the Orkneys and the rock stack of the Old Man of Hoy is quite superb. Below the lighthouse, the teeming seabird population nest on perilous sandstone ledges: puffins and petrels, kittiwakes and gulls. ★

From **Castletown** the A836 continues arrow-straight across five miles of flat moorland to Thurso; about half-way along you can make a detour to **Murkle Bay**, beautiful and sheltered. **Thurso** has been a thriving township ever since the 14th century when it was the chief port for Scottish trade with Scandinavia. Within the deep curve of Thurso Bay the estuary of the River Thurso provides a long sheltered fishing harbour; in the oldest part of the town are narrow 17th-century streets and cottages. Inland are wide grey 18th-century streets, laid out by Sir John Sinclair, and much modern development. It's the second largest town in Caithness and it has a small **Folk Museum** (open from June, closed Sun and lunch). The A882 leads to **Scrabster**, Thurso's fishing port from which ferries sail to the Orkneys.

About five miles east along the A836 a side road on the right leads to the roofless ruins of St Mary's Chapel at **Crosskirk**. It was built in the 12th century; its unusual feature is the low and narrow doorway between nave and chancel. In a further four miles the great white dome of the Dounreay Fast Reactor (DFR) draws the eye; turn right again off the main road to visit the Atomic Energy Authority's **Dounreay Exhibition** (closes at 4pm) which includes audio-visual displays and models. Free tickets for conducted tours of the prototype fast reactor (PFR) can be obtained from the Tourist Information Centre at Thurso.

After Reay the A836 crosses the old boundary into Sutherland before reaching **Melvich**, at the mouth of the River Halladale. From here on the coastline is beautiful and much more varied, but often inaccessible. You can however drive the twisting couple of miles to **Strathy Point**, for tremendous views from Britain's newest lighthouse, built in 1958, and the compelling thought that there is nothing now but sea between you and the North Pole. The bays at Armadale and Kirtomy can be achieved with a little walking. **Bettyhill** is named after Elizabeth Countess of Sutherland, who founded the village for the far from grateful crofters she had

evicted. Today it is a thriving place with good sandy beaches at Farr
Bay and Torrisdale Bay (where there is a bird sanctuary). To the
east, the old church of Farr has been converted into the **Strathnaver
Museum** of folk history (open from June, Tue, Wed, Thur only).

In a further 12 miles the A836 reaches **Tongue** (see previous
chapter). Return instead through Melvich and turn south along the
A897. The single-track road runs 12 miles through fertile Strath
Halladale to **Forsinard**. Road and railway keep close company
through **Kinbrace** and the wide **Strath of Kildonan**, an area
severely hit by the Clearances (though a gold rush brought a brief
influx of optimists in the 1860s). At the south end of the strath there
are many remains of brochs, cairns and stone circles. The road
reaches the east coast at **Helmsdale** (see previous tour).

The A9 winds its way up to **Ord of Caithness**, a well-known
viewpoint on the border of Sutherland and Caithness, over the bare
moors and down to tiny **Berriedale**, set by contrast among trees.
Dunbeath has a broch and a clifftop castle (not open) with a
15th-century keep. **Laidhay Croft Museum**, two miles north, is a
thatched 18th-century croft with byre and stable and winnowing
barn. At Latheron a right turn leads to **Latheronwheel**, a small,
photogenic harbour set in a cove at the foot of cliffs. **Lybster**, an
important fishing port, is most attractive too.

A mile east of Lybster take the Watten road to the left and in five
miles you reach the **Grey Cairns of Camster**. The two Neolithic
burial tombs are among Britain's finest prehistoric sites. The
Round Cairn, 55 feet in diameter and 12 feet high, is entered
through the original entrance passage; there is a skylight. The Long
Cairn is 200 feet long and 65 feet wide, and is being restored to its
original state. Three miles further along the main A9 a turning on
the left brings you quickly to the **Hill o'Many Stanes**. This Bronze
Age monument consists of 22 rows of small standing stones.

In a further three miles you can see one of the most remarkable
sights in Caithness, the 365 **Whaligoe Steps** up which the women
used to carry the loaded fishermen's creels. They're a challenge to
find as well as to climb – off the A9 beside a single house and a
telephone box, just south of **Ulbster**. Four miles up the coast little
Sarclet, with another cliff-surrounded cove, was planned and laid
out in the 18th century as a herring fishing centre: the ruin of the
processing building remains. You reach this cove from **Thrumster**;
five more miles of the A9 takes you back to Wick.

185

Accommodation

There's not a great deal of accommodation in this area and booking ahead is advised. For an overnight stop, Wick and Thurso have a fair number of hotels. For a longer stay, Dornoch offers a reasonable selection. Elsewhere the choice is limited to the occasional hotel in villages, or out in the countryside, and a scattering of bed and breakfast places. We found only one hotel which we are happy to recommend for both comfort and food.

LYBSTER
Bayview Hotel (GFG)
Tel: Lybster (059 32) 346
A tiny pub/hotel in a side street of the small coastal village of Lybster. Its cosy bar and dining room are popular with locals, who come to sample over a hundred malt whiskies, and for the good home cooking. The pine-panelled upstairs lounge is attractive, and the bedrooms comfortable and in good condition; colour TV available on request. The atmosphere is relaxed and informal, and the service friendly.
Open all year; 3 bedrooms; £

General Information

Activities
BOAT TRIPS J M Carney, Tel: Bettyhill (064 12) 229; from Skeray.
P A Matheson, Tel: Barrock (084 785) 332 or Bettyhill (064 12) 326; daily trips in summer to seal island of Ron and Isle of Neave cliffs.
J Simpson, Tel: John O'Groats (095 581) 252 or 315; trips to Stroma Island.
I and D Thomas, Tel: John O'Groats (095 581) 353; trips in summer to Duncansby Head or Stroma Island.
For trips to Orkney see 'Ferries'.
FISHING Brown trout in numerous lochs, including Calder, St John's and Watten. Salmon and sea trout in Loch Wester and the River Wester. Salmon in the rivers Berriedale, Thurso and Wick. Fishing boats can be chartered at Castletown, John O'Groats, Scrabster, Thrumster, Thurso and Wick.
GOLF Bonar Bridge, Brora, Dornoch, Golspie, Helmsdale, Lybster, Reay, Thurso and Wick.
PONY-TREKKING Latheron, Melvich and Rogart.
SQUASH Helmsdale, Thurso and Wick.

SWIMMING Golspie, Thurso and Wick.
TENNIS Bettyhill, Brora, Dornoch, Golspie, Helmsdale, Lairg, Thurso and Wick.

Entertainment
No cinemas. Lyth Arts Centre, near Wick, stages music, dance and theatrical events. Pipe bands in Dornoch; discos etc in local hotels.

Events
JULY Highland Gatherings at Dornoch, Halkirk and Thurso; Caithness County Show, Wick; Sutherland Agricultural Show, Dornoch; Wick and Thurso Gala Weeks; Thurso Folk Festival.
AUGUST Dornoch Festival; Wick Festival of Poetry and Jazz.
SEPTEMBER Highland Gatherings at Invercharron and Rosehall.

Ferries
P&O Ferries, Tel: Thurso (0847) 62052: from Scrabster to Orkney.
Thomas and Bews, Tel: John O'Groats (095 581) 353: from John O'Groats to Orkney, passenger only, 4 times daily in summer, takes 45 min.

Tourist information
Caithness Tourist Office, Wick, Tel: (0955) 2596
Sutherland Tourist Office, Dornoch, Tel: (0862) 810400
Centres open summer only: Bonar Bridge, Tel: (086 32) 333;
Helmsdale, Tel: (043 12) 640; John O'Groats, Tel: (095 581) 373;
Lairg, Tel: (0549) 2160; Thurso, Tel: (0847) 62371

Index

188

190